Galatians

Other Founders Study Guide Commentaries

- *Malachi: Founders Study Guide Commentary*
  Baruch Maoz
  expositional comments on the book of Malachi

- *Acts: Founders Study Guide Commentary*
  Curtis Vaughan
  expositional comments on the book of Acts

- *Romans: Founders Study Guide Commentary*
  Curtis Vaughan & Fred Malone
  expositional comments on the book of Romans

- *1 Corinthians: Founders Study Guide Commentary*
  Curtis Vaughan & Thomas D. Lea
  expositional comments on the book of 1 Corinthians

- *Galatians: Founders Study Guide Commentary*
  Curtis Vaughan
  expositional comments on the book of Galatians

- *Ephesians: Founders Study Guide Commentary*
  Curtis Vaughan
  expositional comments on the book of Ephesians

- *Colossians: Founders Study Guide Commentary*
  Baruch Maoz
  expositional comments on the book of Colossians

- *Colossians and Philemon: Founders Study Guide Commentary*
  Curtis Vaughan
  expositional comments on the books of Colossians and Philemon

- *James: Founders Study Guide Commentary*
  Curtis Vaughan
  expositional comments on the book of James

- *1,2,3 John: Founders Study Guide Commentary*
  Curtis Vaughan
  expositional comments on the books of 1 John, 2 John and 3 John

FOUNDERS STUDY GUIDE COMMENTARY

Galatians
He Did It All

Baruch Maoz

Founders Press

Cape Coral, Florida

Published by
Founders Press

P.O. Box 150931 • Cape Coral, FL 33915
Phone (239) 772–1400 • Fax: (239) 772–1140
Electronic Mail: founders@founders.org or
Website: http://www.founders.org

©2019, 2021 Baruch Maoz

Printed in the United States of America

ISBN: 978-1-943539-20-8

Contents

Preface

This commentary is based on my translation of Paul's letter to the Galatians, and my translation is based on the British and Foreign Bible Society's Nestle and Aland's New Testament text of 1904. All other quotes from Scripture are taken from the English Standard Version (ESV).

Using my, somewhat literal, translation of the text will hopefully accord the reader something of a more direct access to the Apostle's terse language without having its edges rounded off by the conventions of modern translations, with their cultural and literary expectations. It will also spare readers the need to read extended exegetical arguments.

This is a *devotional* commentary. It was not written for scholars. Still, I hope scholars will derive more than devotional benefit from what I have written. There is one exegetical argument I believe important to make because it constitutes a departure from most translations and commentaries. I leave it to the wiser and more learned to evaluate, affirm or contradict it. Read on and you will discover what I mean.

The letter to the Galatians, probably the earliest of Paul's letters, carries the seeds of his later, more mature thinking. The parallels with his letter to the Romans are striking. There is nothing in the Apostle's later writings that are not to be found here in seed form. Paul's love for the Messiah, his pastoral concern and his exhilarating view of the finality of Messiah's accomplishments are all evident. It is fascinating to note how thoroughly the Apostle embraced such a full-orbed Gospel at so early a stage in his apostolic ministry. It is no less challenging to measure ourselves by that and other characteristics, evidenced in this letter.

Paul was a man of God, in love with God in the Messiah and therefore in love with the church. His language mellowed somewhat over the course of the years, as he imbibed more and more of the Gospel's principles and applied them in the course of his ministry. But the Holy Spirit used his more terse language for the good of God's church. Paul's understanding of the Gospel likewise broadened. While his guiding principles remained the same and his love for the Messiah was as white-hot at the end of his life as it was when he penned the words we are about to study.

Writing this commentary became a painfully searching process. I was repeatedly forced to ask myself: How well do I trust the Messiah for my salvation? How much dare I attribute to myself? I am moved by Paul's piercing challenges: "Are you so foolish? Having begun by the Spirit, are you now being perfected by the flesh?" (Galatians 3:3). "I do not nullify the grace of God, for if righteousness were through the law, then Messiah died for no purpose" (Galatians 2: 21).

My hope and prayer, dear reader, is that you would likewise be moved.

Baruch Maoz

Introduction

To the Book of Galatians

When was this letter written?

Scholars disagree as to when the letter to the Galatians was written. Some affirm it was the first of Paul's many letters. Others recognize the many similarities in content and terminology between the letters to the Galatians and that to the Romans. On those grounds they insist that the letter to the Galatians was written closer to the time when he penned his letter to the Romans.

Two issues arise in connection to the dating of this letter. How we handle them will determine the date we consider most appropriate. The first has to do with the decisions of the council in Jerusalem, usually dated somewhere around 48/49 AD. This council determined that Gentile believers were not obliged to the ceremonial aspects of the Torah (Acts 15). It seems unlikely this council could have taken place prior to the composition of Paul's letter to the Galatians (written to churches founded in the years 43/44 AD), otherwise, Paul would have naturally referred to the council's decision. After all, its position exactly supported Paul's. It is, therefore, reasonable to conclude that this letter was written prior to the council in Jerusalem, although we are unable to say exactly how much earlier.

Some insist to the contrary, that Paul was anxious to establish his authority in the eyes of the Galatian churches, which is why he chose not to refer to the decision arrived at in Jerusalem. This seems rather forced, more the product of a desire to determine a later date than the product of an objective view of facts. The council's decision could have served well to buttress Pauls' authority over against that of his opponents far more than his neglecting to refer to it.

The second issue has to do with the identity of those to whom the letter is addressed. This is largely due to the difference between Luke's terminology in Acts and that employed by Paul in his letters.

Galatia was a Roman administrative province in central and north of what is now modern Turkey. It included the cities of Iconium, Lystra and Derbe, mentioned in Acts (14:1–20). Paul and Barnabas visited these cities in the course of their first journey for the Gospel. However, the term "Galatia" also referred in those days to a vaguely-defined region in the northern part of modern Turkey, also included within the borders of the Roman administrative province but not encompassing it. Some hold to the view that this letter was addressed to churches in the northern region. However, there is no evidence Paul ever preached there, although we do read that he "went through" it (Acts 16:6). The region was in habited by Gauls (some of whom later settled in France and in Britain), which is how the region and later the province came by its name: Galatia means "the land of the Gaul's."

Luke consistently prefers to refer to cities and regions, not to provinces. Paul, on the other hand, generally refers to provinces. Paul's reference to the Galatians is, therefore, reference to the churches founded in the province of Galatia during the stage of his and Barnabas' first journey for the Gospel. This, of necessity, makes it likely that the letter to the Galatians is one of Paul's earliest letters, if not the earliest. That, in turn, confirms the assumption that it was composed prior to the council in Jerusalem.

The churches in Galatia were founded in 43/44 AD, some 5 years earlier than the council. Paul would have had to be away from Galatia for at least a short period before those whose views he opposes appeared. It would have also taken some time for the teachers of those views to have heard of the founding of the churches in Galatia, to organize and arrive on the scene. At least a few more months would have had to pass for Paul to hear of their teaching and decide to respond. Assuming something like a year after Paul and Barnabas left Galatia before the other teachers arrived, and about six months before Paul sat down to write the Galatians, it seems reasonable to say that this letter was written somewhere between 46–48 AD.

If those who prefer a later dating are right, then the only periods in which we might think that Paul preached the Gospel in northern Galatia would be in the course of his second evangelistic journey (50–55) or the third (55–57). This letter would, then be dated 52/53 AD at the earliest.

As to the similarities between this letter and that to the Romans, these would naturally arise out of the fact that the Apostle was dealing with the same matters. It is highly likely that, while writing to the church in Rome, he would refer to his earlier letter to the Galatians.

One of the features that distinguish this letter is that it is not addressed to an individual (such as Philemon, Timothy or Titus), nor to believers in a specific church (Such as Romans, Corinthians, Ephesians, Colossians and Philippians) but to the churches of Galatia (Galatians 1:1). Even the letter to the Ephesians, apparently a circular letter addressed to a number of churches, the copy we have on hand is addressed to the church in Ephesus.

Assuming the earlier date is correct, we may further conclude that the letter to the Galatians was addressed to the churches in Iconium, Lystra and Derbe. It is also possible that other churches had been established in the province, of which we know nothing.

There is no way to determine where the Apostle was when he wrote this letter. Various plausible suggestions have been made but none of them aid our understanding of what he wrote, so there is no point in reviewing them.

Why was this letter written?

Pauls' letter to the Galatians was written in response to a claim made by some who arrived in Galatia after he and Barnabas had preached there. These teachers held to the view that faith in the Messiah needs to be supplemented by adherence to the Mosaic Law and Jewish tradition. Here we come to the exegetical argument mentioned earlier.

There is an obvious, compelling logic to such a view. After all, faith in the Messiah is a distinctly Jewish affair, the product of the covenants, law, promises and actions of God in the history of the Jewish people. In other words, non-Jews who believe in Jesus have come over to the faith of the Jews. They believe in the God of Israel and now share the Faith that distinguished Jews from Gentiles for centuries. Should they not, therefore, embrace the fullest implications of that Faith, thereby bringing it to its fulfillment by submitting to laws and traditions that are so much part of it?

Paul thought otherwise. He believed that the fullest implications of the Faith of Israel, of its law and the promises made to the nation are to be found in the Messiah, and that the fulfillment of Israel's Faith is to be found in faith in the Messiah and in Him alone.

He further understood that another issue was at stake. It was not only an issue of Messiah versus the Law of Moses and Jewish tradition; it was an issue of God's work or ours, and therefore of law—any law, law in principle—and the accomplishments of the Messiah. So far as Paul was concerned, the Messiah did all that was necessary. There is no need or room to supplement His work by ours.

Paul therefore draws a careful distinction, arguing from the greater to the least. He argues against reliance on law of any kind for a greater spirituality, and therefore against reliance on keeping the Law of Moses and/or Jewish tradition. He does so by a careful, almost imperceptible distinction between law (without the definite article) and the Law (with the definite article). The first is law in principle—any law. The second is the Law of the covenant (the Torah) God made with Israel at Sinai.

This is most simply illustrated by what the Apostle has to say in 4:21, which literally says, "Tell me, you who wish to be subject to law, do you not listen to the Law?" In verse nine of the same chapter Paul speaks of the Galatians, who were being encouraged to embrace the Torah and Jewish tradition, as wanting to "return" to law-keeping. Of course, the Galatians were never subject to the Torah or to Jewish tradition. They had no previous share in the covenant of which the Law of Moses was a major part. In their inclination to submit to the Torah and to Jewish tradition they were reverting to a general law that is part and parcel of all false religions, including the error that had crept into Jewish thinking about the role of the Torah. That law dictated the relationship between people and the gods: divine goodwill and blessings were to be obtained by individuals obeying the law. *That* is the idea to which the Galatians were being encouraged to subscribe, and *that* is the view to which they were in danger of reverting.

The literalistic translation on which this commentary is based seeks to draw that attention by carefully following Paul's Greek and inserting the definite article only where Paul inserted it. As a further aid, when Paul speaks of the Law of Moses, I will capitalize, thus: Law. By this medium I hope we shall better understand why this letter was written. It is not a treatise against the Law of Moses or Jewish tradition; it is a clarion call to recognize the fact that salvation—all of it—is God's doing, not ours.

I have chosen to translate the Greek *Christos* by the Hebrew *the Messiah*, not because I object to speaking of our Lord as Christ (as my previous books clearly indicate) but because I believe doing so will help convey a sense that the more familiar *Christ* does not. People nowadays treat the title Christ as if it is a proper name. The significance of the title—almost always preceded in Greek and always in Hebrew by the definite article—is therefore lost and, in the case of this letter to the Galatians, it is a meaningful loss. The term Messiah intimates something important about our Lord. It points to Him as the fulfillment of the demands of the Law and the promises of the prophets. In context of the letter to the Galatians, that is an important truth.

One more point needs to be made about Pauls' language. Paul's letters were not written in lofty, classical Greek; they were written in everyday Greek, the kind used in the markets and in the course of human communication. For that reason, where the option was open to me and in an effort to stay as close to the text as possible, I preferred to translate into spoken, common-place English, rather than otherwise.

Finally, following the example of Scripture, I distinguish between faith (an attitude of trust, Matthew 6:30, Mark 11;22, Acts 6:5, Romans 3:25, 2 Corinthians 5:7) and the Faith (the content of the Gospel, what one believes, Acts 6:7, Galatians 1:23, Ephesians 4:13). I make that distinction by speaking of the attitude with a small f (faith) and of the content by a capital F (Faith).

LET'S SUMMARIZE

- This letter to a group of churches in the province of Galatia was probably written between 43–49 AD and is very likely the first of Paul's letters.

- The principles enunciated in the most mature of Paul's letters—that to the church in Rome—are already evident here, indicating a remarkable consistency as well as a development in understanding.

- The primary issue Paul addresses in this letter is the grounds of spiritual blessing: human merit or those of the Messiah. Human merit is mistakenly thought to be obtained through keeping the Mosaic Law and Jewish tradition. Paul insists that Jesus' merits are enjoyed through faith.

LET'S PRAY

Almighty God of grace and of mercy, You have given us Your Word to teach us how to think and live for Your glory. You have chosen to love us in spite of our sins. We long to love and serve You in response. Grant us the grace to understand Your Word, apply it to our hearts and live out its principles in our daily lives. Teach us to find our all in Jesus, Your Son and our Savior and Messiah, so that we never rely on ourselves but put the whole of our trust in Him, who is able to save to perfection. May Your Holy Spirit guide us, strengthen us, rebuke us as we study Your Word and encourage us by the sweet comforts of the Gospel, to the praise of Your name and for Jesus' sake. Amen.

QUESTIONS FOR DISCUSSION AND STUDY

1. What do you think would be the implications if this letter was written after the Acts 15 council in Jerusalem? If it was, why do you think Paul did not reference it here?

2. Create a list of the fundamentally essential doctrines of the Gospel. Can you find these taught—directly or indirectly—in the Old Testament? If so, where?

3. What is the relationship between the Faith and faith? Can one have the second without the first? Is the first of any use without the second?

Paul's Letter to the Church in Galatia
A Translation

¹ Paul, an apostle appointed, not by men and not through men but by Jesus the Messiah and God the Father, who raised Jesus from the dead, ² and all the brothers who are with me, to the churches in Galatia: ³ grace to you and peace from God our father and the Lord Jesus the Messiah, ⁴ who, in accordance with the will of God the Father, gave himself for our sins to bring us out of this present evil generation, ⁵ to whom the glory is due for age of the ages, Amen.

⁶ I'm surprised that you so quickly leave him who called you by the grace of the Messiah to a different gospel, ⁷ which isn't a similar one, only that there are those who are unsettling you and who want to distort the Gospel of the Messiah. ⁸ but even if we or an angel from heaven would proclaim to you a Gospel contrary to that which we proclaimed, let him be cursed. ⁹ Like we said before I say again now: if anyone is proclaiming to you a Gospel contrary to the one we proclaimed to you, let him be cursed. ¹⁰ And now: Is it men's approval I am seeking or God's? Am I trying to please men or God? If I were still trying to please men, I would not be a servant of the Messiah.

¹¹ I inform you, brothers, that the Gospel proclaimed by me is contrary to man, ¹² because I did not receive it from a man, nor did a human teach it to me, rather, I received it by way of a revelation of Jesus the Messiah. ¹³ You heard of the way I conducted myself previously in Judaism, that I was radically persecuting the church

of God and destroying it. [14] I advanced in Judaism beyond many countrymen of my age because I was all the more zealous for the traditions of my fathers. [15] But when he who chose me from my mother's womb and called me by his grace wanted [16] to reveal his Son in me to that I would proclaim him to the nations of the world, I immediately did not consult with flesh and blood. [17] Nor did I go up to Jerusalem, to the apostles who preceded me, but I went away, to Arabia and again returned to Damascus. [18] Then, after three years, I went up to Jerusalem to make Cephas' acquaintance, and I remained with him 15 days, [19] but I did not see any other apostle, except James, the Lord's brother.

[20] Take note, I am writing to you, I write in the presence of God. I am not lying.

[21] Then I went to the areas of Syria and Cilicia. [22] I was personally unknown to the churches in Judea, [23] only that they heard again and again, "he who persecuted us in the past is now proclaiming the Faith he tried to destroy," [24] and they praised God for what he did in me.

Chapter 2

[1] Then, after 14 years, I went up to Jerusalem again, with Barnabas. I also took Titus with me. [2] I went up in accordance with a revelation and I presented before them the Gospel that I proclaim among the nations of the world. I did this privately, in the presence of those respected among them, lest I be running or had been running to no end. [3] But even Titus, who was with me, who was a Greek, they did not force to be circumcised [4] because of false brothers who stole into the church undetected. They stole in to spy out our liberty, which we have in the Messiah, in order to enslave us. [5] Not even for an hour did we give in to them, and that so that the truth of the Gospel would continue with you. [6] And those who seemed to be respected (for whatever it was, I don't care. God does not differentiate between people), those "respected ones" added nothing to me. [7] To the contrary. They understood that I was entrusted with the proclamation of the Gospel to the uncircumcised just as Peter was entrusted with the proclamation of the Gospel to the

circumcised, 8 because he who worked through Peter in his mission to the circumcised worked through me in relation to the nations of the world.

9 James, Cephas, and John recognized the grace that was given me. Therefore, those who are apparently considered to be pillars in the church in Jerusalem gave me and Barnabas the right hand of fellowship, that we should go the nations of the world but they to the circumcised. 10 They only requested that we remember the poor, and I was eager to do the same thing.

11 But when Cephas arrived in Antioch, I opposed him to his face because he was guilty. 12 For before certain people arrived from James, he ate with non-Jews. But upon their arrival he withdrew and was separating himself from them because he feared the circumcised. 13 The rest of the Jews also acted hypocritically, so that even Barnabas was swept away by their hypocrisy.

14 But when I saw that they were not behaving in strict accordance with the truth of the Gospel, I said to Cephas in the presence of everyone: "If you, a Jew, live like a non-Jew and not like a Jew, why do you force the non-Jews to Judaize? 15 We, by nature, are Jews and not "Gentile sinners," 16 and we know that men are not justified by keeping a law but only through faith in the Messiah, Jesus. We too have believed in the Messiah Jesus, so that we would be justified through faith in the Messiah and not by law-keeping, because by law-keeping no one is justified.

17 "But if, by seeking to be justified in the Messiah, it turns out that we also are sinners, is the Messiah serving sin? It can never be! 18 But, if I reestablish what I have torn down, I make myself out to be a sinner!

19 "For I, through a law, died to law in order that I should live for God. 20 I was crucified with the Messiah, alongside him, and it is not me who is now living but the Messiah living in me, and the life that I now live in the flesh I live through faith in the Son of God, who loved me and gave himself for me. 21 I do not make the death of the Messiah into nothing—because if righteousness is by way of law, then there was no need for the Messiah to die."

CHAPTER 3

[1] Stupid Galatians! Who bewitched you, before whose eyes Jesus the Messiah was pictured crucified? [2] This is the only thing I want to learn from you: did you receive the Spirit by keeping some law or by hearing the Gospel in faith? [3] Are you so stupid? — You've begun in the Spirit and now you achieve perfection by the flesh?! [4] Have you suffered so many things for nothing—if it was in fact for nothing? [5] He who gives you the Spirit and works miracles among you, does he do it because a law is kept or through a hearing with faith?

[6] Abraham also "believed and it was attributed to him as righteousness." [7] So you should know that those who have faith are the sons of Abraham. [8] And the scripture, having seen in advance that God would justify the nations of the world through faith, announced the Gospel to Abraham: you will be a blessing to all the nations of the world. [9] So then, those who believe are blessed with Abraham, the believer, [10] and law-keepers are subject to a curse because it was written: "whoever does not continue in all the matters written in the scroll of the Law and do them is cursed."

[11] Well then, it is clear that no one is justified before God by a law because "by faith do the righteous live," [12] and the Law is not of faith, but whoever fulfills its commandments live by them. [13-14] The Messiah redeemed us from the curse that the Law imposes by becoming a curse for us (because it was written, "everyone who is hanged on a tree is cursed"), so that the blessing, that blessing promised Abraham, will reach the nations of the world through Jesus the Messiah and we would receive by faith the promised Spirit.

[15] Brothers, I speak in human terms: once a will, even a human one, is confirmed, no one cancels it or adds to it, [16] and the promises were given to Abraham and his seed. It was not written "seeds," referring to many, but to one, "and to your seed," who is the Messiah. [17] In other words, after God confirmed the will in the Messiah, the Law which came 430 years later cannot cancel it. If the Law had, in fact, cancelled it, it would have also cancelled the promise [18] because, if the inheritance is conditioned on law, the inheritance is no longer a promise. But God gave Abraham a promise.

[19] Well then, what was the Law for? It was added because of trespasses, until the seed for whom the promise was intended should come. It was given by means of angels and thorough a mediator ([20] and a mediator is not for one person, but God is one).

[21] So then, is the Law contrary to God's promises? It could never be! If there was a law that was capable of giving life, then righteousness would indeed come from law. [22] But the scripture imprisoned everything to sin so that, in Jesus the Messiah, the promise by faith would be given to those who believe.

[23] Before the coming of Faith we were held in custody, imprisoned for the Faith that was about to be revealed, [24] so that the Law was our mentor until the Messiah came, so that we would, by faith, receive righteousness. [25] But since the Faith has come, we are no longer subject to a mentor [26] because you are all sons of God through faith in the Messiah Jesus, [27] because every one of you who was baptized into the Messiah has clothed himself with the Messiah. [28] It is not possible that there still would be a Jew, nor a Greek. It is not possible that there still would be a slave, nor a freeman. It is not possible that still there would be male or female because you are all one in the Messiah Jesus, [29] and if you belong to the Messiah, you are the seed of Abraham, inheritors in accordance with the promise.

CHAPTER 4

[1] But, I say, for as long as the heir is a small child, he is no different in any way from a servant although he is the owner of everything, [2] rather, he is subject to a guardian and to house managers up to the time that the father determined in advance. [3] So too we. When we were little children we were subject to the most basic things of the world, [4] but when the fullness of time arrived, God sent his Son, who came into the world through a woman and was subject to law, [5] in order to redeem those who are subject to law so that we would be adopted as sons. [6] And because you are sons, God has sent the Spirit of his Son into our hearts, crying, "Abba! Father!" [7] so that you are no longer a slave but a son, and if a son then, through God, an Heir.

[8] In the past, when you did not know God, you served those who by nature are not gods. [9] But now, when you know God, or rather, now that you are known by God, how is it that you are turning again to the fundamental, weak and empty basics? Is it to these that you want to be enslaved again? [10] You take note of days and months and seasons and years! [11] I'm afraid for you, lest I exerted myself among you for nothing.

[12] Be like me because I am like you, brothers, I plead with you. You have not wronged me in any way. [13] And you know that because of a weakness in the flesh I proclaimed the Gospel to you in the past, [14] and you did not make light of the test to which you were put because of my flesh, nor did you despise me, but you received me as a messenger of God, like Jesus the Messiah. [15] Well then, where has your happiness gone? I testify concerning you that, if it were possible, you would have plucked out your eyes and given them to me— [16] and now, in telling you the truth, have I become your enemy? [17] They are zealous for you, but not for a good purpose. They want to separate you, [18] so that you would be zealous for them. It is always good to be zealous for a good thing, and not only when I am there with you.

[19] My children, for whom I experience the pains of childbirth again until Messiah is formed in you! [20] I want to be with you right now and to speak to you in a different way because I'm confused about you.

[21] Tell me, you who want to be subject to law, don't you listen to the Law? [22] It was written that Abraham had two sons, one was born from the slave woman and the other from the free one. [23] But he who was born from the slave woman was born according to the flesh, and the one who was born from the free, through the promise.

[24] These things are an illustration, because there are two covenants, one from Mount Sinai who gives birth to the enslaved, and who is Hagar, [25] and this Hagar is Mount Sinai, which is in Arabia, equal to the Jerusalem of today because she and her children are enslaved. [26] But the Jerusalem that is above is free, and she is the mother of all of us, [27] because it was written, "rejoice, barren one who did not

give birth, break out in songs, you who have not experienced the pains of childbirth, because the children of the desolate woman are more than those of the one who has a husband."

28 And you, brothers, like Isaac, are children of the promise, 29 and exactly as he who was born according to the flesh persecuted the one who was born according to the Spirit, so too now. 30 And what does the scripture say? "Send this slave woman and her son away, because the son of this slave woman will not take part in the inheritance alongside the son of the free woman." 31 For that reason, brothers, we are not from the slave woman but from the free.

Chapter 5

1 In the freedom to which the Messiah freed us stand firm and don't get entangled again in a yoke of slavery. 2 Here, I, Paul, tell you that if you become circumcised, you will gain nothing at all from the Messiah. 3 I testify to every circumcised person that he is obliged to keep the whole of the Law. 4 You, who are justified by law-keeping, have been cut off from the Messiah, you have fallen from grace. 5 We, in spirit, through faith, enthusiastically await the hope of righteousness. 6 Because, in the Messiah Jesus, circumcision affects nothing, nor does uncircumcision, only faith acting through love.

7 You were running well, who hindered from obeying the truth?

8 This conviction is not from him who called you.

9 A little bit of yeast causes the whole lump to rise.

10 I have confidence with regard to you in the Lord that you will not think differently, and that whoever is bothering you will bear the punishment he deserves, whoever he may be. 11 But I, brothers, if I still proclaim circumcision, why am I persecuted? In such a case the offense of the cross would be abolished. 12 I really wish that those who are unsettling you would cut themselves [off], 13 because you were called to freedom, brothers, only not to a freedom that becomes an opportunity for the flesh. Instead, serve one another in love, 14 because the whole of the Law is summarized in

one word: "love the other like you love yourself." [15] but if you bite and consume each other, be careful that you are not consumed by each other.

[16] And I say: behave according to the Spirit and you will under no circumstance gratify the desires of the flesh [17] because the flesh desires against the Spirit, and the Spirit against the flesh. These two oppose each other so that you are unable to do what you want to do. [18] But if you are guided by the Spirit you are not subject to law.

[19] What the flesh does is obvious: fornication, impurity, lewdness, [20] idolatry, sorcery, hostility, quarrels, jealousies, competitions, divisions, factions, [21] envy, drunken parties, and the like of which I warn you in advance as I warned you before, that those who are doing these kinds of things will not inherit the kingdom of God.

[22] But the fruit of the Spirit is love, joy, peace, patience, generosity, kindness, faithfulness, [23] humility, self-restraint—against such things there is no law, [24] and those who belong to Messiah have crucified their flesh with its desires and lusts. [25] We live by the Spirit, so we should conduct ourselves by the guidance of the Spirit. [26] Let's not be taken up with empty boasting, provoking one another, envying one another.

CHAPTER 6

[1] Brothers, if someone is caught in some trespass, you, the spiritual ones, restore him while looking humbly at yourselves, and be careful so that you are not tempted. [2] Each of you, carry the burdens of the other and in this way fulfill the Law of the Messiah, [3] because if someone thinks he is really something while he is nothing, he is deceiving himself.

[4] Everyone should examine his own actions, and then he would be able to boast, he and no one else, in what he has done. [5] Each will carry his own load.

[6] Those who are taught the message should share all good things with whoever is teaching him. [7] Don't be fooled: God must not be mocked, because whatever a person sows, that is what he will also

reap. [8] He who sows to his flesh, from the flesh will reap rot, but he who sows to the Spirit, from the Spirit will reap eternal life. So, let's not become tired of doing good [9] because, when the moment comes, we will reap if we do not tire. [10] For that reason, so long as we have opportunity, let's do good to all, and especially to those who belong to the household of faith.

[11] You see how I have written you with large letters by my own hand. [12] Those who want to look good in the flesh are the ones who force you to be circumcised, with the sole purpose that they not be persecuted for the sake of the cross of the Messiah Jesus, [13] because the circumcised are not law-keepers but they want you to be circumcised so that they would be able to boast in your fleshly circumcision. [14] But so far as I am concerned, it will never be that I would boast in anything but the cross of our Lord Jesus the Messiah, by which the world is dead so far as I am concerned, and I am dead so far as the world is concerned, [15] because circumcision and uncircumcision amount to nothing. The only important thing is a new creation. [16] Peace and grace to all who live according to this principle, and to God's Israel.

[17] And now, no one is to cause me trouble because I bear the scars of Jesus on my body. [18] May the grace of our Lord Jesus the Messiah be with your spirits, brothers, Amen.

CHAPTER 1

Opening Words
(GALATIANS 1:1–5)

[1] Paul, an apostle appointed, not by men and not through men but by Jesus the Messiah and God the Father, who raised Jesus from the dead, [2] and all the brothers who are with me, to the churches in Galatia: [3] grace to you and peace from God our father and the Lord Jesus the Messiah, [4] who, in accordance with the will of God the Father, gave himself for our sins to bring us out of this present evil generation, [5] to whom the glory is due for age of the ages, Amen.

Contrary to his practice in the rest of his letters, this letter opens without greetings, prayers or wishes until we come to verse 3. Paul turns to the issue that concerns him immediately after introducing himself. He is concerned with defending the Gospel that he preached to the Galatians over against efforts to distort it. In an effort to justify their views, certain teachers who arrived in Galatia raised doubts as to Paul's understanding of the Gospel and to the validity of his apostleship. The matter at hand is urgent, too important to leave room for niceties. There will be time for that later. Paul opens by declaring that he is an apostle appointed, not by men and not through men but by Jesus the Messiah and God the Father, who raised Jesus from the dead.

The apostle considers it important for his readers to recognize that he is not the founder of a new religion. He did not determine the content of the message he was preaching, nor is he the messenger of some great thinker. Plato did not send him, nor did Socrates. The apostles in Jerusalem did not send him either, nor did wise men or leaders of some religion. Paul's mission was not given to him by humans, although much-respected humans acknowledged his calling and ordained him publicly (Acts 13:2, Galatians 2:1-10). He had been appointed to preach the Gospel by Jesus the Messiah and God the Father, who raised Jesus from the dead.

Knowing that is what gives the Apostle such obvious confidence, leading to the ability to withstand efforts to persuade or influence him, regardless of all dangers and threats. Paul writes knowing that he is a messenger of the Messiah, a messenger of God. He therefore knows that the message he proclaims is the truth, the absolute truth, committed to him by the Messiah and by God the Father.

That being so, and in spite of the temptation to do otherwise, Paul does not dare deviate to the slightest degree from the truth committed to him. We will do well to ask ourselves if we are disciples of a human being, some influential teacher, for example, or if we really and truly examined our views in the presence of God. Are the conclusions at which we arrived truths that stand on their own, or have we embraced them because they serve us in some way? In other words, are we servants of the truth, or have we embraced a so-called truth to serve ourselves? If our conclusions are truly valid, they are objective truth. They stand above us and unequivocally oblige us. Indeed, they oblige all mankind to dedication and sacrifice.

Relative truth, "our" truth, lacks such validity. It is subject to every man's preference. It changes with the tide of opinion. The truth of God stands over us all, obliges us all, demands the obedience of us all with a dedication that knows no bounds and an ongoing sacrifice that never thinks in terms of loss or gain.

The apostle speaks of Jesus the Messiah and God the Father, who raised Jesus from the dead, in that order—a surprising one. He references the Messiah before God the Father! Imagine someone saying he was sent by Moses and God. How could one place God and Moses one beside the other? All the more so would it be unacceptable to place Moses *before* God, unless they are in some sense on par with one another.

The order in which Paul mentions the two is an expression of how the Apostle views the Messiah, and it is all the more impressive because it is incidental. Paul has a high view of the Messiah, and he takes that view so much for granted that he does not comment on it; he simply assumes it.

On the one hand the Messiah is Jesus, that is to say, He has a human name, He is a man among men. But He is not only man. He is equal to God (see John 5:18). Paul believes as does John: "In the beginning was the Word, and the Word was with God, and the Word was God ... And the Word became flesh and dwelt among us, and we have seen his glory, glory as of the only Son from the Father, full of grace and truth" (John 1:1, 14). By virtue of His sonship He is also the Messiah—the object of Israel's hope and the one through whom God is fulfilling all the purposes of His covenant with Israel. As such Jesus has a prior claim on the Jewish people's fealty, obedience and affection. They owe Him double duty by virtue of their Jewishness as well as their standing as humans. However, as we shall see, He is not the Messiah of the Jews only, but also of the non-Jews.

We should also note how Paul describes God. He is the Father, who raised Jesus from the dead. In this connection, the term Father serves to indicate the relationship between the Father and the Son in the one, eternal deity. God is the Father of Jesus in a manner and in a sense that are untrue of His relations with any others. That is why Jesus is also described as Lord. There are many lords in the world, but none as exalted as Jesus, and none whose right to rule exceeds His. He is Lord over all aspects of our lives because His lordship is divine. He is, therefore, not only our Lord but Lord over all creation, the Master of all in heaven, on earth and under the earth, He who determines their fate and is sovereign over their very existence and all that they do.

Paul further tells us that the Father is the one who raised Jesus from the dead. He did so as a testimony to the fact that Jesus' sacrifice was accepted by Him. It satisfied the Father's righteousness and laid thereby purchased the salvation of all for whose it was intended. The Messiah "was delivered up for our trespasses and raised for our justification" (Romans 4:25). God acts in the course of human history: the resurrection took place at a point of time, when God reversed the natural order of things and brought the Lord Jesus the Messiah up from the dead. The God of which the Gospel speaks is not a god far away, remote and disinterested from the course of events. He molds those events, guiding them with a sure hand in the direction to which He would have them go. He is not subject to history but its Lord.

As for Paul, he is no maverick, no lone ranger. His views are common among the believers. That is why he mentions that others—all the brothers who are with me—share what he is writing to the Galatians. Paul insists that his mission was given him by the Messiah and God the Father, but the test of that claim and of the message he proclaimed was to be found in confirmation received from the church of the Messiah of that day. He will later make sure to clarify that his message also received the approval of the Apostles in Jerusalem.

No one should dare ordain himself. No one should presume to be free of accountability to the church. Woe be to the person who is not subject to the watchful, authoritative eye of others in the Messiah. When Paul embarked onto his mission before the approval of the church to which he belonged (in Damascus and later in Jerusalem, in the first period of his walk with God), he wreaked havoc and no recorded good was accomplished.

Acts 9:28–31 indicates as much. Paul, driven by the urgency of his new discovery and the excitement of a new convert, thrilled with what he knew to be his calling, pre-empted the church's confirmation of that calling, embarked on a campaign in Jerusalem. He preached "boldly in the name of the Lord," "disputing with the Hellenists," yet no indication of any fruit of those efforts is given. The only indication of a response to his preaching is that his hearers "were seeking to kill him." The church in Jerusalem was by this time well acquainted with persecution, but "when the brothers learned" of the result of Paul's eager efforts, "they brought him down to Caesarea and sent him off to Tarsus." "Sent him off" the text says. Apparently, they made every effort to ensure this young, well-intentioned but misguided trouble-maker not only left the city, but was shipped off to Tarsus, his home-town. There, presumably chastened by his experience, he remained for an extended period, with no reported Christian activity, until invited assist to Barnabas in Syrian Antioch. Only then did the Holy Spirit speak to the church: the time had come and Paul was to accompany Barnabas in what turned out to be the first of his missionary journeys.

As a result ("So," as the Scripture puts it in Acts 9:31), "the church throughout all Judea and Galilee and Samaria had peace and (in contrast to the short period during which Paul was in Jerusalem) was being built up. And walking in the fear of the Lord and in the comfort of the Holy Spirit, it multiplied."

All that Paul is said to have achieved in the early days of his ministry is a name for himself (They heard again and again, he who persecuted us in the past is now proclaiming the Faith he tried to destroy. Galatians 1:23). It was later, when the Holy Spirit spoke to the church and Paul was ordained by the church for the mission (Acts 13:1–3), that his labors were manifestly blessed by God.

Paul learned to keep himself from the arrogant presumption that motivated many in his day and motivates many in ours. God taught him the advantage of self-effacing humility that recognizes the importance of submitting his views and sense of mission to the scrutiny of others. He learned that initiative, energy, talent and good intentions are not enough, nor is a sense of call by the Messiah. The church's acknowledgement of one's gifting and calling is necessary. Until such an acknowledgment was granted, "the brothers brought him down to Caesarea and sent him off to Tarsus. So the church throughout all Judea and Galilee and Samaria had peace and was being built up and, walking in the fear of the Lord and in the comfort of the Holy Spirit, it multiplied" (Acts 9: 30–31).

That is the logic of the standards God determined and Paul set forth in his letters to Timothy and Titus for those whom the church is to enlist for spiritual service. That is also the logic behind the fact that he provided the churches with those standards. Under guidance of the Spirit, he came to disbelieve in situations when an individual identifies his own good intentions and talents, recognizes an opportunity, and enlists in the service of the Gospel. In the providence of God, he had gone that way and saw its error. Most of the standards he set to Timothy and Titus were fundamentally moral, measured over the course of time by those who know the candidates best. God used Paul's own experience to inform him, and then guided him by His Spirit to write as he did to Timothy and Titus.

Paul writes to the churches in Galatia. We discussed this statement in our introduction. This letter was not addressed to a church but to a group of churches in the province of Galatia, which we identified as Iconium, Lystra and Derbe, the first churches Paul and Barnabas established in the course of their journeys for the Gospel. They visited these three cities during what turned out to be Paul's first of three such journeys. Apparently, sometime after they left Galatia, unnamed individuals arrived and sought to supplement what Paul and Barnabas taught by adding Jewish practices to the Galatians' faith. This letter to the Galatians is a response to such efforts.

As soon as the truth is proclaimed, counterfeits of all kinds emerge, which serve in the hands of Satan to divert us from the truth, often by way of apparently innocent additions. Such false teaching is often presented as helpful for the spiritual life but it, in fact, erodes true spirituality by changing the essence of the Faith simply by adding to it. We ought to be careful with what we hear, as with what we teach.

Paul goes on to write, grace to you, and peace from God our Father and the Lord Jesus the Messiah. Note the fact that he is reverting to the natural order: God the Father is mentioned before the Lord Jesus. The traditional greetings, commonplace in Paul's day, are transformed by the Apostle into an opportunity to proclaim the Gospel and present its essential features.

Paul repeats this greeting, with minor changes, in most of his letters. Here they serve as an introduction to what he has to say to the Galatians later on. The churches of Galatia were inadvertently inclined to deviate from the grace of God. Such a step would inevitably cause them to lose that sense of inner peace and the knowledge of being reconciled with God, both of which are the fruit of grace, and grace is the only valid basis for salvation, its one and only source.

As noted, the churches in Galatia were founded something like a year or so before this letter was composed (see the Introduction). Immediately following their founding, certain people arrived and embarked onto a campaign that sought to persuade the Galatian Christians to supplement their faith in the God of Israel with obedience to the Law of Moses and Jewish tradition.

There was a certain logic to their argument: after all, the Galatians had embraced what was distinctly a Jewish faith. They attributed their salvation to Israel's Messiah and viewed the Scriptures delivered to Israel—the Law, the Prophets and the Writings—as God's living Word. It would only be natural to expect them to subject themselves to the commandments of God in the Law, as well as to the interpretational precepts dictated by the wise men of Israel. It would make sense for them to be circumcised and become part of the nation of Israel.

In spite of its logic Paul stood firmly against such a perception because it implied that the Messiah had merely affected the initial salvation of sinners and, possibly, an assurance of their eternal future. Their holiness, God's presence, their relationship with Him and the measure of their understanding of Scripture were all made contingent on their willingness to proceed from the initial stage of faith and repentance to the supposedly higher, more advanced stage of conducting themselves in accordance with Israel's traditions.

Another reason Paul opposed such a view was that it divided the church of the Messiah into two groups: those who remained at the lower level of spiritual life, and the more advanced, whose righteousness and spiritual supremacy were to be seen in their observance of Israel's traditions: circumcision, celebration of the Holy Days, maintaining the dietary laws, and so on.

In so doing they undermined the Gospel, which teaches that salvation, sanctification, blessing, and enlightenment are the product of God's grace, and that the objects of that grace are all—equally—full-fledged equal members of the body of the Messiah. They all enjoy God's presence and receive his blessing, and their only merit before God is that obtained by the Messiah through his sacrificial death and resurrection—in other words, Messiah did it all. There was nothing more to add.

Grace, of course, means favor one does not deserve. The grace of which the Gospel speaks is expressed in the forgiveness of sins, freedom from bondage to sin, the transformation of sinners' hearts, God's ongoing blessing in their lives and eternal blessing in the presence of God. All this is given to sinners, to rebels against God who broke His commandments, defiled, abused and misused the world He created, and shaped their lives to please themselves instead of pleasing Him.

Peace is the absence of hostility and the existence of good-will between two or more. The peace of which the Gospel speaks has two aspects. The first is the absence of hostility toward men on the part of God and His good-will toward them in spite of their sin. The other is man's acknowledgement of God's right over man, all he is and all he has, and the lack of hostility on man's part toward God, replaced by a sincere desire to honor Him and do His will.

Both are what the Apostle wishes the believers in Galatia, and what we should wish ourselves. Nothing more is necessary.

The Lord Jesus the Messiah who, in accordance with the will of God the Father, gave himself for our sins to bring us out of this present evil generation. These words of the Apostle are so full of meaning they exceed anything we imagine.

The words, gave himself for our sins, refer of course to what Messiah did for the redeemed. The reference is not only to His death but to the whole fabric of His life from that moment in eternity when the Father, Son and Spirit decided to act for the salvation of sinners, through Messiah's conception in Mary's womb, His birth, amazing life, death in our place bearing the guilt of our sin, His resurrection, ascent to heaven where He now sits at the right hand of the Father, ruling the universe and interceding for us as our sovereign king, our faithful priest and our wise, all-knowing prophet, the Lord of salvation.

Every one of these acts of giving are necessary for our salvation. The Lord Jesus, in spite of His amazing glory, willingly gave Himself for our sakes. He is not only the messenger of God the Father's love; He acted out of His own love, not only for the Father but for us. But note! Paul does not say the Messiah gave Himself for everyone's sins (if He had done so, everyone will assuredly be saved), but that that He gave himself for our sins—the sins of specific individuals. Paul will reiterate this amazing truth at the end of Chapter Two of his letter.

The focal point of the Lord Jesus the Messiah's giving Himself is that He took upon Himself the guilt of our sins and died the death we deserve, so that we would have life (or should I not rather say, LIFE!) based upon His merits. He took our place and became the object of God's terrible, righteous hatred of sin. He purchased life for us by His life and death. He purchased an assured, a perfect salvation to which nothing is lacking. By virtue of His merits, we are reconciled to God.

There is more. Paul says that the Messiah gave Himself for our sins to bring us out of this present evil generation. The salvation He purchased for us consists of more than just the forgiveness of our sins. The apostle will write of this again when, in his letter to the Christians in Rome, when he will point to the power of God to save and then describe the consequences of that salvation, including his own inner transformation by the work of the Holy Spirit, so that he earnestly loves God's law and longs to shape his life according to it (Romans 1:16, 7:14 to the end of the chapter).

In other words, salvation includes a complete change in the direction of our lives. It includes freedom from Satan's shackles, from the power and influence of this present evil generation. If we truly have been saved, we are no longer subject to this world. We are no longer obliged to its standards. We are no longer bound to its point of view; we have been born again. The Holy Spirit lives in us. We have tasted the grace of God and recognized His right to be honored in everything that happens in this, His world. He has become the focus of our lives and His grace the foundation of our joys. All we have from Him is given by grace.

This present evil generation to which the Apostle refers was (and is, down to the present day) the generation that worships, power, success, money and influence, that despises the weak, that admires achievers and measures achievement by material and physical standards rather than moral and spiritual ones. Such a generation believes it is more important to make money than to love God, that it is more impressive to run faster than anyone else than to be kind, humble and honest. In such a generation, only those thought to be naive are kind, humble and honest. God is, at best, to be used and displays of devotion to Him serve as a cloak for self-indulgence: "God in not in all their thoughts."

Such is the generation that worships man, whose heroes are superman, iron-man, wonder-woman, free of human limitations and excused of obligations, at liberty to do whatever he wishes: he defines his gender regardless of moral and physical realities. He determines his values. He chooses the course of his life. He denies God and sees in himself and in his enjoyments the purpose of all things.

The Gospel runs contrary to such a view. The Gospel reminds us that man's value is the product of the fact that he is created by God, not the happenstance consequence of a blind chemical or physical reaction. His moral value is not the product of his own achievements or his place in the evolutionary ladder (can someone tell me why an amoeba has moral value at all?) but the fruit of God's grace, who formed man in His image and placed him above all the creatures. There is no room for human presumption, no grounds for pride, no basis on which to boast. If man glories, he should glory in the Lord.

The Gospel places God at the head of all things, while this present evil generation places man there. The Gospel informs us that man is unable to save himself, nor can he contribute anything to his salvation, not even a little. Nor can he secure his ongoing salvation or the ultimate level of spiritual life. The Gospel insists that all we have from God is unmerited: we do not deserve it. It is a gift of God's grace. The Lord Jesus the Messiah gave himself to bring us out of this present evil generation, which is evil precisely because it dares to think otherwise.

The Messiah acted for us in accordance with the will of God the Father. The title Father here refers to the relations between the God the Father and God the Son, not to His fatherhood of all mankind. There was, is, and ever will be full agreement between the Father and the Son (as there is with the Spirit), because the three are one. The Father sent the Son and the Son came of his own volition. Our salvation is the consequence of the will of the Father, the Son and the Holy Spirit, the fruit of the one act they perform together. They may be distinguished the one from another but they can never be separated. God the Father, Son and Spirit is our savior, in all the majesty and greatness of His being.

To whom the glory is due for age of the ages, Amen. It is not altogether clear from this passage whether it is God the Father or God the Son who is to be glorified. The syntax seems to indicate that the reference is to the

Father, because He is the last to be mentioned in the previous statement. In any case, the glory of one is the glory of the other. The Father is glorified in the Son and the Son in the Father. The Father would have all men glorify the Son, and all the Son does has as its purpose that the Father might be glorified in Him.

The will of the Father is that all mankind should honor and glorify the Son as they do the Father. "If anyone does not honor the Son, he does not honor the Father, who sent him" (John 5:23). Jesus, the Son of God, honors the Father, and we honor the Father by honoring the Son. Therefore, it is ultimately immaterial whether Paul is saying that the Father should be glorified, or that the Son should be. The result is the same, and our salvation is intended for the glory of both Father *and* Son.

Contrary to what is often thought, the beating heart of the Gospel is not man's happiness but the glory of God. Jesus gave Himself for our sins to bring us out of this present evil world because that is the way God chose to be glorified. Man's salvation does not begin with man's need, nor does it end in his happiness. It begins with God's right to be glorified and ends with God receiving the glory that is His due for all generations, to eternity and beyond.

The essence of what lies in the future is the glory God will receive. The song of the kingdom is a song of praise to God. Our eternal blessing in the Messiah is that we will at last be enabled to love, value, worship, and praise our Creator, Sustainer, and Savior with cleansed, sincere hearts. This should also be the essence of our hope, the goal to which we aspire, the focus of our service and the purpose of our lives.

Let's Summarize

- Paul insists that the Gospel he preaches was taught him by God rather than through the instrumentality of man. It is, therefore, absolute truth. We should trust it, believe in it and live by it. Do we? Do we really?

- Paul recognized the importance of being subject to scrutiny. He was not self-appointed, nor did he labor alone. Others testified by their support to the validity of his calling. Are we willing to serve alongside others and under their oversight?

- Truth is important in order to true spiritual life. We should labor to know and understand truth, and then shape our lives by it.

- The Messiah is equal to God the Father. He too is to be worshipped.

- We have ample reason to worship and praise Him because He secured every part of our salvation. He did it all. Nothing need be added.

- The Messiah freely gave Himself for our salvation, a salvation which consists of more than forgiveness and wistful hope; it includes actual deliverance from the rule of sin and complete confidence as to the future.

- It was God the Father's will to glorify Himself by saving us. He sent the Messiah for that purpose. Ours must now be to bring Him glory.

LET'S PRAY

Eternally glorious God, Master, Ruler, and Savior of all, three in one and one in three, we adore You for Your amazing beauty. We thank You for the kindness You have shown us in the Gospel. You have granted us solid truth on which to build our lives. You have granted us the fellowship, encouragement and oversight of the church, in which You work by Your Holy Spirit. Teach us to understand and love the truth until it becomes a vital part of our thinking. We cannot stand on our own; move us to seek the scrutiny of others. Teach us to sincerely worship and obey the Son, our Messiah, and to seek in Him alone in the fullness of Your grace. Grant to us the ability to live to Your glory, as those who have been delivered from the power of sin and handed over to righteousness. Glorify Yourself in us, we plead, in Jesus' name, Amen.

QUESTIONS FOR DISCUSSION AND STUDY

1. Discuss: Is truth relative (or is it our understanding that is relative)? Can we arrive at a reasonable measure of knowledge of the truth? If we can, how? If not, by what standard should we live?

2. Enlarge on the importance of serving the Lord within the context of the church's oversight.

3. Consider ways in which our view of truth shapes our spiritual life.

4. To what extent and how do we evidence our deliverance from sin, rather than mere forgiveness, in daily life?

5. Discuss the implications of God's glory being the ultimate object of the plan of salvation.

CHAPTER 2

No Other Gosepel
(GALATIANS 1:6–10)

6 I'm surprised that you so quickly leave him who called you by
the grace of the Messiah to a different gospel, 7 which isn't a similar one, only that there are those who are unsettling you and who
want to distort the Gospel of the Messiah. 8 but even if we or an
angel from heaven would proclaim to you a Gospel contrary to
that which we proclaimed, let him be cursed. 9 Like we said before
I say again now: if anyone is proclaiming to you a Gospel contrary
to the one we proclaimed to you, let him be cursed. 10 And now:
Is it men's approval I am seeking or God's? Am I trying to please
men or God? If I were still trying to please men, I would not be a
servant of the Messiah.

I'm surprised that you so quickly leave him who called you by the grace
of the Messiah to a different gospel, which isn't a similar one. A short while
had passed from the first days of the Galatians' faith in the Messiah. Already, there were among them those who sought to twist the Galatian's
understanding of the Gospel. They sought to divert them from a complete reliance on the grace of God to avenues of human presumption by
relying on law-keeping and adhering to traditions.

Paul considers this a grievous deviation because it not only turns
devotees away from the principles of the Gospel, from a Christian world
view and from a long list of biblical truths; it is also a direct affront to

God, who had called them to himself by the grace of the Messiah. Unwittingly, the Galatians are in danger of turning away from God and His grace to presumed spiritual abilities that purport to earn merit in His sight.

Mankind's relationship with God is, and can only be based on grace, and on grace alone, because the gap between God's holiness and human beings is so colossal that it cannot be bridged by any other means. Man's very existence is fruit of the grace of God, because it is by grace that God created him. It was grace that accorded man status, ability, and a calling apart from which there would be no reason for his existence. Even if man had never sinned, the absolutely perfect, eternal, and uncontingent holiness of God, before whom the angels of heaven hide their face in loving and adoring terror, is like a consuming fire that would obliterate puny man in but a moment.

All the more obvious is that sinful man cannot approach God on the grounds of merit. Had he committed but a single sin in the course of his life, there would be no way he could atone for it. God is too pure to look upon sin. He cannot bear the presence of wrong-doing (Habakkuk 1:13). He is utter, unimaginable, beautiful, terrifying holiness. "What is man, that he can be pure? Or he who is born of a woman, that he can be righteous? Behold, God puts no trust in his holy ones, and the heavens are not pure in his sight" (Job 15:14–15). Man can approach God only on the basis of grace.

Yet, Paul says, God in His grace calls man to approach. The Galatians are reminded that God called [them] by the grace of the Messiah. This calling is not universal. The majority of mankind never even hear it. Paul says that God called them, the Galatians (called you). It was a call directed at particular individuals in a particular place at a particular time. Paul is speaking of a divine initiative, executed by the Holy Spirit that not only causes individuals to hear the Gospel but also to heed it. The Holy Spirit works in the secret recesses of people's hearts, regenerates them, moves them to acknowledge their sin and inability, and causes them to turn to God in honest repentance that recognizes the simple fact salvation is dependent on God and on God alone.

That is the calling of which Paul wrote in his letter to the Romans (8:29–30), when he pointed out the exact parallel that exists between those appointed to salvation and those who are brought to enjoy its fullness (see also Romans 1:6, 9:24, 1 Corinthians 1:2, 7:17, Galatians 1:15, 5:13, Ephesians 4:4, 1 Thessalonians 2:4, 2 Thessalonians 2:14, 1 Timothy 1:9,

1 Peter 1;5, 2:9, 5:10, 2 Peter 1:3, Jude 1). This call is not heard merely in one's ears; by the secret, powerful workings of the Spirit of God, it resounds in one's heart and accomplishes the purpose for which it was made. It is the first stage in the new birth.

God has called the Galatians to one Gospel, yet they had left if for a another. This is a highly significant statement and we will be wise to dwell on it. Some deviations are more significant than they appear to be. After all, the Galatians were not inclined to deny the deity of the Messiah, did not claim to be able to atone for their sins and did not ignore other truths found in Scripture or proclaimed by the Apostles. On the contrary, they admired Jesus, recognized Him to be the sole Savior of sinners and longed to be faithful members of their congregations. They considered themselves true believers and would have undoubtedly been deeply offended if anyone doubted the sincerity of their faith or their affection for the Messiah.

And yet, Paul describes the teaching to which they were inclined as a different gospel, contrary to the true Gospel of Jesus. As we shall see more clearly later, they were, in fact, denying the Gospel of God's grace although they had no intention to do so. It is worth reminding ourselves at this juncture how important it is to ensure we understand the Gospel correctly, and that great caution is needed if we wish to continue in God's ways. The very best intentions could become the occasion for a departure that will lead us, unintentionally, to a different gospel.

Paul says that the Galatian Christians were inclined to follow what he described as a different Gospel. He now explains there is a stark difference between the Gospel Paul and Barnabas proclaimed in Galatia and that being taught by the false teachers against whose views the Apostle is writing. Their Gospel isn't a similar one. It is, in fact, dissimilar in spite of the surface similarities of which it boasts. Only that there are those who are unsettling you and who want to distort the Gospel of the Messiah. It is a wholly dissimilar, gospel. Different, not the same. Paul employs two Greek words, indicating an important lesson: similarity does not necessarily mean identity. In fact, similarity can be misleading. When dealing with important issues, caution is necessary.

Different gospel does not mean the same Gospel in different terms but a different one in similar terms. Two very different Gospels are in view. They differ from one another at the very core. One is a counterfeit. It apes the true Gospel but lacks its power, just as a counterfeit bill is similar to a real one but lacks its buying power. It uses the same terminology, but with a different emphasis and, ultimately, a different meaning. Due to the external similarities, we are in danger of thinking that we are following the Gospel proclaimed by the Messiah and His disciples, but the similarities are misleading. The shell of the Gospel is retained, but its essence has been replaced by something very different.

These words convey a warning. An ancient Hebrew saying instructs us: "Don't look at the bottle but at what's in it." There is a good deal of wisdom in such advice. Similarity can be deceptive. The content of the message, the principles and practical implications that emerge from the content are all-important and should be measured by their implications. Every action has conceptual implications, just as every concept has practical consequences.

We are called upon by the Gospel to be thoughtful people whose views and actions are the product of information that we examined, proved reliable, and understood as thoroughly as possible. We are not to be blind followers. We are not to be groupies. It is simply not enough to have firm opinions, they must be the product of an acquaintance with facts, in this case, with the facts of Scripture, and of a considered, balanced, and courageous comprehension of what is stated.

Among those who sought to persuade the Galatians of the validity of the views they presented the Apostle says, there are those who are unsettling you and who want to distort the Gospel of the Messiah. Of course, none of them consciously chose to distort the Gospel. They had no premeditated intention to teach what they knew to be false. To the contrary. They viewed their version of things to be the peak of Gospel spirituality, its inevitable consequence. They aspired after the most and the best of God's praise, and they taught as they best understood. It would be a mistake to doubt their sincerity.

But sincerity is no defense against error. Many err sincerely. Rather than consciously denying the Gospel, they distort it unwittingly. Regardless of their sincerity, the greater their error, the greater the distance between their gospel and that of the Messiah.

Paul is telling the Galatians that the newly-arrived teachers, who distorted the Gospel, were unsettling them. That is to say, they were robbing them of the only basis for true stability. So long as any part of our salvation, however tiny, is up to us, we have no solid basis on which to rest. If the initial stage of our salvation comes from Christ, but it is up to us to proceed beyond that stage, to achieve any kind of "fullness" or to ensure that we "remain saved," we can never know if we have done enough (nor will we ever be able to do enough). According to this theory, God's grace was the commencement of our salvation. The rest depends on us. What we do or do not do are the determining factors—and it does not matter if the reference is to moral deeds, evangelistic efforts, Sabbath-keeping or anything else.

Our confidence must be established on solid, immovable rock that cannot be moved—ever! Such a basis exists only in the grace of God through Jesus the Messiah. No chain is stronger than its weakest link. Whatever depends on us is unreliable because we are the weakest link in the chain of our salvation.

But even if we or an angel from heaven would proclaim to you a Gospel contrary to that which we proclaimed, let him be cursed. Like we said before I say again now: if anyone is proclaiming a Gospel contrary to the one we proclaimed to you, let him be cursed. The apostle's language is razor-sharp. He believed, contrary to the view so common today in certain circles (including Christian circles), there is a stark difference between truth and error, true and false, light and darkness.

While our understanding of truth is inevitably relative, truth is not. The message of the Bible is certainly not relative. Not only so, but some deviations from the truth are so serious that they must be publicly exposed and made the object of a curse. The apostles believed that every individual is entitled to his own opinions in relation to one another (Romans 14:1–4, 1 Corinthians 8:1–12, 10:29). But they also believed that, before God, we are entitled to no opinion but the truth. Every individual is duty-bound by God to embrace the truth. Should he prefer a lie, he will give account for that to God. He will bear his just punishment and will have no excuse—*that* is how important truth is. That is how important it is that we understand the Gospel correctly.

We should, therefore, be very careful with regard to the truth, even if it turns out to be inconvenient. We would do better to suffer loss and pain on earth for the sake of truth than to suffer eternal lack and endless pain without end. We would do better to lose an eye, a hand, or a foot than to go down to hell with our body intact.

Paul was convinced as to the truth he proclaimed precisely because it was not his but that which God in his grace forced upon him. After all, Paul had been engaged in persecuting the church for the truth it maintained. He sincerely believed he was rendering God faithful service. At first he was a passive but enthusiastic supporter of Stephen's murder, stoned to death for his faith in Jesus. Later, Paul became violent in his treatment of believers. Having sought and obtained authorization from the Chief Priests, he was on his way to Damascus to arrest believers there and bring them to face the wrath of the authorities in Jerusalem.

He was determined to do all in his power to destroy the fledgling church, but God stopped him in his tracks—literally, conquered his heart, and transformed him into a messenger of the very Gospel he previously hated. As Paul proceeds in this letter to the Galatians, he will detail additional reasons why he is so confident of the truth of Gospel he proclaimed, so much so that he is willing to lay a curse on those who oppose it.

We are not the messengers of a movement or of a religious leader. We do not call on people to believe in Christianity. We are messengers of God, conveying His message and calling on people to put their trust in Him. We are not interested in adding the scalps of souls to our belt, members to our church or subscribers to our religious teachings. We long for all mankind—Jews and non-Jews, men and women, young and old, free and bound, from every race and people—to love God, honor Him, and live their lives as He would have them live. To that end we tell them that they must turn from themselves and their sin, ask God to forgive them for Christ's sake, to change their hearts by the power of the Holy Spirit. Then, receiving such gracious forgiveness, we call them to embark on a new way of life, very different from the way they now live.

If you think otherwise, you had better examine your heart: have you truly repented? Has God worked in your heart and changed it? Are you, in fact, saved? Forgiven? Made new? Have you been born again by the grace of God and become a child of God?

It would be good for us to ask: do we love the truth like Paul loved it? Are we faithful to the truth as he was? Will we defend the truth at any cost, or will we prefer to have people like us and therefore saw off the sharp corners of the Gospel, so they do not offend those who hear us? Dare we say with the Apostle, even if we or an angel from heaven would proclaim to you a Gospel contrary to that which we proclaimed, let him be cursed. Like we said before I say again now: if anyone is proclaiming a Gospel contrary to the one we proclaimed to you, let him be cursed!?

Paul goes on, challenging his readers and reminding them of an important reality: and now: is it men's approval I am seeking or God's? Am I trying to please men or God? If I were still trying to please men, I would not be a servant of the Messiah. The Apostle understood full well what we need to understand, of which we need to remind ourselves repeatedly:

we ought not adopt views or do things to find favor with men but with God. All too often there is a fundamental contradiction between pleasing people and pleasing God. We have to choose between the two.

A person who lives for this world has but one standard by which to measure reality because he is unaware of the existence of any other but the immediate, the visible and the tangible—an existence that has but a limited time-span. Ultimately, such a person can only make short-term decisions, valid for 30 or 40 or 70 years. But there is another aspect to reality, more real than the one in which we now live: eternity, to which there is no limit. Whoever recognizes that reality also recognizes a universe of values in which there is a tremendous difference between good and evil. Such a person has a system of values that far exceed immediate needs or wants.

The fear of God provides life in the present with depth and breadth that are not possible where such fear is not found. It gives eternal meaning to the life we live while equipping us to lead lives of value and of meaning. It also enormously increases our understanding of the implications of our actions. A life conducted for eternity impacts life on earth in fundamental ways. Paul knew this to be true. That is why he sought to be faithful to the Gospel of the Messiah and to please God, even at the cost of popularity.

We value being liked. A good measure of the way we view ourselves does not issue from the Word of God—from the fact that we were created in God's image, that we are called to serve God, that our talents and the limits of our abilities were determined by God, that He shaped the circumstances of our lives so as to equip us for His service. Instead, they are the product of how other people view us, especially whether or not they like us.

That is why we often hesitate or even avoid doing the right thing. We fear that those around us will react negatively. We want to belong. We market ourselves by way of the electronic media which our modern world provides, publicize our successes, make light of our failures and try by all kinds of means to be appreciated by others. We consider it important to know how many "likes" we've received on FaceBook, how many views on Instagram, how many actually read the inanities we shared or were impressed with the photos we posted.

Anyone so deeply involved in being liked by people enslaves himself to them. He is no longer his real self, ultimately; he comes to be disliked precisely because people are attracted to individuals who dare be honest and act morally in spite of social risks. They find it hard to respect a flatterer, someone who lacks a moral backbone. They are willing to make use of his weaknesses and present the façade of friendship that is really just a means to take advantage of him, another expression of their lack of respect. Sadly, this needs to be said to many of us who claim to be disciples of Christ. We're much better Christians when others are around to observe us.

Paul understood all that, even though he did not think in modern terms. That is why, he here posits the question: and now: is it men's approval I am seeking or God's? Am I trying to please men or God? and then dares to say: If I were still trying to please men, I would not be a servant of the Messiah.

That is the choice we need to make. Will we conduct our lives for the glory of God or for the fading glory to be had from fellow-humans? Will we dare live courageously, humbly, purely, and in the happy fear of God in spite of the world's reaction? Will we dare be identified as those who fear God and put their trust in the Messiah, or will we prefer the praise of men and the short-term successes this world offers over against blessing in the world to come? Whom do we serve? Let there be no mistake: if we seek to please men, we cannot serve the Messiah.

Let's Summarize

- Do we understand that God is terrifyingly holy? Do we perceive the beauty of His holiness? Do we worship Him, or have we bought into the modern idea of "celebrating" Him as if God is not a person but some kind of event?

- Appearances may be deceptive. Are you a carefully thoughtful Christian? How can you develop more Christian thoughtfulness?

- Are you willing to stand for the truth, even when it is unpopular, when it might cost you? Think back on times when you could have been more faithful to the truth and seek the Lord in respect to those occurrences.

Let's Pray

Awesome, beautiful, holy God, Lord of all grace and truth, open our eyes and enlarge our hearts so that we have a vivid sense of Your endless greatness. Teach us to fear You lovingly and to love You with sincere passion. Grant us to fear and adore Your holiness, so that we fashion our thoughts and our conduct according to the Gospel. May we always prefer Your truth to ours, Your ways to ours, Your will to our own. For Jesus' sake, forgive our failings and teach us to rest on Your grace rather than on our purported merits, so that our lives reflect the wonder of the Gospel and others be drawn to love and serve You. Through Jesus the Messiah, Amen.

QUESTIONS FOR DISCUSSION AND STUDY

1. Why and to what extent does the holiness of God necessitate grace? What does this mean in practical terms?

2. Find three biblical examples of God unilaterally calling people to Himself. What may be learned from these instances.

3. Discuss the importance and practical value of truth in the spiritual life. We cannot serve the Messiah and serve men at the same time. Why is that true?

CHAPTER 3

The Confirmation of Paul's Gospel
(GALATIANS 1:11–24)

[11] I inform you, brothers, that the Gospel proclaimed by me is contrary to man, [12] because I did not receive it from a man, nor did a human teach it to me, rather, I received it by way of a revelation of Jesus the Messiah. [13] You heard of the way I conducted myself previously in Judaism, that I was radically persecuting the church of God and destroying it. [14] I advanced in Judaism beyond many countrymen of my age because I was all the more zealous for the traditions of my fathers. [15] But when he who chose me from my mother's womb and called me by his grace wanted [16] to reveal his Son in me to that I would proclaim him to the nations of the world, I immediately did not consult with flesh and blood. [17] Nor did I go up to Jerusalem, to the apostles who preceded me, but I went away, to Arabia and again returned to Damascus. [18] Then, after three years, I went up to Jerusalem to make Cephas' acquaintance, and I remained with him 15 days, [19] but I did not see any other apostle, except James, the Lord's brother.

[20] Take note, I am writing to you, I write in the presence of God. I am not lying.

[21] Then I went to the areas of Syria and Cilicia. [22] I was personally unknown to the churches in Judea, [23] only that they heard again and again, "he who persecuted us in the past is now proclaiming

the Faith he tried to destroy," ²⁴ and they praised God for what he did in me.

Paul now reverts to describing the source of the Gospel he proclaimed. Its authority was the product of the fact that it came from God. It was not the fruit of any man's religious ideas, however sincere or wise. The Apostle is describing the circumstances due to which he can make such a claim.

There is little room for doubt that Paul first heard the Gospel, even if it was a distorted version, from its opponents. What he heard is what motivated him to persecute the believers in the first place. Obviously, then, he rejected the Gospel and, when he was brought to faith by an extraordinary divine intervention on the way to Damascus, he did not sit at the feet of some believing teacher to study the Gospel's deeper implications. He could sincerely say of the Gospel, I did not receive it from a man, nor did a human teach it to me.

A short while after his baptism, Paul went out to the Arabian desert, studied, thought, prayed, read, corrected, and deepened his acquaintance with the facts of the Gospel and his understanding of their implications. God worked in his heart, confirming what he read. That is how he received it by way of a revelation of Jesus the Messiah. Only afterward did he return to Damascus and fling himself into proclaiming the Gospel which he now embraced. He makes no claim here to visions or to extraordinary means of revelation. Although he was gifted with some such in the course of his life, never did they have anything to do with the contents of the Gospel. In that sense, Jesus reveals Himself to us by the same means He revealed Himself to Paul.

At this early stage he did not understand the role of the church in a Gospel calling. That is why he took it upon himself to act independently, motivated by a zeal untempered by knowledge. Doing so only caused damage to the believers in Damascus, who had to repair that damage, among other ways by sending Paul back to Jerusalem. Sincerity and zeal are necessary, but they are far from enough.

The transformation Paul underwent was revolutionary: You heard of the way I conducted myself previously in Judaism. Paul uses the past tense here because one aspect of that revolution was that he came to understand that the way to God was not through Judaism, nor even through meticulous adherence to the Law, but through the Messiah. For that reason, he broke away from Judaism, reverting to the Bible and therefore to the Messiah. Judaism became a matter of the past.

It is worth noting that Paul speaks of his devotion to Judaism, that is to what he will describe in just a moment as the traditions of my fathers. He now understands what he did not understand then: regardless of his best intentions, his devotion at that time was not to the service of God and his worship, but to a religion and its traditions.

As a result of his devotion to Judaism, he says, I was radically persecuting the church of God and destroying it. He viewed every departure from Jewish things in terms of a departure from God's ways. Because he was so devoted to his religion, he set out to defend it against its opponents, real or imagined, whom he viewed as threatening its role in the life of the nation. He contrasted Judaism with the church of God, and now prefers the latter to the former.

Before he had come to put his trust in the Messiah, Paul says, I advanced in Judaism beyond many countrymen of my age because I was all the more zealous for the traditions of my fathers. Again, note that Paul speaks in the past tense and that his devotion was not to God but to his national traditions. Now, at the time of writing, he is no longer zealous for those traditions.

In the past he was altogether given to their defense. Tradition took the place of truth. The tradition of Paul's forefathers and his nation took precedence over God. He was so devoted that he advanced in Judaism beyond many countrymen of his age. He became a disciple of one of the most famous Jewish Rabbis in history. He left Tarsus, the city of his birth, and travelled to Jerusalem to sit at the feet of Raban Gamliel. When the Gospel began to be proclaimed, he enlisted in the fight against it and was on his way to wreak havoc on the believers in Damascus.

But when he who chose me from my mother's womb and called me by his grace wanted to reveal his Son in me to that I would proclaim him to the Gentiles ... That is how Paul describes the act of God that completely altered the course of the Apostle's life. God overcame his opposition, conquered his heart, and made him subject to the Messiah.

Salvation is always an eternally predetermined act of God. Like Paul, we are all chosen before the foundation of the world. Our salvation is never the product of convincing arguments, the attractiveness of people's lives or of their ability to appeal to our emotions. The new birth is always from above, by the Spirit, at God's initiative—and God is not limited in any way, certainly not by man. He changes men's wills and moves their hearts as He sees fit. Yes, we explain, we persuade, we seek to reflect the Gospel in our lives, but we ought never exert pressure, never manipulate or mislead anyone in an effort to bring him to faith; salvation is God's work. Nor ought we draw back when faced with opposition. The Gospel is God's power to save. We trust it. We believe in it. We make room for it to do its own work.

Immediately, Paul says, following his baptism, he did not consult with flesh and blood. Nor did I go up to Jerusalem, to the Apostles who preceded me. Paul arrived at an intentional decision not to follow the most natural course anyone would have chosen, namely, to return to Jerusalem and ask the Apostles of our Lord to teach him the Gospel. Why he made that decision we can only surmise because there is no information on which to build a theory, and when it comes to the Word of God there is no room for imagining things. Our interest is in the truth.

What is clear is that, consequent to his decision not to turn to the Apostles, Paul says, I went away, to Arabia, and again returned to Damascus. By the time he arrived in Damascus, he knew beyond all doubt that it was God's Gospel that overwhelmed his heart and became the core of his life. This Gospel was all from God, altogether true, and it therefore obliged all mankind.

From that moment on, Paul's life was altered. Of course, there was still a great deal he had to learn. The sincere convictions of his heart were not enough, nor was his devotion. He had yet to learn to channel his enthusiasm into productive channels by submitting them to the authority of a church. We learn more of that elsewhere in Scripture. But this much is clear: rather than continuing in the traditions of his forefathers, he gave himself whole-heartedly to the Messiah and to the Gospel of Messiah's grace. His eager zeal was from that moment on engaged in seeking an ever-increasing understanding of the Gospel and to its spread in the world.

Paul continues to describe his first years in the Faith of the Messiah. He does so because he wants to confirm in the minds of his readers a recognition of the authority of the Gospel he proclaimed. This was necessary because the new teachers in Galatia were promoting a different view of the Gospel and sought to raise doubts as to the validity of the message he preached. After insisting that his Gospel came from God, he brings further evidence of its validity.

Then, after three years in Arabia and after having returned to Damascus, and only then, I went up to Jerusalem to make Cephas' acquaintance

(Peter's Aramaic name was Cephas. Unlike some today, Paul did not insist on using Jewish names. He did not attach spiritual significance to speaking Hebrew), and I remained with him 15 days. But I did not see any other apostle, except James (who was not one of the twelve—the title Apostle is not reserved in Scripture for the twelve), the Lord's brother. Obviously, in that short space of time, Cephas and James did not have opportunity to teach Paul the principles of the Gospel, nor did anyone else.

Take note, I am writing to you, I write in the presence of God. I am not lying. Paul again insists on the truth of his statements, calling God Himself to witness to their veracity and drawing his readers' attention to that claim.

Not only had Peter and James not taught Paul but he goes on to say, Then I went to the areas of Syria and Cilicia. I was personally unknown to the churches in Judea, only that they heard again and again, "he who persecuted us in the past is now proclaiming the Faith he tried to destroy." In other words, Paul did not learn his Gospel from any other member of the churches in Judea. On the other hand, his message received repeated confirmation in that the churches repeatedly heard he was preaching the very same Gospel he earlier tried to destroy. No inkling of criticism was expressed with regard to what they heard. Rather, they praised God for what he did in me.

There you have it. That is how Paul was saved. That explains the change that came over him. Paul describes it in terms of what he (God) did in me. The churches of Judea did not praise Paul for the wisdom of his decision, nor for the courage, devotion and energy that he displayed after the course of his life was changed so radically. They praised God, because it was God who overcame Paul, conquered his heart, caused him to be born again, changed the course of his life and wrote His holy law in his heart.

Salvation, we have said, is from the Lord, from beginning to end. God is the one who did every bit of it. After all, man's decisions and actions are ultimately under God's control. He rules over everything. He directs man's heart and thoughts and he determines their actions. He works in visible and invisible ways in the hearts of men, moving them to choose freely as he wills. He covertly moved Paul to set out on the way to Damascus, and he overtly revealed himself to him in the course of that journey. That is what God did in him.

At the same time, man is responsible for what he does. He is called upon to obediently dedicate himself to God, love Him and make His honor the first priority. Paul never played down the heinousness of his persecution of the church prior to his conversion.

When the moment comes, this apparent contradiction will be resolved. Then we will see the beauty of its wisdom because we will be able to recognize the majesty of God's surprising ways.

LET'S SUMMARIZE

- Sincerity and devotion are not enough. Paul's conduct before his conversion illustrate zeal without knowledge. Examine your heart: are you zealous? Is your zeal informed and directed by the truths of the Gospel?

- Do we preach the Gospel, relying on God to persuade, or do we use means that are inappropriate to the Gospel? Think of practical ways in which you should rely on God in the way you preach the Gospel. What should you do? What should you avoid?

- Do people who know you well praise God for what He did in you by means of the Gospel? How can you most convincingly evidence the work of God in your life?

LET'S PRAY

Lord of every human heart, governor of all that is and was and shall be, You are glorious beyond compare. We bow before You in loving adoration. Search our hearts, Oh God, and purge them of all self-seeking. Make us zealous for Your honor. May our hearts yearn for You to be glorified. Teach us to preach the Gospel in the fullness of its power and the awesomeness of its truth. Change us by the Gospel. Move us to live humbly, to preach humbly, and to rejoice in your majesty as it is reflected in the Gospel. The Jesus our Lord and Messiah, Amen.

QUESTIONS FOR DISCUSSION AND STUDY

1. Explain the significance of the word "but" in verse 15. Note what Paul is contrasting here.

2. On the basis of scriptural evidence, try to reconstruct the course of Paul's life from Stephen's stoning to the Jerusalem visit described in this passage.

3. Discuss appropriate and inappropriate ways to preach the Gospel. Discuss God's role in the promotion of the Gospel.

4. Consider: Paul was confident that the Gospel which he preached was given him by the Lord Himself. Why, then, did he seek the Apostles' approval?

CHAPTER 4

Paul's Gospel Further Confirmed
(GALATIANS 2:1–10)

¹ Then, after 14 years, I went up to Jerusalem again, with Barnabas. I also took Titus with me. ² I went up in accordance with a revelation and I presented before them the Gospel that I proclaim among the nations of the world. I did this privately, in the presence of those respected among them, lest I be running or had been running to no end. ³ But even Titus, who was with me, who was a Greek, they did not force to be circumcised ⁴ because of false brothers who stole into the church undetected. They stole in to spy out our liberty, which we have in the Messiah, in order to enslave us. ⁵ Not even for an hour did we give in to them, and that so that the truth of the Gospel would continue with you. ⁶ And those who seemed to be respected (for whatever it was, I don't care. God does not differentiate between people), those "respected ones" added nothing to me. ⁷ To the contrary. They understood that I was entrusted with the proclamation of the Gospel to the uncircumcised just as Peter was entrusted with the proclamation of the Gospel to the circumcised, ⁸ because he who worked through Peter in his mission to the circumcised worked through me in relation to the nations of the world.

⁹ James, Cephas, and John recognized the grace that was given me. Therefore, those who are apparently considered to be pillars in the church in Jerusalem gave me and Barnabas the right hand of fel-

lowship, that we should go the nations of the world but they to the circumcised. [10] They only requested that we remember the poor, and I was eager to do the same thing.

We noted earlier that Paul provides us with information about his activity that is unavailable anywhere else. The period spent in Arabia and his return to Damascus are mentioned only here. This text is also the source from which we learn that 14 years passed before Paul returned to Jerusalem after having been sent away by the brethren. On the other hand, the Apostle makes no mention of his short stay in Jerusalem after he left Damascus and of which we learn from Acts 9:23–31, nor does he mention the rather embarrassing circumstances of his departure from Damascus.

We have no idea what Paul did during most of these 14 years. We read in Acts 11:19–26 that, after some 13 years, he was invited by Barnabas to serve alongside him, ministering to the church in Syrian Antioch (the New Testament references two cities called Antioch, one in Syria, the other in the Pisidian part of Galatia). In Acts 11:27–30 we read of Agabus, who arrived in Antioch from Jerusalem and prophesied of a coming famine that would affect "all of the world." This is possibly the revelation to which Paul refers in this letter ("I went up according to a revelation"). Apparently, Agabus' prophecy motivated the Christians in Antioch to enlist themselves on behalf of the church in Jerusalem.

A collection was made. Barnabas and Paul (at that stage still known by his Hebrew name, Saul) were commissioned to convey the collection, and Titus, a resident of Antioch, was to accompany them. This was a practical way in which the church in Antioch chose to express its oneness with the church in Jerusalem and the sense of mutual responsibility that churches have one for another. Later, Paul will act in a similar way and raise a contribution for the church in Jerusalem from the churches he will have established (1 Corinthians 16:1–4). The unity of the church was a major theme in Paul's ministry, and for good reason: as we shall see and as he will make so very clear in his later letters to the Ephesians and to the Colossians, he believed that such unity was a reflection of the sufficiency of the Messiah's work.

Having been sent to Jerusalem, Paul took the opportunity to present to the Apostles and the elders the Gospel he had preached to Jews and non-Jews alike, at this stage in Syrian Antioch. But we can be reasonably sure that he spoke up for the Gospel during the years he lived in Tarsus.

He tells us that he presented his Gospel, "privately," and that he did so for a purpose: lest I be running or had been running to no end.

Three lessons are implied in these few words. First, although Paul believed he had heard directly from God Himself, he was not so confident of himself that he was unwilling to submit that conviction to the test of others who had likewise heard from the Lord. We no longer have living Apostles today, but their words are preserved for us in Scripture. It is our duty to submit every view, even views we believe to be the very truth of God, to the test of those apostolic standards.

Second, in spite of his extra-ordinary calling, Paul was sincerely humble. He did not exalt himself. He did not put himself above others although he had heard from the Lord Himself and was appointed by Him to the Gospel ministry. He subjected his teaching and therefore the substance of his ministry, to that of the Apostles. Had they shown him to be wrong, he would have mended his views. The fact that God called him directly did not free him from the obligation to be subject to the scrutiny and approval of others in the Lord, all the more so to the scrutiny and approval of the Apostles. We ought never appoint ourselves to any spiritual role, nor ever think that the message we proclaim is free from the scrutiny of those older than we are in the Lord, or of those to whom authority has been given in the church.

Third, Paul chose to submit his teachings to the Elders' and Apostles' examination privately so as to avoid the possibility of confusion and misunderstanding on the part of those he had taught. He did not wish to unsettle them. Once his teaching received the approval of those respected among them, as Paul describes them, he could embark afresh onto his mission, no one having valid grounds on which to question what he taught.

Paul acted wisely, humbly, and out of a love for the truth rather than a desire to be proven right. He acted in concert with the church and its officers, submitting himself to their authority. In this heightened individualistic age, we would do well to follow his example. We would do well to be less engaged with our sense of value—even of calling—and submit ourselves to the authority of the church and its officers.

But even Titus, who was with me, who was a Greek, they did not force to be circumcised because of false brothers who stole into the church, undetected. They (the false brothers) stole in to spy out our liberty, which we have in the Messiah in order to enslave us.

We sometimes think that the early church was perfect. It is worth remembering that this letter to the Galatians is most likely the earliest of Paul's letters. It was composed a short while after his first missionary journey and the only one he conducted in the company of Barnabas. That being the case, it will have been written somewhere around 44–45 AD, about a year after that first journey and less than two decades following the crucifixion of the Messiah and his resurrection. Already, at that early stage, there were false brothers who stole into the church.

Wherever truth is to be found, the enemy of truth will endeavor to insert error. The early church had to struggle with the same issues with which we struggle today. That is why we can learn from the history of the church's struggles and from the solutions she framed under the guidance of the Spirit, so we too can effectively contend with the challenges that face us.

Those false brothers, Paul says, stole into the church. They appeared to belong but did not. Of course, the Elders and Apostles in Jerusalem did not know they were false brothers. The individuals spoken of entered the church surreptitiously, undetected. Had they been detected, they would not have been allowed to present themselves as brothers. So then, the Apostles were not perfect, nor were they enlightened by the Spirit in all matters. They were not possessed of mystic powers; they were enlightened on occasion by the Spirit. But they still had to make evaluations and did not always make the right ones.

One reason why these false brothers were able to steal into the church was that the Apostles and Elders in Jerusalem had not arrived at a full understanding of the implications of the Gospel of God's grace as to the equal standing of Jews and non-Jews in the Messiah. The realities under which they labored sheltered them from the need to consider these issues. For that reason they did not understand that all who believe are free from the ceremonial aspects of the Law, not to speak of their freedom from Israel's interpretive and applicatory traditions. They did not distinguish between the national-cultural value of traditions on the one hand and their purported spiritual weight on the other.

Even later, after the council in Jerusalem (Acts 15), they were not altogether clear on the matter. It takes time for truth to sink in and impact one's life. It takes time for theory to become practice for doctrine to be translated into reality. We need to be patient with each other, far more than is often the case. We are too quick to exclude or separate from those who differ with us, purportedly on the grounds of objective truth, forgetting that the application of grace is as important as its doctrinal validity. It is not without reason that our Lord said that we are to be known as His disciples by our love for one another rather than by our theological exactitude.

This is to be expected because the circumstances in which they lived, proclaimed the Gospel, and applied its principles enabled them to continue very much in the same way they and their forefathers had lived up to that point. They were in Jerusalem, among their own Jewish people. They did not need to make the evaluations and arrive at the understandings with which Paul had to contend. God the Spirit reserved these for Paul, who labored under different circumstances, through which the Spirit gifted the churches with a clearer comprehension of its freedom in the Messiah by the instrumentality of Paul's ministry.

So long as the church is on earth, it will never be perfect. Its Pastors and Elders will always be liable to err. Those who expect otherwise are mistaken because they too have not yet been brought to perfection. The church is not all it will be in the future. Perfection is our goal. We should strive for it. But we ought not expect any human or any institution—not even the church—to achieve perfection now. There must be room for grace in our relations one with another and with the church of the Messiah. We must make room for grace!

These false brethren stole into the church to spy out our liberty, which we have in the Messiah in order to enslave us. Whether this was their conscious intention or not, whether they were sincerely mistaken or otherwise, the result was the same, and the Apostle took a firm stance against it. These apparent but not true brothers wanted to snuff out the freedom enjoyed by Christians.

To what freedom is Paul referring? Obviously, he is speaking of freedom from the demands that the false brothers sought to impose. And what were those? The ceremonial law and Jewish tradition.

Note the "we" in Paul's wording when he speaks of freedom from the ceremonial law. It is premeditated. It is the fruit of inspiration, of the guidance of the Spirit. Paul is not speaking of a freedom limited to non-Jewish believers. He includes himself alongside the Galatians. He speaks of *our* liberty, which *we* have in the Messiah. He does so because there were those who insisted that Christians are obliged to keep the Mosaic Law and rabbinic tradition, or at least advantaged if they do, whereas non-Jewish believers are free from such obligation. But Paul expressly includes himself and—remember—he is Jewish. If he is free from such duties, inevitably, so are non-Jewish believers. The teachers of this false doctrine were trying to bring the Galatian believers to submit to the ceremonial commandments of the Law and rabbinic tradition. But Paul insists that both Jews and non-Jews in the Messiah are free.

Among those false brothers there were some who demanded that Titus, who accompanied Paul and Barnabas to Jerusalem, be circumcised. The Apostles and Elders were therefore forced to discuss the matter. Paul describes their conclusion when he says, but even Titus, who was with me, who was a Greek, they did not force to be circumcised.

Note the circumstance under which Titus was not forced to be circumcised. He was a Greek, not Jewish. Timothy, on the other hand, was Jewish because his mother was Jewish (Acts 16: 1). He was, therefore, circumcised, so as to avoid giving Jewish people grounds for the charge that the Gospel negates Jewish national identity (Acts 16:3). Scripture contains not a hint of his being obliged to do so, but it was a wise and generous step to take.

The facts speak for themselves. Will we hear their voice? Will we heed what they are saying? That is the measure of our liberty, which we have in the Messiah, whether we be we Jewish or Gentile. The circumcised are to remain circumcised and the uncircumcised are to remain such, without thinking that their respective states confer or withhold spiritual advantage. In the Messiah, neither circumcision nor uncircumcision matters. Because Jesus did it all, the only thing necessary is that we put our trust in Him.

Having referred to the Apostles' and Elders' decision that Titus was not bound to be circumcised, nor advantaged by undergoing the rite, Paul makes it clear that the Apostles' and Elders' decision upheld the freedom of all who are in the Messiah. Verse 5 makes it clear that a strenuous discussion had taken place over the matter, in the course of which, Paul says, not even for an hour did we give in to them, and that so that the truth of the Gospel would continue with you. And those who now seemed to be respected (for whatever it was, I don't care. God does not differentiate between people), those "respected ones" added nothing to me. Apparently, more than one opinion was represented, a vigorous discussion ensued, and Paul refused to compromise. So far as he was concerned, nothing was to be added to what The Messiah achieved. He did it all. This was Paul's message, and it was one to which the Apostles and Elders in Jerusalem gave their approval.

Such discussions, often strenuous, are one way we draw closer to the truth, and there is often more than one way to avoid it and therefore miss an opportunity to grow. It is legitimate for believers to disagree, even vigorously, so long as they are engaged in a mutual search for the truth rather trying to win an argument. There is room for discussion, not for politicking. None of us can comprehend the whole body of truth. Every one of us experiences difficulties when it comes to understanding—or even accepting—one aspect of truth or another. One reason for this is in the inclination of our sinful hearts. Another is the sheer comfort of habit and lack of the moral courage necessary to admit we're wrong, and change our ways. That is why we need each other: so we can be challenged, corrected, and encouraged to grow by correcting our mistakes, broadening our views or discovering subtleties of which we were not aware.

But we must never allow differences of opinion to become personal conflicts. We must never conduct discussions over matters of principle by way of personal affront. Most differences of understanding are not a valid reason for separation, and we have no right to separate from any who are our true brethren in the Messiah. We shall see this all the more clearly later, in our discussion of Paul's conflict with Peter.

We can and should speak clearly, but what we must not do is give or take offense because someone says we are mistaken. After all, we're all liable to err, far more than we care to admit. Love for God and therefore love for his truth, should guide us. When such love is our motive, we will more often discover that we erred than that we have not.

Compared to the Apostles and Elders, Paul was young in the Faith. The apostles had been with the Lord Himself some three wonderful years, hearing Him teach and witnessing His life. Was that enough to ensure they would not err? Not at all. They did not cease being as human as any of us, and what we read about them in the Gospels makes that very clear. Even after the extraordinarily wonderful work of the Holy Spirit on the day of Pentecost, they remained human and fallible, except in those instances when the Spirit guided them or inspired them to write what ultimately became Scripture.

The question whether or not Titus was to be circumcised was not determined merely on the basis of the authority given to the Apostles but in the course of a discussion between them and the Elders and on the basis of the Gospel itself. On that basis, the Apostles, the Elders of the church in Jerusalem, Paul and Barnabas all stood on equal footing.

What counted was the authority of the truth, and all involved recognized that. Their conduct was characterized by a humility that brought them to listen to Paul, take his arguments into consideration, and change their minds in spite of their seeming advantages over him. We all remember the time when an ass taught a prophet, challenging his ways.

Those who teach or who lead us in God's ways would do well to conduct themselves in a similar fashion, and we will all do well to prefer the truth of God to our pride. So long as they teach God's Word and conduct themselves accordingly, we ought to follow them.

Paul, as we said, is defending our liberty, which we have in the Messiah. He therefore does not insist that non-Jewish believers are free of obligations to the Law and to Jewish Tradition but that we—Jews and non-Jews in the Messiah—are equally free of the two, naturally leading to the conclusion that not only are non-Jewish believers free in this respect, but Jewish believers are as well.

Were there an inkling of spiritual advantage to be found in the observance of the duties the Law and Jewish tradition imposed, the Apostles and the Elders in Jerusalem would have said as much, as would have Paul here. But there is no hint of any such advantage. Instead, Paul says in verse 7, that those who now seemed to be respected (referring to the Apostles) ... added nothing to me. Why did they not? Because all we have in the Messiah is the fruit of God's grace, and we have in the Messiah all of the fruits of that grace.

The Apostle refused to budge on this matter, so that the truth of the Gospel would continue with you. In other words, the issue raised by the false brethren touches the very the truth of the Gospel (this too will become clearer as we study what Paul said to Peter in Antioch). Why? Because the Gospel is essentially a message of God's unilateral grace (grace is inevitably unilateral): We are saved by grace. Our salvation—all of it—is dependent on grace.

Salvation is not merely forgiveness of sins. It is much more. It has to do with forgiveness and leads to the eternal glory we shall be granted when we stand in the presence of God, beautified with his beauty, clothed with the righteousness of the Messiah as the fruit of God's actions for and in us. The redeemed are destined to be remade into the image of Son of God, so that he might be the firstborn among many brothers and that God would be glorified through his amazing, unilateral grace. That is a summary of the Gospel. That is its essence. To add anything to it is to subtract from it. Either Jesus did it all, or He did not.

Those who now seemed to be respected (for whatever it was, I don't care. God does not differentiate between people), those "respected ones" added nothing to me.

Paul presented to the leading figures of the church in Jerusalem the contents of the Gospel he proclaimed, and they confirmed his message, adding absolutely nothing to it. Absolutely nothing can be added to the achievements of the Messiah. Believers from among the Gentiles were not required to keep the Mosaic Law, all the more so they were not required to maintain the Jewish traditions. No such requirements can add anything to the quality of our spiritual lives or to our understanding of the Scriptures. Whoever comes under their yoke distorts his understanding of the Gospel.

To the contrary. They understood that I was entrusted with proclamation of the Gospel to the uncircumcised just as Peter was entrusted with the proclamation of the Gospel to the circumcised. Paul does not speak here of two Gospels, one for the Jews and one for all the rest. He has already told us, in Chapter 1, that there are not two Gospels. Here, again, his language is clear.

When Paul speaks of, those who now seemed to be respected (for whatever it was, I don't care. God does not differentiate between people), he is in no way making light of the Apostles. We ought never disrespect those who serve in the church, especially those whom God has entrusted with the task of leading. No disrespect is meant by Paul's words. Had he not respected them, had he not recognized their role in the church, he would not have gone to the trouble of submitting his message to their scrutiny and seeking their affirmation. He is using language that is meant to disparage the claims of those who sought to sway the Galatian believers away from the pure Faith of the Messiah and toward the Law and Jewish tradition. In order to do so, they made light of Paul and, over against him, emphasized the status of the Apostles and Elders in Jerusalem: "Paul? Who's he? Did he ever meet the Messiah in person? The Apostles accompanied Jesus for three years, during which they learnt directly from him. They, not Paul, are the ones He appointed to proclaim His message to the world—and they are careful to observe the law and the traditions. Where did Paul get the idea that believers are not obliged to do likewise?!"

Well, those respected ones did not alter Paul's message one bit. Nor did they add to it. Rather, they understood that Peter and Paul received different commissions. He and Peter were to preach the same Gospel in different contexts, and the Apostles lent their support to both. From that moment on, Paul not only knew that he had been called to the service of the Gospel, that not only the church in Antioch lent support to that calling, but the Apostles and Elders in Jerusalem stood behind him as well. Everyone could now know that he and they are of the same mind. He was an ambassador for the whole church, by virtue of which he was to be recognized as a messenger of God. His mission was firmly established on the basis of the approval of those respected ones and the appointment of the church from which he and Barnabas eventually embarked onto the Gospel mission.

> Because he who worked through Peter in his embassage to the circumcised worked through me in relation to the Gentiles. James and Cephas and John recognized the grace that was given me. Therefore, those who are apparently considered to be pillars in the church in Jerusalem gave me and Barnabas the right hand of fellowship, that we should go the Gentiles but they to the circumcised.

In the paragraph above Paul explains why the Apostles and elders in Jerusalem affirmed his mission to the Gentiles. They saw that God had worked through Paul exactly as he had done through Peter. They therefore accorded the two the same approval: they saw how the loving fear of God spread among the Gentiles. They saw the marked changes that came over the lives of Jewish and non-Jewish believers alike: their moral conduct, their affection for God and his Messiah, their willingness to submit to the authority of Scripture. They saw the new believers' openness to anything that served to exalt God, or that claimed to be able to do so. It was impossible to ignore what had happened in Salamis, Paphos, Iconium, Lystra and Derbe, where Paul and Barnabas preached the Gospel in the course of their missionary journey that preceded this letter. If there was any room for doubt in the minds of the Apostles and Elders, Barnabas, who enjoyed their confidence (having been sent by them to Antioch), dismissed it by supporting Paul's narrative of that journey.

Nor could they ignore the fact that Peter himself had visited Antioch (Galatians 2:11) witnessed God's blessing there and, in the long run, came to see things as Paul did with regard to this issue. Even if the Apostles and Elders thought Barnabas was prejudiced, Peter's testimony clinched the matter.

God had so arranged the order of things, apart from human intervention, that everything pointed to the one possible conclusion: the Apostles and Elders in Jerusalem acknowledged Paul's mission and supported it because he who worked through Peter in his embassage to the circumcised worked through me in relation to the Gentiles. For that reason James (the brother of the Lord and the leading light among the Elders of Jerusalem) and Cephas (Peter) and John (the author of the Gospel of John) recognized the grace that was given me. Therefore, those who are apparently considered to be pillars in the church in Jerusalem gave me and Barnabas the right hand of fellowship, that we should go the Gentiles but they to the circumcised. Different persons, different missions, different circumstances, but one Gospel for all, incumbent on all and proclaimed to all.

They only requested that we remember the poor, and I was eager to do the same thing. Matters now become significantly, impressively clear. Just as our Lord drew a sharp distinction between the ceremonial and moral duties the Law imposed (Matthew 23:23, Mark 7:9–13), so did His apostles. They recognized the fact that believers are free from the dietary laws, circumcision, the feast days and all other ceremonial aspects of the Law, while they insisted that the moral duties of the Law are binding.

Caring for the poor is a moral duty that the Law and the prophets repeatedly address:

> You shall not strip your vineyard bare, neither shall you gather the fallen grapes of your vineyard. You shall leave them for the poor and for the sojourner: I am the Lord your God (Leviticus 19:10).

> When you reap the harvest of your land, you shall not reap your field right up to its edge, nor shall you gather the gleanings after your harvest. You shall leave them for the poor and for the sojourner: I am the Lord your God (Leviticus 23:22).

> You shall not oppress a hired worker who is poor and needy, whether he is one of your brothers or one of the sojourners who are in your land within your towns. You shall give him his wages on the same day, before the sun sets (for he is poor and counts on it), lest he cry against you to the Lord, and you be guilty of sin (Deuteronomy 24:14–15).

When the people of Israel sinned by taking advantage of the poor, the prophets castigated them in no uncertain terms:

> Seek the Lord and live, lest he break out like fire in the house of Joseph and it devour, with none to quench it for Bethel, O you who turn justice to wormwood and cast down righteousness to the earth! ... because you

trample on the poor and you exact taxes of grain from him, you have built houses of hewn stone, but you shall not dwell in them; you have planted pleasant vineyards, but you shall not drink their wine. For I know how many are your transgressions and how great are your sins— you who afflict the righteous, who take a bribe and turn aside the needy in the gate (Amos 5:6–12).

Isaiah adds to these, saying,

The Lord has taken his place to contend; he stands to judge peoples. The Lord will enter into judgment with the elders and princes of his people: It is you who have devoured the vineyard. The spoil of the poor is in your houses. What do you mean by crushing my people by grinding the face of the poor?" declares the Lord God of hosts (Isaiah 3:13–15).

Jeremiah said,

Woe to him who builds his house by unrighteousness, and his upper rooms by injustice, who makes his neighbor serve him for nothing and does not give him his wages, who says, "I will build myself a great house with spacious upper rooms," who cuts out windows for it, paneling it with cedar and painting it with vermilion. Do you think you are a king because you compete in cedar? Did not your father eat and drink and do justice and righteousness? Then it was well with him. He judged the cause of the poor and needy; then it was well. Is not this to know me? Declares the Lord. But you have eyes and heart only for your dishonest gain, for shedding innocent blood and for practicing oppression and violence (Jeremiah 22:13–17).

We conclude with Malachi's stern rebuke (note the company in which God puts those who abuse the poor and ignore their need):

I will draw near to you for judgment. I will be a swift witness against the sorcerers, against the adulterers, against those who swear falsely, against those who oppress the hired worker in his wages, the widow and the fatherless, against those who thrust aside the sojourner, and do not fear me, says the Lord of hosts (Malachi 3:5).

Note Jeremiah's words: "He judged the cause of the poor and needy; then it was well. Is not this to know me? Declares the Lord. Note those of Malachi: those who oppress the hired worker in his wages, the widow and the fatherless, against those who thrust aside the sojourner, and do not fear me, says the Lord of hosts."

Awareness of others in their need and a vivid sensitivity toward others characterized Paul and his ministry. Just think of the scores of personal references he makes in his letters. Those who came to know the Gospel through him internalized that principle and later amazed the selfish, lustful, arrogant Roman world by their generous, often sacrificial kindness. Are we in any sense like those first believers?

A sincere fear of God is always sensitive to the needs of others. James said as much when he wrote, "Religion that is pure and undefiled before God the Father is this: to visit orphans and widows in their affliction, and to keep oneself unstained from the world" (James 1:27). We ought not be surprised therefore, when James, Peter and John asked Paul to conduct himself exactly in that light.

All who are in the Messiah are free from the ceremonial duties the Law imposed. But they are obliged—as is all mankind—by its moral duties. No one is a law unto himself. No one has a right to make law for himself, no one is lord of himself, and no one has the right to live for himself. We are obliged to take the needs of others into consideration. We are all obliged to love one another as we love ourselves.

The world may try to convince us that God does not exist, and then turn each one of us into a god around whom everything revolves. This generation is especially characterized by such idolatry: "As long as you're happy," "as long as you feel good about it," "if that is what you want to do." The truth is that the "long" of which they speak is not so long; it is barely a speck in eternity.

Ours is a generation in which people create virtual realities of themselves in a futile effort to obtain a Facebook "like" instead of maintaining true friendships. Momentary, lustful satisfaction is spoken of as "making love" by individuals who have forgotten what true love is. People dare try to alter the very foundations of nature in a cynical effort to transform their desires, their honor, their riches and their beastly pleasures into the ultimate goal of life. As a result we trample on each other in our headlong rush to enjoy ourselves.

The apostles thought otherwise. In the spirit of Israel's Law, in response to Israel's prophets and in obedience to Israel's God, they insisted that Paul, Barnabas and all who claim to be followers of the Messiah remember the poor, and, at the same time they excused them from those temporary duties that were meant to represent the essence of the Faith and are not that essence itself.

It is appropriate that we ask ourselves another important question: remembering the poor doesn't only mean that we think of them and pray for them. It means that we make an effort to meet their needs. Love that is not expressed in deeds is hypocritical. Are we actively involved in reaching out to the needy? If we are, is it because we sincerely care for them or, God forbid, as a way to feel good about ourselves or promote our religious agenda? Woe to us if our motivations are impure. Doing the right things with the wrong motives is not serving God.

LET'S SUMMARIZE

- Whatever we know, from whatever source we believe it has come, should always be willingly subjected to the scrutiny and confirmation of the church.

- God grants various people varying enlightenments. We are therefore in need of each other.

- The unity of the church between various nations, cultures and personal backgrounds is expressed, among other ways by our ensuring that there is no essential difference between us in terms of the essence of our spiritual life. We must be careful not to assume or create any such difference.

- We should never compromise on essential truths, regardless of who promotes them.

- Doctrinal controversies should never be allowed to become personal conflicts.

- There is one Gospel for Jews and for non-Jews. There is no room for any distinction of duties, privileges or status.

LET'S PRAY

Beautiful God of all truth, You who are served by truth and hates all falsehood, teach us to love Your truth and to put it before any comprehensions we might have. Teach us—if need be, force upon us—a humility that is willing to learn from others and to submit our understandings to the scrutiny and wisdom of others. Enable us to understand that all of grace is in the Messiah, that there is nothing more to be had beyond Him; that He is our all in all, the grounds of our salvation, our sanctification and our glorification, the sole and sufficient grounds of our fellowship. In Him we are one with You and with each other. Our great God, we revel in the glories of Your Son our Savior, and rest in the perfection of His accomplishments for us. In Him You are glorified, and it is in His glorious name we dare address You in prayer. Hear us for Jesus' sake, Amen.

QUESTIONS FOR DISCUSSION AND STUDY

1. What is the difference between truth and "our truth"? How are we to discern between the two?

2. Describe three important areas of imperfection in the church of the Apostle's day (base your findings on Scripture).

3. Why was it important for Paul to prove he had the support of the Apostles and Elders in Jerusalem? How did this fact serve his argument? How does Paul's example in this apply to our lives today?

4. What is the relationship between the sufficiency of the Messiah's work and the unity of the church?

5. Should we help the needy because we want to pave the way for evangelism or from another motive?

CHAPTER 5

Peter and Paul in Conflict
Part 1
(GALATIANS 2:11–14)

[11] But when Cephas arrived in Antioch, I opposed him to his face because he was guilty. [12] For before certain people arrived from James, he ate with non-Jews. But upon their arrival he withdrew and was separating himself from them because he feared the circumcised. [13] The rest of the Jews also acted hypocritically, so that even Barnabas was swept away by their hypocrisy.

[14] But when I saw that they were not behaving in strict accordance with the truth of the Gospel, I said to Cephas in the presence of everyone: "If you, a Jew, live like a non-Jew and not like a Jew, why do you force the non-Jews to Judaize?"

Paul continues to counter the teaching of those who sought to bring the Galatian Christians around to the view that they were in some way obliged to, or could be advantaged by, subservience to the Law and Jewish tradition. Paul has insisted on the validity of the Gospel as he preached it and indicated its divine source and the approval of the Apostles and Elders in Jerusalem. He now turns to describe an event that occurred sometime earlier, and that related to the issue dealt with in this letter. By so doing he provides the Galatians with yet another reason to reject the teachings of those who had come among them. True, those who sought

68

to promote such views arrived as emissaries of James and, most likely, claimed to teach what he taught. But their teachings did not enjoy the support of the Apostles and Elders in Jerusalem, James included.

At some stage during the time that Paul and Barnabas served the church in Antioch, most likely prior to their joint missionary journey, Peter arrived in the city. After some time, a problem arose, similar to that addressed in the letter to the Galatians.

Paul was at the very beginning of his Gospel ministry, serving as Barnabas' protégé, without status or public recognition beyond the confines of the church in Antioch. Barnabas, on the other hand, was an emissary of the twelve apostles in Jerusalem and of the church in that city. He was well-known and much respected among the believers. Peter was senior among the Twelve.

Upon his arrival, Peter conducted himself like any other Christian in the city, without distinguishing between Jewish and non-Jewish believers or between kosher and non-kosher foods. Sometime later, a group arrived from Jerusalem, sent by James the brother of the Lord. From what Paul says later (3:5, 4:8–10), as well as from James' approval of Paul's understanding of the Gospel described earlier, it seems that the group that arrived from Jerusalem exceeded the mandate James committed to them and attempted to persuade the Galatian Christians to undergo circumcision and embrace Israel's traditions.

Peter, fully acquainted with the conservatism of many in the church in Jerusalem, and intimidated by the new arrivals, made a complete turn-about and began acting as if he always maintained a kosher diet. He therefore avoided eating in the homes of believers from among the nations. Barnabas and other Jewish Christians in the city were swept along with him and began following his example.

Paul viewed such conduct, even at this early stage of his ministry, as contrary to the essence of the Gospel because it implied a denial of grace and of the only basis on which sinners can be acceptable to God. It therefore constituted a *de facto* repudiation of the Messiah's sacrifice. Needless to say, Paul protested in no uncertain terms, for good reason.

At first glance, it is difficult to understand why Paul should be so unequivocal about this matter. After all, from an Old Testament perspective, there is obvious logic to the expectation that those who believe in Israel's Messiah would follow Israel's traditions, all the more so when the source of many of these traditions is in the Old Testament. Jewish Christians are certainly not required to cease being Jewish following their faith in the Messiah. How, then, can they be Jewish in any practical sense apart from the traditions of their forefathers? Do non-Jewish Christians have a different set of duties?

This argument suffers from a failure to distinguish between a national heritage, in which religious customs, on the one hand, play a large role even when they have been emptied of religious content (such as Christmas in the west, for example), and religious duties on the other. Jewish Christians are, of course, free to observe any aspects of their national heritage that do not conflict with the Gospel. They are free to do so as an expression of their national and cultural identity (in which non-Jewish Christians do not share). But they ought not view those customs as if they are an aspect of spirituality. In some cases, national traditions might even serve as a means to express spiritual life, but they are never essential or advantageous to it. They are always a matter of liberty in the Messiah, never of obligation. No one should attribute to those traditions spiritual value, an ability to provide one with spiritual advantages or as having spiritual authority.

True, many Jewish customs have their roots in the Word of God. But they were never of the essence of the relationship between God and man. That is why they were not required by God of our father Abraham, let alone of Adam in the Garden. They were given at a certain moment, for a certain purpose and meant to apply up to a certain time (as Paul will say later). That being so, they fulfill no role in the relationship between God and those who lovingly fear Him today.

It is worth noting the considerable risk Paul took when he stood up to Peter, Barnabas and the rest of the Jewish Christians in Antioch. As noted, he was at the very beginning of his ministry in the service of the Gospel, having been rejected earlier for over-enthusiastic, unwise, and incautious conduct in Damascus and in Jerusalem (Acts 9:19–31). Recognition of his authority was naturally limited and rather tenuous.

At the same time, he knew himself to be called by God to preach the Gospel to the Gentiles, a call he received on the day of his conversion. Paul loved God and His Gospel dearly. He was willing to sacrifice everything, to be unpopular in the church that commissioned him and among those of spiritual and moral authority, so long as he was true to the Gospel. He was willing to oppose anyone although he knew full well that those who do so are usually hated and persecuted. May we all, like Paul, be faithful to God and to God's Gospel. May we prefer God's honor first and foremost.

Let us, now, turn to Paul's description of his conflict with Peter.

But when Cephas arrived in Antioch, I opposed his to his face because he was guilty because before certain people arrived from
James, he ate with non-Jews. But upon their arrival he withdrew
and was separating himself from them because he feared the circumcised. The rest of the Jews also acted hypocritically, so that
even Barnabas was swept away by their hypocrisy.

Paul, having described the approval his message received from
James, Peter, and John, the Apostle says, "but." Why the juxtaposition?
Because he is about to describe Peter's conduct, which stood in contrast
to his previous position visa vie Paul's message, which he had approved.

When Cephas arrived in Antioch, instead of consistently applying the
principles he enunciated with James and John, he acted contrary to those
principles: Before certain people arrived from James, he ate with non-Jews.
But upon their arrival he withdrew and was separating himself from them
because he feared the circumcised. Paul will later speak of Peter's dining
in the company of non-Jews in terms of his conducting a non-traditional
Jewish life, living like all other believers from among the Gentiles.

Peter was no more than human. He suffered from weakness as do
we all. He feared the circumcised and, for that reason, acted contrary to
what knew was right. We ought not idolize the Apostles or any of those
described in Scripture. We ought not think they were cut from a different
cloth. They were like us. One moment they were courageous and dared
take a stand for the Messiah in the presence of an outraged crowd or of
the High Priest, the next moment they quaked with fear when faced with
conflicting views within the church.

Who are the circumcised of which Paul speaks? They were believers,
at least apparently so. But what characterized them here was not their
faith in the Messiah but their insistence on circumcision and other Jewish practices rather than on the Messiah. What made them stand out
among other believers was the attachment to Jewish tradition.

Peter feared them. Why? They could not do to Peter what the San-
hedrin could do. His life and limbs were not in danger. The only thing at
stake was his position among the Apostles and of many in Jerusalem, yet
Peter caved rather than standing for the truth.

Paul uses very strong words to describe Peter's behavior. That behavior was obviously wrong, unworthy of the Gospel, and Paul did not
hesitate to describe it as such. But, are *we* free of cowardly fear? Do we
never compromise the truth in an effort to find favor? Is the gap between

what we know and how we live as large as that between Peter's conduct and his knowledge? Before we dare condemn his conduct, we should examine ourselves.

Paul took issue with Peter. He dared oppose him. Peter was one of the Twelve, the senior among them, and Paul was but a relative babe in the Messiah and a young Gospel emissary. Peter had spent some three years in the company of the Lord, witnessed what he did, heard what he taught, saw him die, discovered he was alive and saw him ascend into heaven, whereas Paul had only seen the Lord in a vision. But Paul was not as impressed with people or their status as he was with the authority of truth, and it is the truth that he was determined to defend, even at the cost of Peter's approval or of how the other Apostles will come to view him. The fear that found a place in Peter's heart found none in Paul's. If it did, Paul overcame it.

In fact, Paul chose to take issue with Peter in public, in the presence of others, rather than pulling him aside. He did so because Peter was a public figure, and because his sin was public and therefore had public consequences: others were being led astray by the example Peter set. Public error ought to be corrected publicly and truth must be made clear to all.

The days in which Paul and Peter lived were not characterized by the delicate, easily offended self-love that is common today, that transforms every disagreement into personal conflict. People then knew how to distinguish between "he disagrees with me" and "he doesn't like me." They did not view every person who held a conflicting opinion as an enemy. We would do well to learn from their example.

Before certain people arrived from James, he ate with non-Jews. That is to say, Peter did not maintain the traditional dietary laws. Anything served on a non-Jewish table would not be kosher, among other reasons because there was no separation of dairy and meats, and plates on which non-kosher meat was served would have become ceremonially unclean to a Jew. Instead, he acted on the principle that, in the Messiah, there is no distinction between Jews and non-Jews, nor should any distinction be made. All are one in the Messiah. The claim that the Apostles continued to maintain the traditions and to follow a strict Jewish lifestyle after Jesus died and rose has no leg on which to stand. Peter ate with non-Jews.

But upon their arrival, that is, upon the arrival of the group from Jerusalem, he withdrew and was separating himself from them. He ceased sharing their meals because he feared the circumcised. By separating himself, he was dividing the body of the Messiah. He did not deny the non-Jewish believer's faith but, without saying a word, he declared in no uncertain terms, intended or otherwise, that there is a difference between them and him; the non-Jewish believers were on a lower level. What distinguished the one from the other was the Jewish lifestyle some maintained. In this way Jewish tradition was considered more highly than the Messiah because tradition was allowed to separate those who would otherwise be united: maintaining Jewish tradition, rather than the finished work of the Messiah, became the grounds of fellowship.

The problem in Galatia was similar to that which arose in later years in the churches of Colossae and Corinth: the Messiah's achievements on behalf of the redeemed were deemed considerable but insufficient to ensure the fullness of salvation. They needed to be supplemented by something that the redeemed were to do.

Of course, those were not Peter's intentions. Nor were they his convictions. He had no intention of exalting Jewish tradition over the Messiah and his accomplishments. Nevertheless, in spite of his best intentions, those were the implications of his conduct. Peter's fear of men clouded his thinking, so that he could not see the implications of his own behavior.

We should derive a number of important lessons from Peter's mistake. Above all, we should weigh the implications of our actions in advance, rather than respond without thinking on the spur of the moment, out of the fear of man or hope for immediate gain. It is our duty to act like the Christians we are by giving the Gospel priority in our thinking. It is our duty to acknowledge the fullness of Christ's achievements. We ought never act as though our actions somehow "add to" the benefits we've been given. Adding to the Gospel always detracts from it.

By the way, the fact that Barnabas was originally sent to Antioch by the church in Jerusalem, and that a group had later arrived in that city from Jerusalem, indicates that the churches maintained some form of meaningful relations. It also indicates that the church in Jerusalem fulfilled a leading role in those relations. Unity between the churches was more than lip service; it was practically expressed. The church in Jerusalem being the oldest, most experienced and best equipped to lead, served the other churches.

However, the Jerusalem church did not control those churches; they consulted with her, and only as to matters of the Faith and moral conduct. For example, the church in Antioch initiated Barnabas' and Paul's mission for the Gospel without seeking the approval or blessing of the church in Jerusalem. Nor did Paul need the Jerusalem church's approval each time he embarked onto a missionary journey. The approval of the church in Antioch sufficed.

The rest of the Jews also acted hypocritically, so that even Barnabas was swept away by their hypocrisy. Peter's behavior influenced the rest of the Jews, meaning the Jewish Christians in Antioch. Jews who did not believe in the Messiah would not have eaten with the non-Jews in any case. Paul is saying that Peter's example caused other Jewish Christians in Antioch to separate themselves from their non-Jewish brothers and sisters in Christ. Instead of brotherly love, unity and hearty cooperation, two groups were formed, even if they recognized each other as brethren over the fences they erected. The distance between them inevitably grew because, when we separate from others, we tend to polarize, and to increasingly emphasize the differences between us as a means to justify the separation. The church in Antioch, having once enjoyed unity, was now divided.

Not only were the rest of the Jewish Christians swept away by Peter's poor example. Even Barnabas was swept away by their hypocrisy. We might recall that Barnabas was sent to Antioch by the church in Jerusalem to encourage and strengthen the church in the city. He was, therefore, a leading light in the church, and his conduct would naturally affect many. But even Barnabas, known as the man of comfort, a kind and soft-hearted man, was swept off his feet by Peter's error. This is the man who defended Paul when Paul returned to Jerusalem following his conversion, who believed in him when no others would. Now he, too, was carried away into error. After all, if Peter, the senior apostle, acted as he did, who was Barnabas to act differently?

Paul describes their shameful conduct in terms of hypocrisy. That is a valid description for two reasons. First, Peter, Barnabas and the Jewish Christians in Antioch acted as they did in spite of their earlier understanding that no distinction is to be made between those who believe in the Messiah. Peter had arrived at that conclusion way back in Caesarea, in Cornelius' home (Acts 10: 34, 47). He defended that position before the Apostles and Elders in Jerusalem (Acts 11:17). That is why Before certain people arrived from James, he ate with non-Jews.

Barnabas, on the other hand, was serving at the time in a mixed congregation made up of Jews and of non-Jews, and there is not a hint of difference being made between the two up to that moment. In fact, he knew how Peter conducted himself until the group arrived from Jerusalem. As much was true of the rest of the Jewish Christians in the city: they had not drawn distinctions nor hinted at the duty of any—Jew or non-Jew in the Messiah—to maintain Jewish tradition.

That being so, their behavior following the arrival of the group from Jerusalem contradicted what each of them knew, as well as how every one of them had behaved up to that moment.

Second, Paul describes their conduct as hypocritical because it was meant to create the false impression that they always insisted on drawing a distinction between those in the Messiah who observed Jewish tradition and those who did not.

Peter behaved in this way because he feared the circumcised and Barnabas was swept away. It is worth saying it again: the two did not act thoughtfully, in a principled manner. They were carried away, driven to behave in a manner that contradicted their convictions for fear of the consequences of being faithful to the Gospel. In this case, we ought not follow their example.

> But when I saw that they are not behaving in strict accordance with the truth of the Gospel, I said to Cephas in the presence of everyone: "If you, a Jew, live like a non-Jew and not like a Jew, why do you force the non-Jews to Judaize?"

Once again Paul commences with a "but," this time in response, or rather in reaction to Peter's conduct. Paul opposed it. Why? He tells us: I saw that they are not behaving in strict accordance with the truth of the Gospel. It is important to understand that the Gospel is not just a message that points out the way of salvation. It is a way of life. It is how we are forgiven, made new, sanctified, guided, encouraged, rebuked, taught and glorified. The Gospel is meant to shape every step we make in the various spheres of life: in the family, in church and in society. The Gospel contains truth on which we are duty-bound to insist humbly, firmly, kindly, without compromise and with a consistency that finds expression in what we say and how we live—above all in the principles that motivate and guide us.

We are to live in strict accordance with that truth. It is therefore important that we understand it, ponder its practical implications and seek for the best ways to live it out in the varying circumstances of reality. That is just what Paul does at the conclusion of most of his letters. He applies the principles taught in the first part. There is an integral connection between the two parts, as there ought to be between what we believe and how we live. The power of the Gospel is shown in the way it changes the hearts of individuals and—therefore! —their lives: in the quality of their relations with their spouses and how they bring up their children, in the priorities that determine what they do with their time and money, in the jokes they tell and are willing to hear, in their work ethic and their relations with neighbors—yes, also in their attitude to Israel's traditions.

That is why Peter previously lived like a non-Jew and not like a Jew. He understood the freedom he had in the Messiah. He knew himself to be free from Jewish traditions. He lived like a non-Jew and thereby demonstrated the beauty of the Gospel and its ability to free individuals from bondage of all kinds and to make the grace of God the basis of their spiritual, familial, congregational and social life.

Paul therefore turns to Peter with a complaint: "If you, a Jew, live like a non-Jew and not like a Jew, why do you force the non-Jews to Judaize?" By so doing he exposes Peter's hypocrisy and challenges him openly, in the presence of James' emissaries and of the church in Antioch. The latter, of course, would have been fully cognizant of Peter's hypocrisy, but none seemed willing to challenge him over it.

Paul says that Peter's behavior actually forced non-Jewish believers to Judaize. How? Why would this be so? Think about it for a moment: Peter was one of the twelve Apostles, the senior among them. He was a Jew, the son of Jews. The believers from among the Gentiles could make no such claims. By separating himself from them Peter had effectually drawn a line that said, "if you want to be like me, you must cross this line and act as I do—be circumcised and observe Jewish tradition." In this way he forced the non-Jewish believers to Judaize. He presented himself and those like him as of a higher, fuller level of spirituality, achieved by maintaining a purportedly higher level of faithfulness. He, as it were, represented the spiritual elite which the Antiochian Christians were invited to join.

Apparently, the examples we set have tremendous import. They speak in terms that are far more convincing than anything we say, so much so that if there is a contradiction between what we say and how we conduct ourselves, no one will hear what we are saying. No one will be persuaded that we really believe what we profess to believe, and for good reason: we act contrary to our profession. Is there an inherent contradiction between how *you* live and the truth you claim to believe?

The unity of the church of the Messiah—the unity of Jews and non-Jews in the Messiah, of those who speak various languages and come from various cultures, the unity between blacks and whites, between Israelis and Palestinians—means that we are duty-bound to relate to one another in the context of one church and in strict accordance with the truth of the Gospel. Whatever our differences, however important, they fade into insignificance in comparison with our Lord the Messiah. Divisions in the church are denials of the Gospel because they attribute more importance to the differences that distinguish us than to the Messiah, who unites us. We ought never divide.

Paul continues his argument with Peter: We, by nature, are Jews and not "Gentile sinners," and we know that men are not justified by keeping a law but only through faith in the Messiah, Jesus. We too have believed in the Messiah Jesus, so that we would be justified through faith in the Messiah and not by keeping a law, because by law-keeping no one is justified. We'll think about that statement, and more, next.

Let's Summarize

- Do you, like Paul, take personal risks for the truth of the Gospel? Think of times you have not done so and seek the Lord with respect to those events.

- You and I should be as personally passionate about the truth of the Gospel as was Paul. Examine your heart. Are you? How does your passion express itself?

- Have you any traditions, yours or those of others, sacrosanct and therefore beyond challenge, modification or replacement?

- Are you guided in your choices by the fear of man or any other form of self-love?

- In what ways does your life reflect the Gospel? Think of three ways in which you can improve on such a reflection.

Let's Pray

You are a God who sees all things, from whom nothing can be hidden. We are sinners, with far too much to hide. The Gospel is contrary to our sinful inclinations. It calls upon us to love You in ways that disrupt our plans, threaten our comfort and refuse us immediate, sweet pleasures. But Your Gospel is truth and life. Work in our hearts, O God of all grace, for Jesus' sake. Forgive us our sins and teach us to hate them. Move us to understand the Gospel and to love its truths with heartfelt affection. Move us to apply the Gospel to the everyday of our lives. Move us to be true to you even when we are visible to none but your fearsome, penetrating gaze. Move us to love You more sincerely, more devotedly, more consistently than we do, and lead us to glorify You, Your Son and Your Spirit in the sight of others. Amen.

QUESTIONS FOR DISCUSSION AND STUDY

1.   What lessons must be drawn from the fact and nature of Peter's conduct upon arrival of the embassage from Jerusalem?

2.   What lessons must be drawn from the fact and manner of Paul's confrontation with Peter?

3.   Summarize Paul's argument so far and indicate 3 practical applications of the argument.

4.   What is the relationship between the Gospel and the patterns of life?

CHAPTER 6

Peter and Paul in Conflict Part 2

(GALATIANS 2:14–18)

[14] But when I saw that they were not behaving in strict accordance with the truth of the Gospel, I said to Cephas in the presence of everyone: "If you, a Jew, live like a non-Jew and not like a Jew, why do you force the non-Jews to Judaize? [15] We, by nature, are Jews and not "Gentile sinners," [16] and we know that men are not justified by keeping a law but only through faith in the Messiah, Jesus. We too have believed in the Messiah Jesus, so that we would be justified through faith in the Messiah and not by law-keeping, because by law-keeping no one is justified.

[17] "But if, by seeking to be justified in the Messiah, it turns out that we also are sinners, is the Messiah serving sin? It can never be! [18] But, if I reestablish what I have torn down, I make myself out to be a sinner!

From this point to the end of Chapter Two, Paul presents to the Galatians the argument with which he faced Peter. He commences, as one ought every time the opportunity presents itself, with areas of agreement.

We (Paul and Peter), by nature, are Jews, that is, we were born Jews. We did not convert. We belonged to the Jewish nation from the very beginning of our families' existence. Paul is referencing Israel's boast, which might mistakenly also be Peter's. We are not "Gentile sinners," as many of the adherents of Jewish tradition tend to think, looking down on those who are not Jewish.

The phrase Gentile sinners expresses a measure of scorn Peter and Paul did not have toward non-Jewish Christians, but some measure of scorn is what Peter's behavior implied even if he did not intend it to do so. There is no way around it: our lives expose the truest motivations of our hearts, the hidden principles by which we live, be they conscious or otherwise. The tendency to separate oneself from another is almost always the product of the conviction that somehow we are better than they. Why else would we be different?

And we, you (Peter) and I (Paul), Jews and the children of Jews, know that men are not justified by keeping a law. This is something we know, clearly, beyond doubt. We don't think, we don't surmise, we don't imagine. We know. How do they know? The answer is at hand: they're Jewish, aren't they? They grew up in a Jewish home and were exposed to the written revelation God gave His people. Not only so, but they were exposed to the relentless demands of the Pharisees, who sought to apply to the whole nation the laws pertaining to the priests, so that the people would be a holy nation of priests. By such exposure Paul and Peter had learned afresh that men are not justified by keeping a law.

They tried. Oh how they tried! But they repeatedly failed. It does not matter if the law in question came from God or was the product of human ingenuity. The Law had taught them that God is so holy and that humans are so sinful that they can never satisfy His holy demands. The Law taught them that sin created a wide, bottomless abyss between man and God that even the divinely-given means of atonement (the tabernacle, the altar, the sacrifices, the priests and the High Priest himself) were defiled, needed both to be atoned for and repeatedly purified, time and again, endlessly, because the problem of sin had not been resolved. They also learned from their experience how easily people sin and how difficult it is to maintain holiness. Did I say "difficult"? It is not difficult, it is impossible!

Peter and Paul learned something no less important. They not only knew that men are not justified by keeping a law, they also knew how people can be justified: only through faith in the Messiah, Jesus. Not by human merit, nor by human effort (which implies that faith in the Messiah is also not something man does, on the grounds of which he is saved.

Faith is the means by which God reaches out to save us, not the grounds on which He does so). The merit, the grounds and the effort are all God's. We should take note of the little word only here. It serves to indicate that there is no other way, not even a half-way. Faith in the Messiah is a stand-alone. No one can be saved but by hearing the Gospel and being moved by God to respond to it in faith, putting his whole trust in Jesus.

Paul was very comfortable in presenting the Gospel from what we call the Old Testament. He could do so by more than merely quoting isolated verses (like those on which we like to rely, often divorcing them from their context and their natural meaning in order to present them as Messianic prophecies). He knew how to draw from central Old Testament themes and perceptions that, brought together, formed the fundamental concepts of the Gospel: God's perfect, uncompromising holiness, His demands of man, the concept of representative atonement by way of sacrifice, forgiveness of sins on the grounds of grace, leading to a renewal of relations.

Paul and Peter knew their Old Testament. More than that; they understood it. They therefore knew how to present its basic ideas and to draw from them the inevitable conclusions. These naturally led to the Messiah, regardless of who might chose to claim otherwise. Undoubtedly, their time under Jesus' tutelage enhanced their understanding of the Old Testament, but the truth is there, on the surface of the text, as Paul later put it, sufficient to equip the man of God for every good work.

Do we know how to read the Old Testament? Are we comfortable with the Old Testament as a revelation on its own, able to equip the man of God for every good work? Do we understand the message of the Old Testament? Do we see how its central themes, its theology, its narrative, its poetry, legislation, wisdom and idiom all lead to the Messiah. Can we show how these, in context, all point to Him, or do we need to resort to some kind of subjective spiritualization in order to arrive at the Gospel?

Yet more: reading the Old Testament, do we recognize our guilt? Are we aware of our uncleanness in the sight of God? Are we conscious of the fact that we deserve nothing from God but condemnation? Do we really understand what it means to be justified by grace, in spite of our sin? Do we understand the Old Testament as did Paul and Peter?

Paul presents a principle that is true of all mankind and of all religions, namely that no one can be justified in the sight of God by the keeping of any kind of law. He then applies this principle to himself and Simon Peter, and therefore to all Jews and non-Jews: Three times in two verses Paul repeats the principle that no one is justified by law-keeping. We still need to repeat this truth—more than merely three times—because it is so difficult to grasp its fuller implications.

First, we know that men are not justified by keeping a law. A person justified by law-keeping is one whose life has been thoroughly examined and in which not an inkling of shortcoming is found. On those grounds, as a reward for his righteousness, he is granted eternal life in the presence of God. But we know that no such person exists. There is not a single individual who can stand in the presence of God's beautiful but terrible holiness, His perfect righteousness and say, "I have done all that is required of me. You now owe me blessing."

It does not matter how much a person might have tried or what law he tried to keep, in comparison with God, even the angels are unclean—all the more so we who are born in sin, delight in iniquity, who are selfish, arrogant, unkind, and boastful. Ever since our first father sinned, our nature has been distorted. We find pleasure in impurity. We break God's law by lying, lusting, stealing, desecrating the Sabbath, refusing to honor our parents, coveting what other people have and leading our lives as if we deserve to be happy, as if we are the center of the universe.

Second, We too have believed in the Messiah Jesus, so that we would be justified through faith in the Messiah and not by keeping a law. Justification here is described are having one's life examined and, in spite of one's sin, being granted eternal life in the blessed presence of God by virtue of the Messiah's merits. In other words, here, "to be justified" means "to be saved." Someone else's merit has been attributed to us, on the grounds of which we are forgiven and blessed eternally. He did it all. We need not add anything to what He has done.

Third, in case we've not gotten the point, Paul reminds Peter, we have turned from ourselves to someone else for justification because by keeping a law no one is justified, not Rabbi Gamliel, nor the Lubavitcher Rabbi, not the most determined monk nor anyone else, however strictly he may keep whatever law.

If no one can be justified by keeping a law, is mankind doomed? Is there no way to be saved? Mankind is *not* doomed. There *is* a way for man to be justified. That way is through faith in the Messiah, only through faith in the Messiah, Jesus. That is the way, and that is the *only* way. It is not enough to believe God exists. It is not enough to mean well. It is not enough to do our best, to be sincere, kind and honest. One can be justified only through faith in the Messiah, Jesus.

But what does faith in Jesus the Messiah mean? It means that we stop trying to stand on our own two feet and put all our trust in Him. It means that we do not try to be justified by keeping this law or that tradition, but pin our hopes on Him; that we expect God to forgive and save us because of what *He* did as the reward of *His* life on earth, *His* perfect sacrifice, *His* resurrection, and *His* ascension to God's right hand where He lives forever serving as our High Priest. The Messiah Jesus fulfilled the Law perfectly, and then died to atone for the sins of all whom the Father gave Him before the universe was called into being.

That is why, Paul says to Peter, We too have believed in the Messiah Jesus, so that we would be justified through faith in the Messiah. He says we too, meaning himself, Peter as well as believing non-Jews. There are not two ways to be justified before God. One can only be justified on the grounds of the Messiah's merits. Paul, Peter and anyone else who ever has, is or will be saved, will be saved by this means alone. In this matter there is no difference between Jews and non-Jews, just as there is none between men and women, slaves and freemen, Israelis, Palestinians, members of any culture, or speakers of any language.

Three times Paul has said that no one can be justified by law-keeping. He has also said three times that justification is through faith in Jesus the Messiah.

Have you believed in the Messiah, Jesus? Have you really, truly believed—or have you been convinced intellectually while, in your heart of hearts, you continue to be driven by other principles? Have you given up on yourselves? Have you stopped thinking you deserve anything and turned to God with the painful recognition of your deceitful heart, asking Him to forgive you because of what Messiah has done and in spite of the fact that you do not deserve to be forgiven? Have you been justified through faith in Jesus the Messiah? No question is more important. Answer carefully because how you answer will determine your fate for all eternity.

Paul continues to present his case to Peter saying, but if, by seeking to be justified in the Messiah, it turns out that we also are sinners, is the Messiah serving sin? It can never be! But, if I reestablish what I have torn down, I make myself out to be a sinner! This statement requires a brief introduction to clarify the Apostle's argument:

The Apostle has just completed presenting a position that directly contradicts an assumption that lies at the foundation of every religion in the world: that by some means of our own doing, by the keeping of some rule, law or custom, man deserves divine blessing. The background is Judaism's assumption that the keeping of the Mosaic Law and the interpretive traditions of Israel accord an individual spiritual advantages. The Galatians were told (as were the Antiochians earlier) that, having received the Faith of the Messiah, they must also assume the yoke of the Law and of Jewish tradition in order to grow in faith and establish their spiritual life on a solid basis. That is the view against which Paul argues in these verses. Let's now turn to the argument itself.

Once again Paul begins with the conjunction but, contrasting the principle of salvation through grace by virtue of the life and sacrifice of the Messiah, with what the Apostle says next: if, by seeking to be justified in the Messiah, it turns out that we also are sinners (because we have stopped viewing the Law and the tradition as the means by which we find favor with God), is the Messiah serving sin?

It is again important to note that Paul uses the first person plural—we (we know, we too have believed, so that we would be justified). Paul is premeditated in his use of pronouns. Here he is saying, "you, Peter, and I, Paul, knowing as we do from the Law and the Prophets that no one can be justified by law-keeping, we've turned away from our previous assumptions and our previous way of worship and conduct. We no longer expect to obtain anything from God by observing the Law or our national traditions. All our expectations now rely on the Messiah, and Him alone, on what He has done for us rather than in anything we do."

He goes on to argue: "Well, if in doing so, and because we have done so in response to what the Messiah taught us, it turns out that we also are sinners, does this mean that He (the Messiah) is serving sin? Is He teaching us to do what ought not to be done, that is, to forsake law-keeping for salvation, or any part of salvation, and to put our whole trust in Him? Is it a sin to give up trying to be justified by the Law and tradition? Could it be that, rather than glorifying God and accomplishing His perfect purposes, the Messiah misled us? Is the Messiah serving sin?"

The answer is ready: It can never be! Before we consider that impossibility, it is worth reminding ourselves that the Antiochian and Galatian Christians were not being called upon to turn from their faith in the Messiah. They were being called to add to their faith obedience to the commandments of the Law and Jewish tradition. Having come to believe in the God of Israel, it seemed natural that they would embrace Israel's customs, or so thought some in Antioch and Galatia. That is the view against which Paul protests in this letter. In spite of the sincerity of those who made such a demand, and although they had no intention of degrading the Messiah or faith in Him, their views contradicted the Gospel. They challenged one of its most fundamental tenets, justification by grace through faith alone. They therefore transformed the Gospel into another form of self-salvation.

Paul answers the question, "is the Messiah serving sin" in the only way possible. It can never be! Such an idea is preposterous. It is illogical. It runs contrary to everything Jesus did and everything the Law, the Prophets, and the Apostles taught. It certainly was not what Paul taught. The Messiah came to fulfill the law, not to annul it. In the course of His life He kept every commandment of the Law to its utmost extent. He was holy even as the Lord our God is holy. He was perfect even as our Father in heaven is perfect, thus providing a perfect righteousness over and above the righteousness that was His by virtue of His divine nature. Then, in response to the Law's demands on us because of our sin, He took on our guilt, died the death the Law prescribes for sinners, and fully satisfied its demands. By virtue of His sacrifice we are now free from guilt and the punishment that it dictates. By virtue of His perfectly righteous life, attributed to us by grace, we stand before God, not only guiltless but righteous. The regenerating work of the Holy Spirit birthed us into a new life in which we are gradually transformed, led from glory to glory, empowered in our struggle with the habits of sin and its temptations. One day we shall be fully transformed, having been re-created into God's glorious image. Salvation is a wonderful thing!

That is exactly where the difficulty in Peter's conduct arises: but, if I reestablish what I have torn down, I make myself out to be a sinner! If, after having put my trust in the Messiah for salvation, I turn around and accord the Law and Jewish tradition a role in my walk with God, I revert to viewing them as a means to obtain spiritual advantage, I make myself out to be a sinner for forsaking the Law. I'm actually implying that I should have never turned in the first place. All I should have done is added Jesus to the mix.

What Paul is telling Peter is that willingness to view the Law and Jewish tradition as means to a spiritual life, to being acceptable to God to any extent, is mistaken because it runs contrary to the Faith of the Messiah. This is nothing new. It was always true, even before the Messiah came. Anyone who thought he or she could satisfy God's demands and earn merit before God simply did not understand the Law or the Prophets, because they taught time and again, in various ways and by various means, the opposite. To the extent that Jewish tradition obscured that fact, it was mistaken, as it is to this day.

That is why Paul says later on, I, through a law, have died to law in order that I should live for God. I do not reestablish what I have torn down. I refuse to revert to the idea that, if I do my best, if I'm sincere in my efforts, I will achieve spiritual merit or obtain spiritual advantage. My obedience is not in order to obtain anything. It is, rather, in response to the fact that I have been given so much so freely. It is an act of love and gratitude. I am dead to law. It does not matter what kind of law is in view. Instead of relying on keeping a law, I put my trust in the Messiah Jesus, and I live for God. I do so, first of all, by trusting Him for what He did for me through the Messiah, and by trusting Him all the way to eternity.

Let's Summarize

- Describe 3 ways in which tendencies to law-keeping as defined here by Paul are expressed today.

- Examine yourself and find 3 ways in which, since your conversion, you incline to self-justification. What should you do about these (think of practical steps you should take)?

- Read again the section on faith. Do you truly trust in the Messiah for every aspect of your salvation, including your sanctification?

Let's Pray

Great God and heavenly Father, all truth is Yours; it all reflects the amazing wonder of Your glory. Your kindness reaches down to sinners and transforms so they are no longer reflections of darkness. Instead, they become reflections of Your light. We are transformed by the Gospel. Move us, dear Lord, to put our whole trust in the Messiah for our salvation. Protect us by Your grace so that we never revert to law-keeping instead of trusting Your Son. Teach us, empower us, and sustain us so that we live for Your and Your glory, never relying on ourselves, never attributing to ourselves abilities that are Yours alone. Grant us the love and the courage to exhort one another in the path of faithfulness, and when we fail—for fail we shall—forgive us for Jesus' sake, Amen.

QUESTIONS FOR DISCUSSION AND STUDY

1. Summarize Paul's argument in verses 1–18.

2. What is the relationship between justification, sanctification, and glorification?

3. Elaborate: why can't people be justified by their efforts? In what ways does sanctification differ from justification?

4. What is included in Paul's use of the term "justification" in this passage? How is this supported from other portions of Scripture?

5. How does the Old Testament teach the Gospel?

6. As Christians saved through grace alone, we are called to obey God, but we have a tendency to view our obedience as worthy of His love. Discuss this tendency. What is wrong with it? How can we avoid it?

CHAPTER 7

Peter and Paul in Conflict Part 3
(GALATIANS 2:19–21)

[19] "For I, through a law, died to law in order that I should live for God. [20] I was crucified with the Messiah, alongside him, and it is not me who is now living but the Messiah living in me, and the life that I now live in the flesh I live through faith in the Son of God, who loved me and gave himself for me. [21] I do not make the death of the Messiah into nothing—because if righteousness is by way of law, then there was no need for the Messiah to die."

For here serves to connect us with what was said a moment ago: We too have believed in the Messiah Jesus, so that we would be justified through faith in the Messiah and not by law-keeping, because by law-keeping no one is justified. The word For here refers to the consequence of Paul's statement, rather than to the cause of what he is about to say.

I, through a law, have died to law. Dead to law—any law—with regard to my salvation. I am dead because the law killed me: that is how Paul described his new way of life, and that is the way he called upon Peter, the Antiochian and the Galatian Christians to live (of course, there is more to it than death to law. Read on and you will see). The law that killed Paul was the Law of Moses, coupled with the Pharisaical interpretive and applicatory traditions (which are the basis of Jewish tradition today and to which Paul considered himself bound until he was brought to faith in the Messiah). That Law, although it came from God, and the tradition, although it claimed to explain and apply God's Law, was not capable of giving life (Galatians 3:21. Compare Romans 8:1–4), nor is it able to do so today.

Laws, if they are good laws, reflect God's holiness and the duties of mankind due to the unequivocal demands that God's holiness imposes on us. But no law, even from God, can change human nature. That is where the root of the problem lies: in the distortion that has come over human nature following the sin of our first father, Adam. That is how laws kill everyone under their authority. Good laws are reflections of "God's righteous decree that those who practice such things (that is, who sin) deserve to die" (Romans 1:32).

That is what happened to Paul, as he tells us in Romans 7:7–11:

> If it had not been for the law, I would not have known sin, for I would not have known what it is to covet if the law had not said, "You shall not covet." But sin, seizing an opportunity through the commandment, produced in me all kinds of covetousness. For apart from the law, sin lies dead. I was once alive apart from the law, but when the commandment came, sin came alive and I died. The very commandment that promised life proved to be death to me. For sin, seizing an opportunity through the commandment, deceived me and through it killed me.

Only the Gospel is capable of changing human nature, because it is God's very power to save (Romans 1:16). That is why the Apostle posits the attempt to achieve spiritual status in the eyes of God by law-keeping and tradition over against the effort to live according to the will of God, for His glory and as a response to His grace: I ... have died to law in order that I should live for God.

It is impossible to do both. We need to choose: either we rely on God for our spiritual lives, from the very beginning all the way to their glorious end, or we rely on ourselves to improve upon our salvation in some way.

The Gospel tells us that the grace of God is the source of our spiritual life. It teaches us to admit that, in spite of our efforts to understand spiritual things, in spite of the hours we might spend studying and thinking, all the books we might read and all the seminars we might attend, if God does not choose to enlighten us, we might become acquainted with facts, but we will never understand them. We might identify principles, but we will not experience their power, nor will we be able to live by them.

True spirituality is the product of what God does in our hearts, not of human effort. We have no ability but that which God grants us by grace. As Isaiah put it, "O Lord, you will ordain peace for us, for you have indeed done for us all our works" (Isaiah 26:12). Spiritual life is not a reward for human effort but a gift of God, the fruit of the sacrifice of the Messiah.

We should be careful not to attribute to ourselves what only God can do. "Shall the axe boast over him who hews with it, or the saw magnify itself against him who wields it? As if a rod should wield him who lifts it, or as if a staff should lift him who is not wood" (Isaiah 10:15). We, who put our trust in the Messiah, are the truly circumcised. It is we who worship God in spirit and in truth and boast in Jesus rather than in anything else (Philippians 3:3). Humility is to be preferred to any claim of merit—and humility is a far more realistic view of things. Dead to law of any kind, we are alive in relation to God, and partake of the endless blessings that are the fruit of his work for and in us.

> I, through a law, have died to law in order that I should live for God. I was crucified with the Messiah, alongside him, and it is not me who is now living but the Messiah living in me, and the life that I now live in the flesh I live through faith in the Son of God, who loved me and gave himself for me.

Paul is saying that he is dead to any law that purports to assure him of anything of spiritual value. Not only is he dead to the law, but law is what killed him. In the first part of the paragraph above he contrasts life by law-keeping against life for God and chooses the later. In the second part of the paragraph he enlarges on that idea, clarifying how and when he died to law and what are the results of that death. Let's look into that:

I was crucified with the Messiah, alongside him. The death of the Messiah marked the death of the Apostle. By His death, Messiah fulfilled all that the law demanded of Paul. How was this accomplished? In spite of his devout religiosity, Paul was a sinner and the law to which all men are subject determines, as does the Mosaic Law, "the soul that sins must die" (Ezekiel 18:4), and that "those who practice such things deserve to die" (Romans 1:32). But the Messiah intervened on Paul's behalf and died the death that Paul deserved. He atoned for the Apostle 's sin and thereby relieved him of the punishment law prescribes. Not only so, but the Messiah's death released Paul from any obligation law can impose as a condition for a relationship with God. God's relation to him is not determined by the extent which the Apostle meets a law's requirements but on God's kindness to him in the Messiah.

Of course, Paul's specific reference is to the Mosaic Law and to the Jewish interpretational tradition. But he uses a more general term because what was true of his relation to the Mosaic Law is true of all human beings' relationship to all and any law, including that to which the Galatians were subject before they were brought to faith. However these various laws may define sin and righteousness, they all prescribed death to sinners and assured blessing to the righteous. Paul is telling us that a law (in this case the Mosaic law) killed him by killing the Messiah. Paul died in the death of the Messiah, thus exhausting all of the law's demands on him. In terms of his standing before God, he is obliged to law no longer.

The death of the Messiah served not only to lay a foundation for salvation; it actually secured the salvation of those for whom it was intended. In other words, the Messiah's death did more than make salvation possible; it accomplished a real, full, complete salvation: I was crucified with the Messiah, not *in potentia* but in reality.

When Jesus died, Paul died, and his salvation was secured there and then, although it was realized later. God created so real an identification between the Messiah and those whom the Messiah represented on the cross, that they all died with Him and therefore inevitably rose with Him.

And it is not me who is now living but the Messiah living in me. The Apostle is not describing a mystical experience of the sort spoken of by eastern religions (and, regrettably, by some Christians). Our identity is not erased by conversion—after all, Paul continues to use the first person singular, "I" and, after he says that it is not him who lives, he goes on to speak of the life he lives in the body, trusting in the Messiah. Paul is referring to what God does in man's nature when He births him again by the power of the Holy Spirit, releases him from bondage to sin and binds him with bonds of love to the divine will.

Paul's seemingly incidental reference to the Messiah living in him serves to indicate its importance: the work of the Spirit and His presence in the heart of man is described in terms of the Messiah lives in me. The Holy Spirit is the Spirit of the Messiah (Romans 8:9, Philippians 1:19). The presence of the Spirit is the presence of the Messiah. That is why Jesus promised He would not leave His disciples orphaned, as it were, that he would come to them, and immediately afterward described His coming terms of the presence of the Spirit. Then, in the same breath He spoke of Himself and the Father coming to them and remaining with them (John 14:1–23).

Where the Holy Spirit is to be found, there too are the Father and the Son, because God cannot be divided. He is one, perfectly glorious, beautifully holy, almighty (that is, able to do all and anything He wants to do) and infinite in His wisdom and grace. Those who think that the Messiah can be received without the Holy Spirit are mistaken, as are any who think God can be divided.

We do not believe in half-gods, just as we do not believe in many gods or in a God made up of parts. There is but one God who is and was and will be all glorious; one to whom there is no equal; the first and the last of all that exists; without a beginning and without an end, immeasurable, unimaginable, unchangeable, indivisible, to whom nothing may be added; unlimited in power, happiness, holiness and glory.

This God is our God, our living Redeemer, our rock and joy in the day of troubles; He is our Captain, the one to whom we flee, our inheritance, the one upon whom we call. He is our Healer and our healing. He watches over us and assists us when we are in need. We gladly place our lives in His hands whether we sleep or are awake, whether we live or die. This God is our God. We fear and love none but Him.

Such is the God for whom and by whom the Apostle lived. Such is the God Paul aspired to glorify, whose will he endeavored to do. Paul labored to show all mankind the amazing glory of this wonderful God's grace and longed for all mankind to love Him sincerely.

> It is not me who is now living but the Messiah living in me, and the life that I now live in the flesh I live through faith in the Son of God, who loved me and gave himself for me.

The Apostle was not focused on being more spiritual but on loving God with all his heart, soul, mind and strength and, in so doing, presented us with an example we should follow. We said Paul is not speaking of a mystical experience in which he loses his individuality and in which, in some way, the Messiah takes over his being. These words make that much clear. Paul continues to be Paul. His nature has changed, that is to say, the direction of his life has been changed, but he remains himself. There is a mystery here, but no mysticism.

In the course of time his personality will also change, and he will become increasingly more like Jesus. But we are speaking of the same person. He is the one who makes decisions, but his decisions are now different because his priorities have changed due to the change that came over his tendencies. He still lives, as he puts it, in the flesh. He still eats and drinks, burps and hiccups, sleeps and awakes, is angry and hurts, rejoices and relaxes. But he now does all that, believing in the Son of God who loved me, who loved me and gave himself for me—and that is what makes all the difference.

Paul no longer relies on his efforts or supposed abilities in the course of his spiritual life. He relies on the Son of God and on what the Son did for him. God the Father loved Paul and gave His Son for him. The Son loved Paul and came willingly for Paul's salvation. He took on Himself all of Paul's guilt, bore his punishment, died for him and in his place. That kind of love obliges all to whom it is directed, which is why Paul mentions it here. He is appealing to Peter's conscience in an effort to draw him back to his previous loyalty to Jesus, who loved Peter as he loved Paul, and who did for him all that he did for Paul. Such an appeal was necessary because Peter's actions in withdrawing from table fellowship with non-Jewish believers and his support of the pro-circumcision group was a *de facto* denial of the Messiah, an act of disloyalty. Paul will say exactly that in a moment.

The Apostle sharpens the point of his appeal when he speaks of the Son of God who loved me and gave himself for me. We should pay attention to the little word "me." Paul is telling Peter that the Messiah did not love a faceless mass of human entities but that he went to the cross because He loved Paul, Peter, and every other individual the Father gave Him before the worlds were called into being (John 6:37,65). Some would depict God in terms of a machine-gunner who lays hold of the Gospel, aims at humanity at large, pulls the trigger and hopes to hit as many as possible. Paul thought of Him rather, in terms of a sharpshooter who zeroes in on his target, takes careful aim, patiently and with full determination squeezes the trigger, and hits exactly whom he wants to hit (John 6:45).

That is quite an amazing thought: God really and truly loved you and me. He loved us from eternity before the universe was created. He loved us unconditionally, for no reason but that which is found in Him. Long before He decided to create the world, before the first star appeared in heaven, in that eternity in which God dwells, He loved us and framed a plan meant to ensure our salvation. God's love is so wonderful! Ought we not love Him in return?!

Now comes the clincher: I do not make the death of the Messiah into nothing—because if righteousness is by way of a law, then there was no need for the Messiah to die. Paul has come to the point of his argument

with Peter and to the reason he has mentioned Messiah's great love. Peter
was known for his ardent, sincere, pure and enthusiastic love for Jesus.
Will he accept the idea that the death of the Messiah was unnecessary?

Paul considered it important for Peter to understand, that in spite of
his best intentions, the way Peter conducted himself with regard to believers from among the Gentiles was a denial of the Messiah's effectually
justifying and sanctifying love because it made light of the value of the
Messiah's achievements. Peter's actions spoke louder than his intended
words. Of course, he was not aware of the contradiction. He certainly
had no intention to belittle the Messiah's achievements. But the way he
behaved with regard to role of the Law and to Jewish tradition was a direct contradiction of the Gospel of grace.

That is why Paul says, I do not make the death of the Messiah into
nothing by separating myself from believers from among the Gentiles
and attributing to myself special status by virtue of being Jewish, keeping the Law and observing Jewish custom. Of course, Paul did not stop
viewing himself as Jewish. Nor did he give up loving his people in a most
unselfish way (Romans 9:1–2). But he loved the Messiah more, and he
understood that, because Messiah freed us from the burden the Law imposed, he freed all mankind from the duty to find acceptance with God
by way of law-keeping. He also understood that to act in a way that gives
the opposite impression is to make the grace of God into nothing.

Why? Because it implies that, by way of law-keeping, we can be justified, or at least add something to our salvation. If we can be sanctified
by works, if we can climb a spiritual ladder by doing things, there is no
reason to think we cannot be justified by the same means—and that can
only mean one thing: if righteousness is by way of a law, then there was no
need for the Messiah to die. His sufferings and death were a waste. Man
can manage on his own, without the sacrifice of the Messiah. Man can
gain by his efforts what Jesus obtained for him by His sacrifice.

It was important for Peter to understand salvation by grace was
meant to bring people to live wholly on the grounds of grace. We are
saved by grace, sanctified by grace, continue faithful by grace, and will
be glorified by nothing but grace. None of this can be the product of
something we may attribute to ourselves. How we live is the clearest testimony of the measure of our understanding of the Gospel and our faithfulness to it: do we live by grace or on the grounds of earned merit? Do
we relate to others on the basis of grace, or must they always be worthy
of our love? Grace is more than a doctrine; it is a way of life.

This is something we desperately need to understand. We can and ought to be faithful to our nation's culture and traditions. But these cannot add a whiff to our spirituality, nor may we allow faithfulness to national laws or traditions to be thought of as a form of faithfulness to God.

LET'S SUMMARIZE

- Did your initial experience of God's grace and its ongoing experience include recognition of sin in the light of God's law? If so, what is the remedy? Think of areas in which you need to improve, for example in relation to others.

- What have you learned from this section about spirituality and what are you going to do with what you have learned? Be specific.

- In what ways do you react to the discovery that God's love is directed specifically toward you in ways that are not true of all mankind? How does that fact oblige you, and to what?

LET'S PRAY

How we love Your law! You have loved us and will love us from eternity to eternity. You sent the Messiah to live and die for our sins, that we might live for You. Your law killed us, and the Messiah gave us life. We long to fulfill Your law. Move us, O God, to love You in real terms, not merely by emotions. Teach us to live in constant, joyous faith even as we strive to keep Your law. Move us never to trust in anything but Your grace and kindness. Help us always remember we are not entitled to anything but by the virtues of the Messiah, and that by His virtues we are entitled to the fullness of Your blessings. Work in us, so we never make light of grace or imply the Messiah died to no purpose, so You might be glorified in us, and we in Your, for Jesus' sake, Amen.

QUESTIONS FOR DISCUSSION AND STUDY

1. Summarize what Paul has to say here about the role of law in the Christian life.

2. What is the relation between living for God and what Paul says in verse 20?

3. Describe the roles of the Father, Son and Spirit in the course of our salvation (especially in sanctification).

4. Define the areas of continuity and discontinuity in our salvation and the process of sanctification.

5. Summarize: how did Peter's conduct annul the grace of God and imply that Christ died to no purpose?

CHAPTER 8

An Example from Abraham
(GALATIANS 3:1–14)

¹ Stupid Galatians! Who bewitched you, before whose eyes Jesus the Messiah was pictured crucified? ² This is the only thing I want to learn from you: did you receive the Spirit by keeping some law or by hearing the Gospel in faith? ³ Are you so stupid? — You've begun in the Spirit and now you achieve perfection by the flesh?! ⁴ Have you suffered so many things for nothing—if it was in fact for nothing? ⁵ He who gives you the Spirit and works miracles among you, does he do it because a law is kept or through a hearing with faith?

⁶ Abraham also "believed and it was attributed to him as righteousness." ⁷ So you should know that those who have faith are the sons of Abraham. ⁸ And the scripture, having seen in advance that God would justify the nations of the world through faith, announced the Gospel to Abraham: you will be a blessing to all the nations of the world. ⁹ So then, those who believe are blessed with Abraham, the believer, ¹⁰ and law-keepers are subject to a curse because it was written: "whoever does not continue in all the matters written in the scroll of the Law and do them is cursed."

¹¹ Well then, it is clear that no one is justified before God by a law because "by faith do the righteous live," ¹² and the Law is not of faith, but whoever fulfills its commandments live by them. ¹³⁻¹⁴ The

Messiah redeemed us from the curse that the Law imposes by becoming a curse for us (because it was written, "everyone who is
hanged on a tree is cursed"), so that the blessing, that blessing
promised Abraham, will reach the nations of the world through Jesus the Messiah and we would receive by faith the promised Spirit.

Stupid Galatians! Paul didn't mince words or hesitate to use strong
language when he thought there was justification for doing so. The Galatians were acting foolishly and Paul states that fact in the simplest, stark-
est terms. Can there be anything more stupid than to think that we can
improve upon what Messiah has accomplished? Can anything be more
foolish than to think that man is saved in spite of what he has done but
sanctified by what he does? And what should we say of those who needed
to be saved in spite of the extreme care with which they kept the Law, and
who, after they are saved, imagine that law-keeping can advance them
in God's ways? Clearly if we disagree with the Apostle, we're making a
serious mistake. As Paul puts it, (and let's not forget that this letter was
written under the inspiration of the Spirit of God) we're stupid.

We love ourselves too much. That is why we tend to attribute to ourselves abilities we do not have, and why we view anyone who thinks of
us otherwise as an enemy. That is why we turn every disagreement into
a personal conflict out of which we must emerge victorious and in the
course of which we are entitled to be offended and to offend. Having
lost an awareness of the importance of truth, and in light of the common
insistence that anyone's views is as good as anyone else's (unless they
disagree with us), we no longer dare speak clearly, and those who do prefer to insult rather than present a case. Everything has become a matter
of "he loves me, he loves me not" —as if we're the center of the universe.

The Scriptures teach us to prefer truth over any imagined honor and
to see our honor in that we are more concerned with truth than with
ourselves. That is why Paul could argue so forcefully with Peter, as we
saw in chapter two. That is also why he does not hesitate to write the
Galatians as he does. And they—both Peter and the Galatians—did not
choose to be offended. Instead, they learned from Paul's rebuke. Peter
corrected his ways and the Galatians preserved this letter, which is how
we have it today.

Paul cannot imagine that the Galatians' willingness to come under
the burden of the Law and Jewish tradition as part of their walk with
God is the fruit of careful study and an informed decision. He knows the

course they have chosen is stupid or the product of some negative influence. He recognizes the complete lack of logic in the Galatians' openness to this newfangled, old idea. If it is not the product of stupidity, it has to be the product of some kind of spell that was cast on them. Why else would they think in terms contrary to the Gospel? So he asks next, who bewitched you?

Over against the false view Paul presents Jesus and His atoning sacrifice: who bewitched you, before whose eyes Jesus was pictured crucified? Of course, he is speaking of the way he and Barnabas proclaimed the Gospel to the Galatians, and there are important lessons to be learned from the way he describes that proclamation.

The first lesson is that Paul and Barnabbas' focus was on Jesus. It was not on any felt need that the Galatians had (Do you have a problem? —Jesus will solve it. Is there no purpose to your life? —the Messiah will give you purpose. Are you unhappy? —Jesus will make you happy. Do you find life difficult? —The Messiah will give you strength). Jesus was the focus because it is through Him that God makes Himself known to people, and through Him that they come to God and learn to love and honor Him. The Messiah is the Savior, not man. He is the point and purpose of it all, the resolution of mankind's difficulties, which are the product of man's love for himself at God's expense, blinding him to God, distancing him from the only kind of happiness that lasts for eternity.

Nor was Paul and Barnabas' focus on the Holy Spirit, the Law, this or the other Christian view, be it Charismatic or Reformed. It was not on End Times or where Israel fits into the picture. The focus was on the Messiah, on His divine and human nature, the beauties of His person, the wonder of the truths He taught, His marvelous achievements by taking on humanity, living perfectly, dying to atone for sins, rising in power, ascending to the right hand of God and ruling in glory for the benefit of the redeemed.

The second lesson that we should learn from the way Paul describes how he and Barnabas proclaimed the Gospel in Galatia is that the Messiah was proclaimed as crucified. His apparent weakness was evidence of His endless strength. His death is the source of eternal life. He alone provides atonement. Only He can save. By His virtues, and His alone, can people be justified, sanctified, grow in faith, broaden their understanding, and deepen their spiritual lives. Every point in a person's favor before God is the product of the fact that Jesus was crucified for that person. Not only so, but Jesus' crucifixion is in itself an indication of

God's grace and kindness. Whatever a person has from God was given in spite of that person's ill desert. It was given because Jesus was crucified for him. The grace of God in the Messiah is the foundation on which a redeemed person's life is built, the source of his happiness and the grounds of his confidence. The Messiah's life and crucifixion have secured that person's ultimate salvation.

The third lesson that we should learn from the terms Paul uses to describe how he and Barnabas proclaimed the Gospel in Galatia (before whose eyes Jesus was pictured crucified) is this: Paul and Barnabas did not merely present the Galatians with a coherent series of facts, like lecturers in a university. They spoke with warmth, with excitement. They described the facts in so vivid a manner that the Galatians could actually see Jesus crucified before their very eyes. Paul and Barnabas knew how to address the mind, the will and the emotions. They really preached!

The Gospel does not address man's mind exclusively, although we should never circumvent the mind. The human mind is meant to serve as the gate through which other aspects of the person are approached. The mind is to examine and filter information, reject or accept it, and only then convey it to the emotions and the will. Truth is ultimately meant to reach the emotions, move them and bring a person to love the truth, embrace it, give himself to it, find his joy in it and make it his honest priority.

That is how truth addresses the will. Man's will must be shaped, motivated, directed and controlled by the truth. Once a message has been recognized to be true and the mind has allowed it to impact the emotions and the will, it is meant to move man to respond, to prefer it over what is not true, to submit to it gladly.

It is wrong to turn the order on its head. It is wrong to circumvent the mind and to manipulate people emotionally, just as it is wrong to force someone's will so that he acts contrary to what he believes is right. Truth must determine the emotions and the will. The will must suppress wrong emotions, rein in and modify exaggerated emotions and redirect them to God. So too it is as wrong to emphasize intellectual comprehension over against emotional acceptance, as it is to emphasize emotional responses over against intellectual and moral perception. Proclamations of the Gospel should be heartfelt, red-hot, intelligent, clear, persuasive and courageous. Those who proclaim the Gospel should respect human beings as God has made them to be and therefore know how to appeal to the whole person with their message.

May there be many such preachers among us!

And why is Paul reminding the Galatians how he and Barnabas proclaimed the Gospel among them? Because the Galatians were inclined to turn from that Gospel, although they did not understand that was what they were doing. They were inclined to oblige themselves to the Law and to Jewish tradition, assuming that doing so would give them some spiritual edge. That tendency worried Paul very much, which is why he writes as he does.

Paul faces the Galatians with four questions. This is the first. This is the only thing I want to learn from you: did you receive the Spirit by keeping a law or by hearing the Gospel in faith?

God wants us to lead lives that are shaped by the Gospel, which is why the Apostle's question brings the Galatians back to the simplest, basic facts of the Gospel: do you remember how you received the Holy Spirit, that is, how you were born again from above? On what basis did that happen? Did you need to do something in order to receive the Spirit? Or did you not, rather, hear the message and respond by believing what you heard—nothing more? Were you required to be circumcised or observe Israel's feasts and dietary laws? Were you required to acknowledge the spiritual authority of Israel's Rabbis and submit to their interpretations? Of course not.

Were you required to sanctify the seventh day, speak the truth, serve God according to his commandments, honor your parents, avoid coveting or do anything else before you could be saved? Again: of course not. Quite the opposite. It was because you did not do what you were supposed to do that you needed to be saved in the first place. The second of the two lists referred to are actually human duties, commanded by God. Those who do not fulfill them perfectly are sinners, objects of Gods' terrible and righteous anger. We have all sinned by not doing what we were required to do.

Well, then, how were your sins forgiven? How were you born again and saved from the righteous punishment of your sins? Paul replies: by hearing the Gospel in faith. You did nothing. Even the fact that you heard the Gospel in faith is not something you did because, if God had not worked in the circumstances of your lives, you would have never heard the Gospel (most people don't), and if God had not worked in your hearts you would not have responded to the Gospel in faith (most of those who hear do not respond in faith). We are not saved because we believe in the Messiah, by virtue of our faith in the Messiah. The virtue is all His. The credit—all of it—is due to the Messiah. He did it all. He bought our salvation by His life, death and resurrection. God gives us faith, and then uses that faith to give us salvation.

According to the Word of God, the way to come to faith is by hearing: "how will they believe if they do not hear?" (Romans 10:14). The Bible does not promote visions, dreams or miracles as the means to salvation but the hearing of God's Word. Faith is the product of such hearing (Romans 10:17). Sharing personal testimonies is nice, but the way to biblical faith is by way of a faithful, powerful, persuasive proclamation of biblical truth, the power being that of the Holy Spirit and the persuasiveness the product of His work in the hearts of those who hear the message. That is the way the Word of God should be proclaimed. That is how it is heard and results in salvation.

Finally, note how Paul describes salvation. He asks them, did you receive the Spirit by keeping a law or by hearing the Gospel in faith? They heard the Gospel, responded to it by faith and received the Spirit, that is to say, they were saved. Salvation is nothing less than being born again, from above, by the Spirit of God. There are not two stages. People receive the Spirit when they are born again, in fact, that is what being born again means. It is wrong to think that the new birth is followed by a second step by which we receive the Spirit. Here is how Paul describes salvation in his letter to the Romans:

> The law of the Spirit of life has set you free in Christ Jesus from the law of sin and death, for God has done what the law, weakened by the flesh, could not do. By sending his own Son in the likeness of sinful flesh and for sin, he condemned sin in the flesh in order that the righteous requirement of the law might be fulfilled in us, who walk not according to the flesh but according to the Spirit.

> For those who live according to the flesh set their minds on the things of the flesh, but those who live according to the Spirit set their minds on the things of the Spirit. For to set the mind on the flesh is death, but to set the mind on the Spirit is life and peace. For the mind that is set on the flesh is hostile to God, for it does not submit to God's law; indeed, it cannot. Those who are in the flesh cannot please God.

> You, however, are not in the flesh but in the Spirit, if in fact the Spirit of God dwells in you. Anyone who does not have the Spirit of Christ does not belong to him. But if Christ is in you, although the body is dead because of sin, the Spirit is life because of righteousness. If the Spirit of him who raised Jesus from the dead dwells in you, he who raised Christ

Jesus from the dead will also give life to your mortal bodies through his Spirit who dwells in you (Romans 8:2–11).

In other words, if you don't have the Spirit, you do not belong to the Messiah. You've never been born again.

This is the time to ask: have *you* received the Spirit? Are *you* saved? The test of your salvation is in the ongoing activity of the Holy Spirit in your heart. Are you guided by the Spirit? In other words, are you focused on cultivating your spiritual life or on meeting the desires of your body? Are you busy with God's will or do you prefer yours? Are you concerned with God's honor or your aspirations? Do you really, sincerely love God when no one is around, or have you heard the Gospel and somehow persuaded yourself that you believe it, and now have to suppress a nagging doubt? Have you been born from above, or are you doing your best to be a Christian? Have you received the Spirit? Have you been born again?

If you have, did you receive the Spirit because of something you did or, having heard the Gospel, were you surprised to discover in your heart a lively, bubbly, life-changing faith?

Are you so stupid? — You've begun in the Spirit and now you achieve perfection by the flesh?!

That is Paul's second question for the Galatians. Two more will follow.

As we have seen, life in the Messiah is shaped, motivated and guided by the Gospel. Whoever began on the basis of grace should understand that grace serves as the basis on which he will arrive at the end, not by keeping a law or a tradition. All who reach the finish line will do so by the strength God provides, and only by the grace of God will they receive the crown God set aside for each of the redeemed. It is nothing less than stupidity to think that a person, unable to save himself, can following his conversion, earn rights in the presence of God. The Gospel is not only for unbelievers; it is the essence of a believer's life. It teaches us constant reliance on the grace of God in the Messiah—in every step we take, in every matter and for every need. In short, sinners are saved by grace, sanctified by grace, grow in grace and receive eternal life by grace. No one is able to add anything to God's grace. Nor is there any need, for Messiah has done it all.

Of course, this does not mean that believers have no obligations, but Paul has purposely put off discussing these to the end of this letter, which is where we will discuss them. At this stage, what we need to internalize is that the principle on which the Gospel is established pertains to the whole of human life. We are never in a position to lay an obligation on God. He is never in our debt. We are never worthy of His blessings.

Instead, we are constantly dependent on his grace. The very best of our deeds are stained with our weaknesses and sins. Our most pronounced ability is but weakness, as is often shown to be the case as we go through life. Psalm 16 says, "You are my Lord; I have no good apart from you." For that reason, and for that reason alone the Psalmist can say,

> The Lord is my chosen portion and my cup; you hold my lot. The lines have fallen for me in pleasant places; indeed, I have a beautiful inheritance. I bless the Lord who gives me counsel; in the night also my heart instructs me. I have set the Lord always before me; because he is at my right hand, I shall not be shaken (verses 2, 4–8).

Some think otherwise. They believe that the Gospel is the threshold by which we enter the king's highway. But, they think, to be spiritually enriched, to broaden and deepen our spiritual lives and to conduct ourselves as Christians, we need more than the Gospel. The Messiah obtained forgiveness of our sins and now it is up to us to obey the Law, keep a tradition, undergo an experience, receive the Spirit, withstand pressures and so on. When and if we manage to do these things, we will arrive at a spiritual level at which we will be free from life's struggles.

Paul puts to all who think in these terms the simple, embarrassing question: Are you so stupid? — You've begun in the Spirit and now you achieve perfection by the flesh?! We need to learn to trust the Messiah for everything we hope to receive from God because all we receive is due to the Messiah's merits. There is no room to pretend we are able to add anything. Perfection is accessible on the same grounds as salvation: grace. The end must be compatible with the beginning.

Have you suffered so many things for nothing—if it was in fact for nothing? The third question with which Paul addresses the Galatians has to do with their initial experience of life in the Messiah. The fourth will have to do with their ongoing experience. The reason Paul faces the Galatians with these questions is that their willingness to turn away from grace to a different gospel (that is actually a no-gospel) not only contradicts everything they learned until the false teachers arrived in Galatia, it contradicted what the Galatians themselves originally believed and for which they suffered.

What did the Galatians suffer? Why did they suffer? They suffered because of the natural reaction of their neighbors and fellow nationals who saw them forsake the worship of Caesar and of the gods of their societies. They suffered because they turned from ancient traditions that governed their lives and defined their national and social standing. They suffered because they dared embrace a widely despised faith that ran contrary to everything the Roman and Jewish world of their day believed.

In the Roman world, one was measured by one's prowess in gaining wealth, in politics, at war or by gaining a following. Rome ruled from the southern border of Scotland in the west to the borders of Afghanistan and Tajikistan in the east, from the borders of the Sahara in the south to the Rhine in the north. Her arenas served for the display of physical strength. Her buildings spoke of might and affluence. Her symbols indicated her seeming invincibility. Her Emperor was considered to be divine. Then, out of the blue, this new religion appeared, one that denied the value and moral validity of human prowess, and conquered by what the average Roman citizen considered to be weakness.

No great conqueror stood at the head of this new Faith. Its leader was a Jew from a small town in troublesome Palestine, who was crucified at the instigation of His own people for rebellion, and whose disciples now spread the ridiculous fabrication that He had risen from the dead. This new religion did not speak of human abilities but of the lack thereof. It spoke of man's spiritual and moral defilement, from which none could rid himself. It spoke of a God who cannot be moved by sacrifices, speeches, mystical rituals or impressive feats. It spoke of humility, moderation in everything but the love of God, of turning the other cheek and of an altruistic, sacrificial generosity that did not serve for gain. The Romans thought of grace in terms of something purchased from the gods: Christians spoke of undeserved grace that accords the divine Giver nothing in return.

As a result, having believed the Gospel, the Galatians' social standing was eroded, friends and relatives viewed them as traitors, they were cast out of the social frameworks that served in those days as the economic and social backbone of everyday life.

Now they were inclined to turn from all that by accepting a purportedly Christian view that pretends to please God through human effort. They were invited to join an alternative social grouping made up of those who spoke of their unworthiness and who dared not claim to be worthy of God's good graces.

That is why the Apostle asks, Have you suffered so many things for nothing—if it was in fact for nothing? In the past you had turned away from yourselves and toward the Messiah. You had despaired of yourselves, put your trust in the Messiah and paid the price of that choice. But now you are turning your backs to the Messiah (although that is not what you intend to be doing) and reverting to trust in yourselves, in your ability to achieve in the spiritual realm what may only be given by grace. You are relying on that of which you had previously despaired, for good reason. Have you suffered for nothing? Were you wrong then? Was your suffering in vain, just as Jesus' death is being seen to be in vain by your actions, or perhaps you understood something then that you now are inclined to forget?

It is true: the Gospel of the Messiah does not meet the world's expectations. It rejects the world's standards, replacing them with very different ones:

> The word of the cross is folly to those who are perishing, but to us who are being saved it is the power of God. For it is written, "I will destroy the wisdom of the wise, and the discernment of the discerning I will thwart." Where is the one who is wise? Where is the scribe? Where is the debater of this age? Has not God made foolish the wisdom of the world? For since, in the wisdom of God, the world did not know God through wisdom, it pleased God through the folly of what we preach to save those who believe. For Jews demand signs and Greeks seek wisdom, but we preach Christ crucified, a stumbling block to Jews and folly to Gentiles, but to those who are called, both Jews and Greeks, Christ the power of God and the wisdom of God. For the foolishness of God is wiser than men, and the weakness of God is stronger than men.

> For consider your calling, brothers: not many of you were wise according to worldly standards, not many were powerful, not many were of noble birth. But God chose what is foolish in the world to shame the wise; God chose what is weak in the world to shame the strong; God chose what is low and despised in the world, even things that are not, to bring to nothing things that are, so that no human being might boast in the presence of God. And because of him you are in Christ Jesus, who became to us wisdom from God, righteousness and sanctification and redemption, so that, as it is written, "Let the one who boasts, boast in the Lord." (1 Corinthians 1:18–31).

Paul's third question (Have you suffered so many things for nothing— if it was in fact for nothing?) is based on the understanding that those who sincerely adhere to the Gospel and live it out will suffer. But that is how truly Christian victories are won: by the blood of the lamb, by the testimony of our lips and by our not loving life—even at the price of death. Not by carrying a Roman military ensign but by taking up the cross daily, trusting in the Messiah rather than ourselves, in the unlimited abilities of our Savior, the sovereign Lord of all, rather than our own.

Now comes the fourth question: He who gives you the Spirit and works miracles among you, does he do it because a law is kept or through a hearing with faith? This question has to do with the ongoing reality of the Galatians' life in Messiah. It is a simple but very pointed question. They had received the Spirit by grace, through faith. They had suffered much for the sake of that grace and in defense of that faith. Now a question arises with regard to ongoing realities: do they, even to the slightest degree, receive any of the Spirits gifts or enjoy any of His workings as the fruit of law-keeping, or are the works of God among and in them not the product of grace, God responding in His kindness to their trust in Him?

Are the miracles that God performs among them by His Spirit the reward of anything they do? Are they rewards for the sacrifices they bring, their adherence to dietary restrictions, their circumcision, observance of biblical feasts or praying with a prayer shawl and phylacteries? Or, rather, does God not act among them because He is kind even to those who do not deserve His kindness?

In other words, Paul is inviting the Galatians—and through them he is inviting us—to examine the realities of life. He does not ask if they feel more spiritual. True spirituality is not felt. Instead, others see its evidence in the sincerity of our love for God, our humble conduct and the purity of our morals. He is asking if they can point to any tangible advantage gained by their coming under the authority of laws, rules, prohibitions and requirements. Do they fear God more? Are their affections for God purer? Are they kinder? Humbler? More generous? Is their unity with other believers warmer, more stable, more solid? In essence, the new ideas the Galatians were inclined to adopt and that some among them apparently adopted claimed to be able to provide spiritual benefits. Has that claim proven to be true? Have the promises of the false teachers been fulfilled?

The Galatians might think that their understanding of Scripture deepened since they accepted the yoke of the Law and of Jewish tradition, but they are mistaken. Their understanding, in fact, was distorted by that yoke. Instead of deepening and broadening their faith, they had actually been impoverished. They bartered true spirituality—which is always the fruit of grace, the product of the Spirits working—for counterfeit spirituality, the product of human effort.

Paul does not answer the questions he posited, although the answers are evident. He posits these questions so that the Galatians would examine their hearts and lives, be reminded of the logic of the Gospel, and draw the necessary conclusions. In so doing, Paul acts as did the prophets of Israel (for example, Isaiah 5:4, 45:9, Jeremiah 2:5, Hosea 6:5, Micah 6:43, Malachi 1:6, 8).

There is great wisdom in this course of action. If the Galatians have the courage to examine themselves sincerely, they will inevitably come to the right conclusion, and there is no better way to change a person's mind than to encourage him to do so himself. Paul believes in his readers. He does not treat them like thoughtless children. He encourages them to think for themselves. We would do well to act as he does because that is the only way to raise mature Christians, stable in their principles, pure in their motives, wise in their decisions and consistent in their lifestyles.

Abraham also "believed and it was attributed to him as righteousness." Paul now turns to show the Galatians that those who claim to be faithful to the Law are, in fact, not what they claim to be because they are running against a principle that the Law itself indicates. Salvation by grace through faith is not a new idea that sprung up in Paul's day, during the Reformation or at any other moment in the course of history. It is a principle that lies at the very foundation of the relations between God and man ever since the world was called into being. For that reason, it is also a principle that lies at the foundation of God's relations with Israel, as can be seen from the days of Abraham. As far as righteousness before God is concerned, of any kind and at any level, man does not achieve it; God attributes it to man. It is not the fruit of man's doing but of God's.

Abraham also, Paul says and then goes on to quote the Law, "believed and it was attributed to him as righteousness." Just as the Spirit is given by grace, so too is an individual's righteousness the fruit of God's grace. What feat did Abraham perform for God to consider him to be righteous? None. To prove his point, Paul references Genesis 15:1–6.

Abraham was elderly and, although he had trusted in God, obeyed him, left his homeland and travelled to a country in which he was not allowed to settle, he was not given a son. His sacrificial obedience had not been rewarded. Then, one day, God revealed Himself to him and said, "Fear not, Abram, I am your shield; your reward shall be very great."

Abraham responded, "O Lord God, what will you give me, for I continue childless, and the heir of my house is Eliezer of Damascus? ... you have given me no offspring, and a member of my household will be my heir." God's answer was sharp: "This man shall not be your heir; your very own son shall be your heir." He then brought Abraham out of the tent and told him, "Look toward heaven, and number the stars, if you are able to number them ... So shall your offspring be."

You will not have a son because you are able to have one but in spite of your inability. You will not have a son because of something you do but because of something I will do. I will do the unexpected, the impossible, what no human is able to do.

And he (**Abraham**) believed the Lord, and he counted it to him as righteousness. God did not consider Abraham righteous because of anything Abraham had done. He attributed righteousness to Abraham because Abraham trusted Him. Abraham put his faith in God, in His infinite goodness and power. That is how righteousness comes to any. That is how all are saved. It is the only way a human being can be made righteous before God.

It was not without reason that God waited until both Abraham and Sarah were beyond the age of childbearing. This way it would be doubly clear that the son born to Abraham was not the product of Abraham's ability but of God's. That is how salvation is given. That is how any aspect of righteousness in the presence of God is possible. The merits are not man's; they are the gift of grace. The effort is not man's; it is God's. The Messiah did it all.

What followed in no way contradicted this principle. For example, Israel was not saved from bondage in Egypt because the people kept God's commandments. They did not even remember who God is and, if it were not for God's insistence and the leadership of Moses and Aaron, they would have remained in Egypt to this very day. The commandments of the Law, given after God brought the nation out, were meant to be the way a redeemed nation was to conduct itself, not the grounds of its redemption.

So then, Abraham believed, and God attributed righteousness to him, and that is how we too may be justified because righteousness in the sight of God is impossible in any other way (the term "righteousness" is meant here to include the whole course of man's life, all the way to his complete redemption in the kingdom of God). It is all by grace. It is all secured, maintained and preserved by grace. God chose to be glorified for the wonder of His grace, given to those who are undeserving. That is the Gospel at its essence. Our lives should be squarely established on the recognition of that truth. Because the Messiah did it all, we need not do anything.

So you should know that those who have faith are the sons of Abraham. All who have faith like Abraham's faith are the children of Abraham, regardless of whether they are Jewish or not.

Of course, Paul is not saying that Jews who do not have the faith that Abraham had are not descendants of Abraham and, as such, they are no longer obliged to the covenant God made with Abraham and his descendants. They continue to be objects of the promises and therefore they are obliged to the Gospel in a sense that is not true of the Gentiles. Just as Abraham had two sons and only of one of them was to inherit the promise, so too in this case. It is not enough to be born a child of Abraham. Being Jewish cannot ensure one's enjoyment of the promised blessing. Even if a Jew keeps all the commandments with utmost strictness, he cannot inherit the blessing unless he has the faith that Abraham had. The reason for this is clear: faith like Abraham's is what counts, not human effort.

On the other hand, just as many from the Gentiles were joined by way of their faith in the God of Israel to the covenant God made with Abraham, so will many believers from among the Gentiles inherit the blessing, while some of Abraham's descendants will not because of their lack of faith.

There is a measure of truth in the statement that all of Abraham's descendants are the objects of certain blessings. Paul does not hesitate to say (note the present tense),

> to them belong the adoption, the glory, the covenants, the giving of the law, the worship, and the promises. To them belong the patriarchs, and from their race, according to the flesh, is the Christ, who is God over all, blessed forever (Romans 9:4–5).

> As regards the gospel, they are enemies for your sake. But as regards election, they are beloved for the sake of their forefathers. For the gifts and the calling of God are irrevocable (Romans 11:28–29).

He later says (note the future tense), "the Deliverer will come from Zion, he will banish ungodliness from Jacob" (Romans 11:26).

This promise was not intended to ensure and therefore cannot ensure the salvation of all Jews. It is simply not true to say, according to the rabbinic dictum, that "all Israel have a part in the world to come." The main thrust of the promise to the descendants of Abraham as a whole does not relate to their personal standing before God, apart from the fact that the Gospel is directed at them in a sense that differs from and exceeds the way it is directed to non-Jews, and that the Gospel thereby obliges them in a way that is not true of non-Jews.

The nation of Israel is the only nation with which God entered into covenant, to which he granted a written and reliable revelation, bound it by His commandments, ordained it to His service and promised it a Savior. That being so, the responsibility and consequent guilt of Jews who break covenant and reject the Gospel is greater than those of non-Jews (Romans 1:16; 2:1–11). They fulfill what Paul speaks of when he says that "not all Israel are Israel" (Romans 9:6). They evidence the reality of which Jesus spoke when he said,

> I tell you, many will come from east and west and recline at table with Abraham, Isaac, and Jacob in the kingdom of heaven, while the sons of the kingdom will be thrown into the outer darkness. In that place there will be weeping and gnashing of teeth (Matthew 8:11–12).

On the other hand, a Jew whose faith is identical with Abraham's faith is fulfilling his calling as a Jew and thereby contributing to the fulfillment of the nation's calling. His faith in Jesus is not a foreign planting; it derives from the very root of the Faith that motivated the fathers, prophets and kings of Israel, and all of those from the nation who were true to God and to his covenant. Jews who embrace the Faith of the Messiah have not embraced a Gentile faith. The shoe is on the other foot: Gentiles have embraced the faith of Israel.

Those of us who are Jewish and put our trust in Jesus have not converted to another religion; those Jews who claim that what counts is the keeping of the commandments and the traditions are deceived. They, not we, have departed from the ways of God. They, not we, have turned their backs to the God of the Patriarchs and are worshipping themselves and their abilities. Abraham believed, and God accounted him righteous. That is what we Jewish Christians do.

> The scripture, who saw in advance that God would justify the Gentiles through faith, declared the Gospel to Abraham: you will be a blessing to all the Gentiles.

Paul is insisting that there is nothing new as far as the contents of the Gospel he proclaimed and what the Patriarchs believed are concerned. The same essence is to be found in both. It is the same Gospel, the same Faith, the same hope, although we are now in a more advanced, clearer stage of the process of revelation. The difference is found in that what was embryonic in the Patriarchs' faith is now full-fledged, what was in the bud has now come to fuller bloom. That is why he wrote elsewhere about "the mystery of Christ, which was not made known to the sons of men in other generations as it has now been revealed to his holy apostles and prophets by the Spirit" (Ephesians 3:4–5).

It is not that the mystery was altogether unknown, but that is was not known "as it has now been revealed." It was there all along. Now it has been made clearer, more pronounced, more fully nuanced. When God said to Abraham, "you will be a blessing to all the Gentiles," he spoke of a blessing both Jews and others from the Gentiles would receive. Paul and Barnabas proclaimed in Galatia, as did the Apostles in Judea, the commencement of that promise's fulfillment, which stated "that God would justify the Gentiles through faith," and that He would do so exactly as He justified Abraham, in the same way he justifies Jews.

In this context we should remember that justification is not merely forgiveness of sins. All the more it is not forgiveness of sins committed up to the moment an individual is born again, as if forgiveness after the new birth is contingent on something sinners must do. Justification is full and final, for all sins from the moment of birth to the moment of death. It includes the blessing of underserving sinners in this life and the assurance of their ultimate purification in eternity. It involves a change of heart wrought in sinners' hearts by the power of the Holy Spirit, the writing of God's law on their hearts and a radical change of the direction of their lives. New values appear, new priorities, real differences in behavior. What was is no longer, everything is made new, and the ultimate, perfect realization in the eternal future is assured—and all of this is accomplished by the grace of God, on the basis of the merits of the Messiah and by the working of the Holy Spirit.

This supra-natural, wonderful change is what remakes people into God's image and transforms human society from being selfish, abusive, hedonistic, short-sighted and focused on itself and the satisfaction of its lusts, into a society in which the loving fear of God motivates people to love one another, sacrifice for each other and exert themselves one for another, for the one and only reason that they are laboring together to love God more and to glorify Him more consistently.

The promise, "you will be a blessing to all the Gentiles," means peace between God and mankind. Such peace leads to peace between individuals and that, in turn, leads to peace between nations. It means a just, generous society in which those who belong are characterized by humility, holiness, industriousness and a wisdom in life that are the fruit of their desire to honor God and to express their love to Him. Such exactly was the vision of the prophets:

> It shall come to pass in the latter days that the mountain of the house of the Lord shall be established as the highest of the mountains, and shall be lifted up above the hills; and all the Gentiles shall flow to it, and many peoples shall come, and say: "Come, let us go up to the mountain of the Lord, to the house of the God of Jacob, that he may teach us his ways and that we may walk in his paths." For out of Zion shall go forth the law, and the word of the Lord from Jerusalem. He shall judge between the nations and shall decide disputes for many peoples; and they shall beat their swords into plowshares, and their spears into pruning hooks; nation shall not lift up sword against nation, neither shall they learn war anymore (Isaiah 2:2–4).

> The wolf shall dwell with the lamb, and the leopard shall lie down with the young goat, and the calf and the lion and the fattened calf together; and a little child shall lead them. The cow and the bear shall graze; their young shall lie down together; and the lion shall eat straw like the ox. The nursing child shall play over the hole of the cobra, and the weaned child shall put his hand on the adder's den. They shall not hurt or destroy in all my holy mountain; for the earth shall be full of the knowledge of the Lord as the waters cover the sea. In that day the root of Jesse, who shall stand as a signal for the peoples—of him shall the Gentiles inquire, and his resting place shall be glorious (Isaiah 11:6–10).

That is how the Gospel transforms families, communities and human society, calling them to glorify God by showing grace one to another and refashioning the image of God in them, previously marred through Adam's sin. The climax of that promise is described in the book of Revelation: "Behold, the dwelling place of God is with man. He will dwell with them, and they will be his people, and God himself will be with them as their God" (Revelation 21:3), which is nothing less than a fulfillment of God's promise to Abraham (Exodus 6:7, Leviticus 6:12). That is what the

Apostle meant when he wrote to the Romans about the promise given to Abraham that his descendants would inherit the world (Romans 4:13).

This delightful, eternal, assured future is wholly the product of God's gracious act on the basis of the Messiah's merits and by the power of the Holy Spirit.

Our view of the Gospel is often far too paltry, too narrow and altogether too shriveled to include its fullness. We tend to focus more than we ought on the salvation of individuals instead of the promised salvation of nations and transformation of creation, a salvation toward which history is inexorably progressing in spite of what meets the eye. God is the Lord of all events. He is guiding them with a sure hand toward their predetermined goal. Being God, He will not fail. Being God, He cannot fail. Paul was not taken up with the salvation of individuals to the extent that he did not think in these biblical terms. That is why he speaks here of the blessing intended for "all the Gentiles," which is also why he did not focus exclusively on the nation of Israel. Even when he thought of God's future saving work in Israel, he thought of it in terms of what it would mean for the world at large:

> If their trespass means riches for the world, and if their failure means riches for the Gentiles, how much more will their full inclusion mean! … if their rejection means the reconciliation of the world, what will their acceptance mean but life from the dead? (Romans 11:12, 15).

This blessing will not be realized in the world because the United Nations will become a transforming power, or because believers pray, do good and evangelize, or because of anything else humans might do. It will be realized through faith. It is a gift of God's grace, the goal of history and the hope of any who properly understand the Gospel promised Abraham and proclaimed by Paul.

Paul now reverts to his argument in verse 7 (those who have faith are the sons of Abraham) and draws the inevitable conclusion: So then, those who believe are blessed with Abraham the believer, and those who are keeping a law are subject to a curse because it was written: "whoever does not continue in all the matters written in the scroll of the Law and do them is cursed."

Paul is making two main points here, in each case proving his argument by reference to Scripture. First, the Apostle says, those who have the faith of Abraham, be they Jews or from the Gentiles, are blessed with Abraham the believer. Contrary to modern fascinations prevalent among some Evangelicals today, the main part of Abraham's blessing was not the promise of a land or of many descendants, certainly not the material wealth his children would amass over the years.

The main part of the blessing was God's promise to be with him, to be his God (Genesis 17:7–8), and the God of his descendants (Exodus 6: 41, Leviticus 11:45, Numbers 15:41). God accorded Abraham the title "my friend" (Isaiah 41:8) and called him to live his life in His divine presence (Genesis 17:1). God revealed Himself to Abraham more frequently than to anyone else mentioned in Scripture apart from Moses. All this was Abraham's lot by grace, without regard to anything he did, merely by way of the faith he had, following which God considered him righteous. That is exactly how the history of the world began, with an uninvited, uncontingent, unilateral, undeserved and sovereign word of God (Genesis 1:3) spoken to nothingness. That is also the essence of God's blessing to Israel over the years (Deuteronomy 29:13, Jeremiah 7:23, Ezekiel 11:20, 37: 23,27). All who believe as did Abraham receive the same blessing, on the same grounds.

The very thought that this should be so conveys tremendous comfort. Few of us are strong. Few are characterized by a large measure of self-discipline. Few are wise, think deeply about the Scriptures and are significantly consistent in our spiritual lives. And yet, those who believe are blessed with Abraham the believer.

We do not need to climb Mount Everest, fast 40 days, put a note in the Western Wall, adopt Jewish custom, crawl on our knees on the steps of the Vatican, have morning devotions, evangelize or do anything else to earn God's blessing. All we have from God is given exclusively on the grounds of grace, through faith, by virtue of the life, sacrifice, resurrection and ascension of the Messiah. That is precisely why those blessings are secure. The day will come when we will be brought into His presence, dressed in the righteousness of the Messiah, beautified with His beauty, to dwell in His presence forever, blessed, made holy and sharing His glory. Even now, in the course of our daily lives, we enjoy His blessing, protection and faithful love on the same grounds and by the same means. The grace of God is the firm foundation on which our lives and hopes are built.

Second, those who are keeping a law are subject to a curse, regardless of what law they keep. They might keep the Mosaic Law, Israel's traditions or the law and regulations of some religion, but by that means they will not obtain anything from God. It is not possible for human beings to be worthy of God's blessing. We shall never be able to put Him in our debt. Those who say otherwise are claiming to be their own saviors. They are declining the yoke of the kingdom of God and seeking to determine the terms on the basis of which they will be blessed.

God's response is sharp and clear: He will,

> punish the speech of the arrogant heart of the king of Assyria and the boastful look in his eyes. For he says: "By the strength of my hand I have done it, and by my wisdom, for I have understanding; I remove the boundaries of peoples and plunder their treasures; like a bull I bring down those who sit on thrones. My hand has found like a nest the wealth of the peoples; and as one gathers eggs that have been forsaken, so I have gathered all the earth; and there was none that moved a wing or opened the mouth or chirped." Shall the axe boast over him who hews with it, or the saw magnify itself against him who wields it?

> As if a rod should wield him who lifts it, or as if a staff should lift him who is not wood! Therefore the Lord God of hosts will send wasting sickness among his stout warriors, and under his glory a burning will be kindled, like the burning of fire (Isaiah 10:12–16).

Those who, in their arrogance, claim to obtain spiritual blessing by their efforts bring a curse on themselves. They are distancing themselves from blessing. We lose by effort what we cannot gain by effort.

Proof of such an understanding is to be found in the Law itself, which states that all who do not persist in keeping each and every one of its strictures are subject to a curse: those who are keeping a law are subject to a curse because it was written: 'whoever does not continue in all the matters written in the scroll of the Law and do them is cursed." It is not enough to sanctify the seventh day, to abstain from lying or fast on the Day of Atonement because

> whoever keeps the whole law but fails in one point has become guilty of all of it. For he who said, 'Do not commit adultery', also said, 'Do not murder'. If you do not commit adultery but do murder, you have become a transgressor of the law (James 2:10–11).

Who among us can claim to have kept any law to perfection? But a perfect God demands perfect obedience. A perfectly holy God demands perfect holiness. Nothing but perfection can satisfy Him because he cannot deny himself. He cannot be content with partial obedience or with spotty holiness, all the more so when such purported achievements are motivated by self-love and a vain effort on the part of man to establish ownership of himself and control of his destiny. If we do not love God with all our hearts, souls, minds, bodies and resources, our love is insufficient. If no spouse would accept a somewhat-love, why should Almighty God? In fact, even if we did love God with all we are and have, we would not love God enough.

The way to God's blessing is not through law-keeping but through reliance on Him, and *that* is exactly what faith in Him means.

Well then, it is clear that no one is justified before God by a law because "by faith do the righteous live." There is no other way: the choice is between justification by law-keeping or by grace through faith—and we should again remind ourselves that justification is far more than mere forgiveness of sins, that it includes the whole of salvation (Galatians 2:17, 5:4. Note that the Apostle speaks of those whose sins *have been* forgiven). A "righteous" person is one who lives his life in faith (by faith do the righteous live), who does not expect to earn blessing by law-keeping. Faith means that we rely on the grace of God, not on human merit, on God's ability to do for us what we cannot do for ourselves, on what God did for us in the Lord Messiah, and not on what we do for Him

No one is justified before God by a law. No one. It does not matter who he is, what he does, how strict he is in observing the law, or which parts he keeps. It does not matter if he is Jewish or not. The perfect holiness of God is so beautifully terrible that no human can approach it. Nor does it allow for compromise. It is not enough to do our best (though none of us do even that). It is not enough to do what we know (though none of us do all we know). The only way one can be righteous before God is by virtue of the atoning, purifying, saving, regenerating righteousness of the Messiah.

And the Law, like any other law, is not of faith, but whoever fulfills its commandments live by them. We cannot live by the commandments because law, by its very nature says, "do this perfectly and earn life. Do this without any imperfections and you will obtain blessing." The Law makes our blessing contingent of perfect conduct. That is how it teaches us how much we need the grace of God. That is how we come to see the extent to which we are dependent on grace. That is the purpose of the Law's emphasis on the need for sacrifice. That was, in fact, the summary of Israel's religious practice, the focal point of its faith and worship, almost the only thing the people did in their worship of God at the temple.

The sacrifices, constantly repeated, offered by priests who themselves required atonement and in a temple (before that, in a tabernacle) that needed to be purified (Leviticus17:6, 11–20), all pointed to the not-yet-provided need for an effective atonement because, as Ecclesiastes put it, "there is not a righteous man on earth who does good and never sins" (Ecclesiastes 7:20).

The Gospel uproots man's empty pride and exalts God. The Gospel puts man in his place and reminds him that he is no more than a creature, made by God for His glory, dependent in every sense on his Creator's good will. Man does not exist by virtue of his power, nor has he the right to himself or to his life. The very essence of sin is the arrogant claim that man is his own master. He is not. God is man's Lord and Master, and the Gospel teaches that lesson time and again by robbing us of the illusion that we are able to merit anything from God. That is exactly why pride is the opposite of the message of the Gospel and why sincere humility is a true expression of it.

> So that the blessing, that blessing promised Abraham, will reach the Gentiles through Jesus the Messiah, and so that we would receive by faith the promised Spirit, the Messiah redeemed us from the curse that the Law imposes by becoming a curse for us, because it was written, "everyone who is hanged on a tree is cursed."

What the Messiah did, He did for the Gentiles, all of them, although He never promised the Gentiles He would do so. That was a promise—and a calling—He gave Israel, not the nations. As Paul puts it, whatever He did involved doing something for us (Jews and non-Jews. Paul includes himself alongside the Galatians), to the end that we would receive from God what He had purposed to give us, and to redeem us from the curse. God acted in the Messiah to the end that the blessing promised Abraham, will reach the Gentiles, not only to Jews.

The blessing of which Paul speaks here is the blessing of salvation, with all that salvation involves. Paul is speaking of the blessing promised Abraham, which includes the promised Spirit, received by faith and not by law-keeping.

Prior to that, we were all subject to the curse that the Law imposes:

> "Cursed be the man who makes a carved or cast metal image, an abomination to the Lord, a thing made by the hands of a craftsman, and sets it up in secret." And all the people shall answer and say, "Amen."

"Cursed be anyone who dishonors his father or his mother.' And all the people shall say, "Amen."

"Cursed be anyone who moves his neighbor's landmark." And all the people shall say, "Amen."

"Cursed be anyone who misleads a blind man on the road." And all the people shall say, "Amen."

"Cursed be anyone who perverts the justice due to the sojourner, the fatherless, and the widow." And all the people shall say, "Amen."

"Cursed be anyone who lies with his father's wife, because he has uncovered his father's nakedness." And all the people shall say, "Amen."

"Cursed be anyone who lies with any kind of animal." And all the people shall say, "Amen."

"Cursed be anyone who lies with his sister, whether the daughter of his father or the daughter of his mother." And all the people shall say, "Amen."

"Cursed be anyone who lies with his mother-in-law." And all the people shall say, "Amen."

"Cursed be anyone who strikes down his neighbor in secret." And all the people shall say, "Amen."

"Cursed be anyone who takes a bribe to shed innocent blood." And all the people shall say, "Amen."

"Cursed be anyone who does not confirm the words of this law by doing them." And all the people shall say, "Amen." (Deuteronomy 27).

The curse of which the Law speaks pertains to all mankind but pertains specifically to the people of Israel by virtue of covenant made at Sinai ("to the Jew first and also to the Gentiles," Romans 2:9). the Messiah redeemed us from the curse that the Law imposes by becoming a curse for us, because it was written, "everyone who is hanged on a tree is cursed." It is worth stopping for a moment to think about the meaning of those words. We are so used to hearing them that we do not give them give sufficient thought.

Jesus took upon Himself the curse directed at those who disobey God. He assumed the curse that was meant for those who worship idols, despise their parents, lay obstacles in the path of the blind, pervert justice, take advantage of strangers, orphans and widows, lie with their father's wives, are guilty of bestiality, murder, bribery and extortion! In spite of His perfect holiness, He identified with such individuals and bore the awful curse that God in His righteousness determined should be their lot.

Think, too, of the nature of that curse. Think of Jesus' distress when God the Father, because of His righteous, His pure hatred of sin, turned His back to His Son. The very heavens darkened in amazement. The earth shook in horror. Yet the Messiah bore this So that the blessing, that blessing promised Abraham, will reach the Gentiles through Jesus the Messiah, and so that we would receive by faith the promised Spirit.

Such is the measure of the grace of God and of his goodness in the Messiah to all without distinction.

Let's Summarize

- How does self-love affect *your* spiritual life and what are you going to do about it?

- It what areas of your life should Jesus be more prominent than He is? Think of practical ways you can give Him the pre-eminence.

- Are there aspects of truth that entertain your mind without engaging your affections and impacting your life?

- We are all liable to stray without noticing. What steps should you take to reduce the likelihood that will happen to you?

Let's Pray

Great God of eternal wisdom, protect us from our foolishness, from ever presuming in Your presence. May we never attribute to ourselves what only You can do. Grant us so to understand the Gospel, so to love and internalize it, that it will become part and parcel of our very being. Having begun, by the working of the Spirit, our walk with You, grant us the grace to continue in the same way, true to You and true to the Gospel.

Faithless as we all are, none of us may legitimately consider himself a true son of Abraham unless You work in our hearts and grant us faith and repentance. Having granted us both, we are wonderfully blessed. By the kindness of Your heart, the Messiah bore the guilt and awful punishment of our sins that we might be given the promised Holy Spirit. We adore the majesty of that grace, we thrill at its sufficiency and we humbly submit to its governance, which we will endeavor to do until you introduce us into the kingdom of the Son of Your love, in whose name we pray, Amen.

QUESTION FOR DISCUSSION AND FOR STUDY

1. Discuss the role of pride in the Galatian error. Why is such pride foolish?

2. How similar was the Roman worldview to that common today? How does the Gospel contradict the world's view of itself?

3. Discuss the role of the mind, the affections and the will in the Christian life and the relations of the three one to another.

4. The truly Christian life is shaped by the Gospel. Why? How? In what areas? Be sure to think in practical terms.

5. Summarize what Paul has to say in this section about Israel, Gentile believers and their relation one to the other.

CHAPTER 9

Testaments Cannot Be Changed
(GALATIANS 3:15–18)

[15] Brothers, I speak in human terms: once a will, even a human one, is confirmed, no one cancels it or adds to it, [16] and the promises were given to Abraham and his seed. It was not written "seeds," referring to many, but to one, "and to your seed," who is the Messiah. [17] In other words, after God confirmed the will in the Messiah, the Law which came 430 years later cannot cancel it. If the Law had, in fact, cancelled it, it would have also cancelled the promise [18] because, if the inheritance is conditioned on law, the inheritance is no longer a promise. But God gave Abraham a promise.

Brothers, I speak in human terms: once a will, even a human one, is confirmed, no one cancels it or adds to it, and the promises were given to Abraham and his seed. Paul provides an excellent example to all who teach the Scriptures. First, he writes to be understood. To that end he enlisted various means to ensure, as much as possible, that his readers would, in fact, understand. After having made an argument from the Scriptures, he chooses to employ examples with which the Galatians would be familiar, taken from common experience. Later, he will illustrate his argument by referencing an event narrated and individuals mentioned in Scripture.

Paul is appealing to the Galatian's mind, to their conscience and their emotions. As a true teacher of God's Word, he uses every valid means at his disposal to assist the Galatians to recognize the truth of what he is teaching, understand its implications and embrace those truths in their walk with God. It is right to address people's minds, but our argument is more than an intellectual one and man is more than mind. Those who teach God's Word should address the whole of man.

Second, God's truth is the main issue. Paul is not attempting to entertain his readers, to curry their favor, meet their expectations or lighten the burden of the implications of the truth. He is not seeking to impress them with personal stories, or somehow enhance his value in their eyes. He is focusing on the Gospel, the truths of the Gospel and the binding implications of those truths. That is why he does not hesitate to insist on the truth and, when justified, use strong words. Because he loves God, he loves God's truth. He knows full well that it is the truth that is capable of bringing the Galatians back to God's ways, and that truth will do so time and again when the need arises.

He does not try to impress his readers with high-flying words, impressive oratory or hints of genius the depths of which no one can plumb. Instead, he takes up examples from daily life, as did the Messiah before him. He is not of those who think that if they speak of matters that exceed the understanding, people will inevitably consider them to be wise and therefore submit to his teaching. He wants them to know and understand the truth, and then respond to the truth, not to him.

Third, Paul is not a post-modernist, swimming with the flow, unwilling to affirm the existence of objective truth. He knows there is but one God and therefore but one truth, and it is on that truth he insists. He is not of the opinion that men are free to follow their hearts and believe as they deem right, but that the one truth of God obliges all mankind and demands the loyalty of all; that all will be judged by that truth and will pay the price of their rejection of it unless they find refuge in the Messiah. He believes in the existence of hell, in the coming judgement, in the Messiah who is both God and man, who lived a real human life, suffered and died and rose from the dead. Although these truths are foolishness in the eyes of those around him, he is not swayed. He will not shy away from truth or to obscure it in any way. He declares the truth with a courage, a clarity and a consistency that evoke admiration.

Fourth, he knows those to whom he writes and does not hesitate to use the realities of their lives to clarify the truth he teaches. He is not cut off from the lives of those to whom he writes. He knows the history of their faith, and he knows the patterns of life with which they are acquainted. That is how he is able to remind them of how they came to faith, and to use examples taken from their everyday life.

Finally, and this too is important enough to mention: we learn that it is simply not enough to know the truth; it needs to be understood. Nor is it enough to understand the truth; it needs to be obeyed. In Chapter Two of Galatians we saw that Peter's conduct conveyed a message that contradicted the Gospel's as well as Peter's intentions. Our conduct must be compatible with the Gospel, and the way to ensure that is the case is to plumb the depths of Gospel truth, discover its implications, and apply them thoughtfully, rather than in accordance with the various pressures brought to bear on us, capriciously, or in response to our prejudices and selfish preferences.

The first example Paul employs is taken from a Roman custom. An individual's last will and testament was thought of in terms of a covenant between a person and whoever was to be heir to that person. As such, terms were laid out: For example, "Justinus will care for me in my old age, protect my home from thieves, offer sacrifice to Zeus on my behalf and see to my burial under honorable circumstances. If he fulfills these obligations, he will inherit my farm in Capua, apart from five goats and three lambs, which I accord the local temple of Diana." Once the will was signed, Justinus could not alter its terms, nor could he demand anything but what was assigned to him in the will, on condition that he fulfilled his duties outlined therein. As Paul puts it, Once a will, even a human one, is confirmed, no one cancels it or adds to it. So, the will often included terms and benefits, the latter dependent on the former, which is precisely what constitutes a covenant. Remnants of that view are still with us, in the common term "last will and testament," because the term testament originally meant covenant.

Paul is utilizing the fact that wills were covenants because this suits what he wants to say to the Galatians. They were being encouraged to accept the yoke of the covenant made at Sinai and of Jewish tradition. Paul, on the other hand, is basing his argument on the covenant God made with Abraham. Contrary to what is often assumed today, Paul viewed the fundamental covenant between God and Israel to be the one made with Abraham, not that made with Israel in Sinai. That is why he references the promises made to Abraham and his descendants rather than the covenant of Sinai, which he will reference later.

> The promises were given to Abraham and his seed. It was not written "seeds," referring to many, but to one, "and to your seed," who is the Messiah.

Before Paul deals with the idea of a last will and testament, he needs to lay groundwork for what he wants to say. To that end he reminds his readers that the promises God made to Abraham were to Abraham and his seed, not just to Abraham. He then draws our attention to the word "seed."

Of course, Paul knows Hebrew. He knows that the word seed, in the singular, is a collective term, much like the words "fruit," "produce" and "deer," in which the one represents the many. In biblical Hebrew, the singular is the only form but in Pauls' day Hebrew allowed for the plural form as well (The Mishnah has a Tractate titled "Appointed Time," in the singular, referring to the biblical appointed times). Paul draws attention to the collective nature of the biblical word, seed in which the one represents the many by stating, It was not written "seeds," referring to many, but to one, "and to your seed," who is the Messiah. The Messiah represents the many. In Him the promises of the covenant find their present significant fulfillment and, in the future, will find their complete fulfillment. All those represented by Him will come to enjoy those blessings by virtue of His merits on their behalf.

In other words, Paul is insisting that the promises God gave Abraham are dependent on the Messiah and focus on Him, and that those who enjoy the promised blessings are individuals whom the Messiah represented in the course of His perfect life, His atoning sacrifice and His resurrection. That is why the promises will undoubtedly be fulfilled. They are not contingent on our obeying commandments but on Him having kept them perfectly; not on our abilities but on the powerful sufficiency of the Holy Spirits work in us. The Israel of God to which Paul makes reference at the end of this letter, the remnant of the people of Israel whom God had preserved for Himself and for whose salvation He acted in the Messiah, is not the church (the larger part of which is far from God), nor the evangelical church (that is far from perfect), nor is it the totality of the people of Israel (most of whom do not fear God), but those in the nation of Israel, alongside many non-Jewish disciples of the Messiah, who by grace are members of the body of the Messiah.

Israel has not been replaced, nor may we place our deeds in place of those of the Messiah. Nor may we place them alongside His accomplishments. God is true even if all mankind denies His existence or refuses the sweet yoke of His lordship; even if all men reject Him and turn away from Him, even if the nation of Israel does so. He will undoubtedly fulfill His promises to Abraham, and He will do so because of what the Messiah did on behalf of the people He represented, not because of anything man can attribute to himself.

So there you have it—a picture of Messiah's central role in the salvation of Israel as in that of any, and of His centrality in the life of faith. You also have an all-important principle for a truly spiritual life: everything in the Messiah, by the Messiah, through the Messiah and by virtue of what He has done. All who are in the Messiah are represented by Him and therefore a recipient of all the blessings of God.

> It is clear that no one is justified before God by a law because "by faith do the righteous live," and the Law is not of faith, but whoever fulfills its commandments live by them. So that the blessing, that blessing promised Abraham, will reach the Gentiles through Jesus the Messiah, and so that we would receive by faith the promised Spirit, the Messiah redeemed us from the curse that the Law imposes by becoming a curse for us, because it was written, "everyone who is hanged on a tree is cursed."

> We therefore thank God and dare not rely on ourselves.

> I'll say more: after God confirmed the will in the Messiah, the Law which came 430 years later cannot cancel. If the Law had, in fact, cancelled it would have also cancelled the promise because, if the inheritance is conditioned on a law, the inheritance is no longer a promise. But God gave Abraham a promise.

We have seen that the fundamental covenant between God and Israel is not the one made at Sinai but the one with Abraham. We have further seen that focusing on the Law given at Sinai at the expense of the Messiah is a grievous error. Now Paul brings yet another argument, connected with the one preceding: no one may cancel or alter a will, not even one written by man. By the same logic, the covenant of Sinai cannot alter the covenant God made with Abraham 430 years earlier. It cannot add conditions that we not part of the earlier covenant, because doing so cancels the promise that was part of that covenant. A promise given without being made contingent on Abraham's descendants' obedience cannot later be rendered conditional without cancelling the promise itself—and God made such an uncontingent promise to Abraham.

It may be that we have tired of hearing about the difference between trusting in the Messiah and observing the Law and Jewish tradition, but Paul does not tire of the subject. He returns to it time and again and it is our duty to hear him out. That, after all, is the subject of this letter.

If a will written by man cannot be altered, how much more so can there be no change to terms of the covenant made by God. It is therefore obvious that the Law of Sinai cannot alter the terms of the covenant with Abraham. It cannot replace trust in God and His ways with law-keeping. Any such change is to cancel the covenant altogether because it affects the covenant's very essence. Abraham was not called because he believed; he believed because he was called. The promise was not given him because he obeyed; he obeyed because he believed. His faith in the promise motivated him to obey. So to with Israel: God led them out of Egypt and then gave them the Law. He did not lead them out because they obeyed the Law. Redemption precedes obedience and leads to it (Romans 16:26); it is not the product of obedience.

Still further, if the inheritance is conditioned on a law, the inheritance is no longer a promise. But God gave Abraham a promise. Israel would have long lost its place in God's purposes if the inheritance is conditioned on a law. As much is true of us. After all, they and we repeatedly break God's law. Israel is far from the ways of God this very moment. Israel's society, like ours, is characterized by selfishness, pleasure seeking, rebellion against God, violence, promiscuity, gender-confusion and a willingness to take advantage of others. Even among some who profess religious faith we see evidence of a hypocritical lack of morality that is nothing short of amazing. God's faithful grace is the only thing that can assure blessing. He is a God who fulfills His promises precisely because He is the God of all grace. His kindness is not contingent on man's obedience.

Any who think otherwise do not understand the Gospel. If God's blessings depended on the level of our performance, we would have lost them long ago because we, like Israel are as unstable as water, as unreliable as sand, we are more consistent in sinning than we are in cultivating holiness in the fear of God.

LET'S SUMMARIZE

- Paul was deeply committed to the truth and used it wisely. Think of ways and specific circumstances in which you can emulate him.

- How central is the Messiah in your daily walk with God? Do you place anything alongside him? To illustrate your answer, give five examples of things you do daily that indicate the centrality of the Messiah in your thinking.

Let's Pray

In spite of our sins, You, gracious Lord, have not left us in darkness. You gave us, in the Scriptures, the light of life. Grant us the wisdom to use the Scriptures rightly, to understand them properly and live by them faithfully. We love Your truth, Oh God. We love Your Scriptures because we love You. We love the beauty of Your faithfulness, in which we find peace and assurance. The Messiah has secured our inclusion among the blessed. We revel in Him and would have Him ever as the focus of our lives. Without Him we have nothing. With and in Him we have the fullness of Your blessings, to be enjoyed in the company of all who put their trust in Him. We bless You for the power of the Gospel and its ability to change our hearts, our hopes and our longings. We rest in the comfort of the knowledge that, however much we fail, Your grace is able to ensure our inheritance because the Messiah has done all that is necessary for our salvation. Amen

Questions for Discussion and Study

1. Summarize Paul's principles of Bible interpretation as shown in this section.

2. Think of the implications to be drawn from the centrality of the Abrahamic covenant rather than that of Sinai.

3. Discuss the place and necessity of the Messiah in the fulfillment of the promises to Abraham.

4. Compare the principle expressed in verse 17 with Romans 5:12–21.

CHAPTER 10

What Was the Law For?
(GALATIANS 3:19–29)

[19] Well then, what was the Law for? It was added because of trespasses, until the seed for whom the promise was intended should come. It was given by means of angels and thorough a mediator ([20] and a mediator is not for one person, but God is one).

[21] So then, is the Law contrary to God's promises? It could never be! If there was a law that was capable of giving life, then righteousness would indeed come from law. [22] But the scripture imprisoned everything to sin so that, in Jesus the Messiah, the promise by faith would be given to those who believe.

[23] Before the coming of Faith we were held in custody, imprisoned for the Faith that was about to be revealed, [24] so that the Law was our mentor until the Messiah came, so that we would, by faith, receive righteousness. [25] But since the Faith has come, we are no longer subject to a mentor [26] because you are all sons of God through faith in the Messiah Jesus, [27] because every one of you who was baptized into the Messiah has clothed himself with the Messiah. [28] It is not possible that there still would be a Jew, nor a Greek. It is not possible that there still would be a slave, nor a freeman. It is not possible that still there would be male or female because you are all one in the Messiah Jesus, [29] and if you belong to the Messiah, you are the seed of Abraham, inheritors in accordance with the promise.

What the Apostle had to say about the grace of God in contrast with law-keeping raises an inevitable question which Paul hastens to reply: Well then, what was the Law for? It was added because of trespasses, until the seed for whom the promise was intended should come. It was given by the means of angels and thorough a mediator (and a mediator is not for one person, but God is one).

If the Law is not essential to the relationship between God and Israel (because the covenant with Abraham fulfills that role), if law-keeping cannot be the means by which believers secure God's blessing, what was the Law for? Why was it given? Did the Apostle's argument not render the Mosaic Law superfluous? If it did, what purpose did the Law serve? Paul replies, "it was not superfluous at all." There was a necessity at that time: it was added because of trespasses. When the people left Egypt, they were far from the ways of God. The nations surrounding them worshiped idols, and morality was not a feature of their lives or their religion. Not only so, but ever since Adam's sin in the Garden of Eden, men's hearts are inclined to evil. The people needed to be redirected to the ways of God. The influence of the nations round about needed to be restricted until something more effective was put in place. The Law served that purpose by establishing a protective barrier between Israel and the nations.

The Law had three aspects that, combined with promises and warnings, formed the terms of the Mosaic covenant and its content: there were laws that had to do with ritual, laws that had to do with government and national political conduct, and moral laws that reflected the divine perfections. The latter were and remain reflections of the image of God in man. As such they existed from the first day of creation and remain valid throughout eternity.

This latter aspect of the Law, the moral aspect, summarized in ten commandments, were always incumbent on mankind and remain so today. By it mankind will be judged. It was reiterated at Sinai and accorded special status in that the moral aspects of the Law and no others were written with the finger of God and deposited in the ark of the covenant.

The other two aspects separated Israel from the other nations, taught Israel the first principles of the worship of God and of orderly national life in accordance with the will of God.

Paul says that the Law was added. Added to what? Added to the promises God had given Abraham, to which Paul referred earlier. The apostle says that the Law was added because it is just that, an appendage, not essential to the promise and therefore not essential to the relations between God and Israel. It served a specific purpose for a specific period, until the seed for whom the promise was intended should come. The fundamental covenant is that made with Abraham. The appended Law was not intended to be eternally binding. It was added a long time after the promise was given, and its authority was to end when the seed came— and Paul has already made it clear that the seed is none other but the Messiah. As the sages of Israel put it, once the Messiah has arrived, the Law of the covenant made at Sinai is no longer binding—and we know that the Messiah has arrived.

The Law of Sinai was given by the means of angels and thorough a mediator. The Old Testament speaks of the giving of the Law in connection with the presence of angels: "The Lord came from Sinai and dawned from Seir upon us; he shone forth from Mount Paran; he came from the ten thousands of holy ones, with flaming fire at his right hand" (Deuteronomy 33:2). Apparently, Moses intended here is to say that the Law was given Israel by means of those "ten thousands of holy ones," presumed to be angels. (It is worth noting what is said in Hebrew 2:2 in this connection). Paul is telling us that the Law is inferior to the promise, because the promise was given to Abraham directly, by God Himself, whereas the Law at Sinai was given through angels and by the means of a mediator, that is, by the hand of Moses.

Of course, the Law had and has value in and of itself. It was God's special gift to Israel, a crown of glory and a path to holiness and to the presence of God. But, just as the light of moon cannot be seen when the sun rises, so does the Law pale in the light of the Messiah. Paul is drawing a contrast between the Messiah and what he describes as "the most basic things of the world" (4:3), and again "the fundamental, weak and empty basics" (4:9). He describes the law in such terms because it teaches important principles but is unable to save. The Law, like any law, cannot secure the salvation of a single individual for the simple reason that no one is capable of keeping it perfectly.

Having mentioned that Moses served as mediator in the giving of the Law, Paul adds, by way of a parentheses, a mediator is not for one person, but God is one. He here departs from the idea a will as such and puts more of an emphasis on its nature as a covenant. Two or more are always involved in a covenant. A mediator mediates between two (or more). Between whom, then, did Moses mediate since God is one? The other party was the seed for whom the promise was intended. That is to say, the

Messiah, serving as the representative of the remnant of Israel and of all those who were joined to that remnant.

The Messiah, as the representative of His people, was bound by the Law of the covenant given at Sinai and, as a representative of His people He lived under that Law (4:4), kept it to perfection and then, on behalf of His people, died the death it prescribed for sinners. In this way He exhausted all its requirements and freed His people from any further obligation to it. Christian obedience today is not to the covenant made at Sinai but to the eternal commandments of God, which reflect His holy nature. As we noted, those were reiterated at Sinai, but they existed long before and will never cease to be obligatory. That is the law God writes on the hearts of the redeemed by the power of the Spirit.

For those brought up on the assumption that the Law of Sinai comprises the essence of Israel's national identity, these ideas are hard to digest. But we must not refuse to embrace them. They are the truth of the Gospel.

The Law does not exceed the promise's importance; it was meant for a period and for a purpose. Now that the seed has come, the Law must leave the stage. Valuable as it is in itself, compared to the Messiah it is but a shadow, basic and powerless, not for any shortcoming in and of itself but due to our human frailty. By way of contrast, in the Messiah and by the Messiah's virtues,

> God has done what the law, weakened by the flesh, could not do. By sending his own Son in the likeness of sinful flesh and for sin, he condemned sin in the flesh, in order that the righteous requirement of the law might be fulfilled in us, who walk not according to the flesh but according to the Spirit (Romans 8:3-4).

We value each of the three aspects of the Law of Sinai as a true and time-oriented revelation of the will of God. We recognize its three aspects and we value beyond all measure the seed for whom the promise was intended, who, by grace, has chosen to share its blessing with us.

> So then, is the Law contrary to God's promises? It could never be! If there was a law that was capable of giving life, then righteousness would indeed come from law. But the scripture imprisoned everything to sin that that, in Jesus the Messiah, the promise by faith would be given to those who believe. Before the Faith we were guarded, imprisoned for the Faith that was about to be re-

vealed, so that the Law was our mentor until the Messiah came, so that we would, by faith, receive righteousness.

So, then, if the Law was intended but for a period, if it was added because of transgressions, and if its value compared to the Messiah is so low, another question inevitably arises: Is the Law contrary to God's promises? Is there a contradiction between the promise to Abraham and the Law given at Sinai, between the Gospel and the Law? Pauls' response is as sharp as can be imagined: It could never be! Indeed, it could not, not even to the slightest extent; the Gospel is the fulfillment of the Law. The very righteousness demanded by the Law is fulfilled in the life and sacrifice of the Messiah and is again fulfilled in the lives of those saved by the power of the Holy Spirit, who moved the redeemed to love the law of God and conduct their lives in accordance with it.

The apostle further explains, If there was a law that was capable of giving life, then righteousness would indeed come from law. We've already learned about the Law's weakness. We've also seen that the Law, like every law, is incapable of imparting life. We reminded ourselves that the fault does not lie with the Law but with us. We are enslaved to sin. We live in a body that is subject to sin. The most natural needs with which we were created have been distorted by sin. They have become lusts that drive us and increase our bondage yet further. Every one of us is driven by lusts of one kind or another. Some lusts are visible: gluttony, drugs, alcohol, sport, chess, FaceBook, Instagram, our cell phone or our tablet. Others are more refined, at least the beginning stage, before they take over and become characteristic of our conduct: the lust for status, approbation, money, influence and the like.

We referred earlier to another reason why there is no law capable of giving life: "the absolute, perfect, eternal, uncontingent holiness of God, before whom the angels of heaven hide their face in loving and adoring terror, is like a consuming fire that would obliterate puny man in a moment." Who is like God in holiness, righteousness and purity? Who is His equal in any sense? If there were such, even one, then righteousness would indeed come from law.

But the scripture imprisoned everything to sin by exposing the sin of all mankind. The Law was given Israel, but Israel shares defilement with all mankind. Scripture repeatedly tell us that there is not a single person who does good and does not sin. That is exactly Paul's argument in chapters 1-2 of his letter to the Romans, summarized in his statement to the effect that "all have sinned and fallen short of God's glory" (Romans 3: 23).

To what end did the Law imprison mankind in sin? So that, in Jesus the Messiah, the promise by faith would be given to those who believe. Now *that* is grace! What humans are incapable of achieving, God achieved for them. But—it is important to note—He did it His way, not in a way that appeals to human pride. Not by way of man obeying a law, observing a tradition or doing something else, but by God keeping a promise given by grace, in Jesus the Messiah, by faith, to those who believe.

That was the purpose of the Law. It was to that purpose it was given. Hence, it is obvious that the Law does not contradict the promise God gave Abraham. To the contrary: the Law is fulfilled in the fulfillment of the promise. In other words, the Law was meant to serve the promise, to pave the way for the promise's fulfillment, to advance, preserve and sharpen recognition of sin until the seed would come. It finds its fulfillment in Jesus the Messiah. He accomplished all it required, and He did so perfectly. Before the Faith we were guarded, imprisoned for the Faith that was about to be revealed, so that the Law was our mentor until the Messiah came, so that we would, by faith, receive righteousness. Not only does the Law not contradict the promise but it serves it, and both find their fulfillment in the Messiah.

> Before the Faith we were guarded, imprisoned for the Faith that was about to be revealed, so that the Law was our mentor until the Messiah came, so that we would, by faith, receive righteousness. But since the Faith has come, we are no longer subject to a mentor because you are all sons of God through faith in the Messiah Jesus.

The Law imprisoned us to the guilt of sin while serving, at the same time, as our mentor. The Greek word is *pedagogos*, from which we get the modern terms, pedagogy, pediatrician and so on. Paul is employing another example from his readers' daily life. Aristocrats and other rich individuals, even middle class members of society, would often engage slaves to serve as mentors for their sons (sometimes their daughters) and teach them reading, writing, poetry, elocution, finances, history and the national myths.

Such children could not so much as leave the house without being accompanied by their mentors, who would oversee their conduct and correct any error. Many of these mentors were known for their strictness. Their duty was to prepare their understudies for adult responsibility at home and in society. As soon as sons reached adulthood, they were granted the legal privileges of sonship. From that moment their mentors became their slaves, often loved and appreciated but void of authority over their former understudies, although the *pedagogoi* would naturally still have much they could teach the adult come-of-age.

Paul compares the Law to such mentors: the Law was, he says, our mentor until the Messiah came. Its role was to prepare us, so that we would, by faith, receive righteousness. Now, with the coming of the Messiah, the Law has fulfilled its role and we are no longer subject to a mentor because you are all sons of God through faith in the Messiah Jesus. The Law's former role has come to an end. We are now sons. By faith we have received righteousness and the Law no longer has authority over us, although it continues to be loved and can still teach us important lessons about God and the way to conduct ourselves.

Note that Paul has moved from the first person plural (us, we) to the second person plural (you). In the first case he includes himself. In the second he refers to Gentile believers. They (you, dear reader?), do not need to strive for equal status with believing Jews by way of some spiritual act such as law-keeping or observance of Jewish tradition. They (you? — if you are in the Messiah) have already been granted such equality: you are all sons of God through faith in the Messiah Jesus. We are all on the same par with Abraham, the father of all who believe, Jews and non-Jews alike. As such they and we are objects of God's amazing grace and all of the wonderful promises He gives His children.

> You are all sons of God through faith in the Messiah Jesus because every one of you who was baptized into the Messiah has clothed himself with the Messiah. It is not possible that there still would be a Jew, nor a Greek. It is not possible that there still would be a slave, nor a freeman. It is not possible that still there would be male of female because you are all one in The Messiah Jesus, and if you belong to the Messiah, you are the seed of Abraham, inheritors in accordance with the promise.

All of you, says Paul, with no exception, without regard to race, nationality, social standing or gender, whether you are Jewish or Gentile, are sons of God through faith in the Messiah Jesus. By grace you (we) have all been accorded this wonderful status. No more needs be done. If you have the Messiah you have everything, all that God accords, because it is all in the Messiah. You are not short of a single spiritual blessing. You are inheritors in accordance with the promise. The reason for that is because every one of you who was baptized into the Messiah has clothed himself with the Messiah.

Paul is not saying that baptism is the means by which we clothe ourselves with the Messiah. On the contrary, only those who are clothed with the Messiah, that is to say, who put their faith in Him, may be baptized. No magic is involved in God's dealings with man. Baptism is not what affects the change; it announces and seals the change publicly by obedience to the Messiah's commandment and accompanied with His blessing. As Peter puts it, in baptism we turn to God and "appeal to God for a good conscience, through the resurrection of Jesus Christ" (1 Peter 3:21). Baptism is itself an act of faith on the part of those baptized.

The implications of Pauls' statement is that, contrary to the practice of many beloved brethren in the Messiah, only those who have been regenerated by the Spirit of God, who have repented, been forgiven and clothed themselves with the Messiah by their faith in Him should be baptized. The righteousness of which they partake is not the reward of action on their part but of the Messiah's perfect work on their behalf and in them by His Spirit. The holiness of their lives is not the fruit of their efforts but of his for and in them. They do not boast in spiritual feats they have done but of those perfect, absolute and final feats He did by His life, death, resurrection and ascent to sit at the right hand of God, His Father and theirs, His God and theirs. They therefore rest confident, not in their abilities but in His determination to remain with them in spite of their weakness and sins.

That is why it is not possible that there still would be a Jew, nor a Greek. It is not possible that there still would be a slave, nor a freeman. It is not possible that still there would be male of female because you are all one in The Messiah Jesus, and if you belong to the Messiah, you are the seed of Abraham, inheritors in accordance with the promise. It is simply not possible. The status in the presence of God granted to all the redeemed is the product of their having put their faith in the Messiah, not in anything that has to do with them. It does not matter what their role or status in society may be, or whether there are male or female. It is not possible to create or maintain distinctions between those who are in the Messiah because God makes none such. Distinctions contradict the Gospel at its most basic, most essential point: the grounds on which we stand before God and are accepted by Him.

Is what we have from God given by grace or by any virtue we can attribute to ourselves? The answer is at hand for all who understand the Gospel: you are all one in The Messiah, without distinctions, apart from any differences, on no grounds but grace, and if you belong to the Messiah, you are the seed of Abraham, inheritors in accordance with the promise. You are no longer under the authority of a mentor. By grace, you are entitled to enjoy the inheritance the Father has reserved for you. By the same grace you are assured that will yet enjoy that inheritance to the full, so that he who boasts should boast in the Lord. This is the goal of the Gospel: that God would have all the glory, world without end. Amen.

LET'S SUMMARIZE

- Think for a moment: we all tend to want to rely on law-keeping. Examine your heart: why is this so. Think of examples when you fell into that trap.

- Grace is a wonderful thing. We all need it. Never rely on anything but grace, and remember that your relationship with others must reflect the grace you have been shown by God.

LET'S PRAY

Holy God of purity and righteousness, You have given us Your law that we might discover our need of You. You gave Israel the Law that it might lead the people to recognize their sinfulness and flee from themselves to You, forsake all efforts at self-justification and rely wholly on what the Messiah has done.

Your law condemned us, but Messiah has granted us a righteousness that cannot be taken from us. We have, by grace through faith, clothed ourselves with Him, who made us all the true seed of Abraham, inheritors in accordance with the promise. We thank and praise You for Your grace. May we always serve You in gratitude for the abundance of Your mercies to us, through Jesus the glorious Messiah, Amen.

QUESTIONS FOR DISCUSSION AND STUDY

1. Summarize what Paul says here about the purpose of the Law. Can you find Old Testament indications of that purpose?

2. Summarize according to this passage: law-keeping versus grace; the Law and the promise; law and grace.

3. Why is it impossible for there to be distinctions in the body of Messiah, such as are common in the world?

4. Discuss: does grace lead to obedience, or does obedience assure us of grace.

CHAPTER 11

No Longer Slaves
(GALATIANS 4:1–11)

¹ But, I say, for as long as the heir is a small child, he is no different in any way from a servant although he is the owner of everything, ² rather, he is subject to a guardian and to house managers up to the time that the father determined in advance. ³ So too we. When we were little children we were subject to the most basic things of the world, ⁴ but when the fullness of time arrived, God sent his Son, who came into the world through a woman and was subject to law, ⁵ in order to redeem those who are subject to law so that we would be adopted as sons. ⁶ And because you are sons, God has sent the Spirit of his Son into our hearts, crying, "Abba! Father!" ⁷ so that you are no longer a slave but a son, and if a son then, through God, an Heir.

⁸ In the past, when you did not know God, you served those who by nature are not gods. ⁹ But now, when you know God, or rather, now that you are known by God, how is it that you are turning again to the fundamental, weak and empty basics? Is it to these that you want to be enslaved again? ¹⁰ You take note of days and months and seasons and years! ¹¹ I'm afraid for you, lest I exerted myself among you for nothing.

But, I say, for as long as the heir is a small child, he is no different in any way from a servant although he is the owner of everything, rather, he is subject to a guardian and to house managers up to the time that the father determined in advance. So too we. When we were little children we were subject to the most basic things of the world.

Paul now turns to his third example, similar in many ways to the first. This is to be expected because his intention is to illustrate the same principle, here with a few differences that serve to clarify issues that were not as clear from the first example.

Paul now speaks of a guardian rather than the mentor spoken of earlier. A guardian is appointed to manage the affairs of a child until he is able to do so himself. For as long as the heir is a small child, he is no different in any way from a servant although he is the owner of everything, rather, he is subject to a guardian and to house managers up to the time that the father determined in advance. The guardian and the house managers determine what the child will do and how he is be treated, what he will be given and when, what will be withheld from him and why. The child is yet to inherit everything. It is all potentially his. But he cannot partake of anything that is legally his unless his guardian permits it under terms determined by the father.

Paul refers to the status of the child appointed heir and to the authority the guardian has over him as an illustration of the condition in which both the Jews and Gentiles were before the Messiah came. Surprisingly and contrary to common assumptions, he perceives no essential difference between the two: So too we. When we were little children we were subject to the most basic things of the world (note the inclusive we). What were those most basic things of the world? Paul identified these earlier in his letter: the Jews were subject by their traditions to the commandments of the Law in a way that contradicted the commandments' original purpose, as a means to obtain the blessing of God. The Galatians were subjected by their traditions to idolatrous ceremonies as a means to obtain the blessing of the gods. The principles that informed Jews and pagans were, at heart, identical. Both viewed divine blessing as the fruit of human effort, which is why Paul was right in saying that we—both Jews and idol worshippers—were subject to the most basic things of the world.

Such a principle has invaded some parts evangelical thinking today. Whenever it does, it distorts one's understanding of the Gospel and of the nature of spiritual life. It robs them of a significant measure of peace and increases their tendency to believe in their own abilities. Sometimes it leads to insecurity and despair of their standing before God, and to a sense of superiority in relation to fellow Christians.

Of course, God blesses efforts made for His glory and according to His Word. But none such can oblige Him. Nothing we can do is capable of making God our debtor. Nothing we are able to do can secure His blessing. Some may faithfully labor in the Gospel for years without seeing results. Some strive to walk close to God and yet contend with depression and a painful sense of spiritual destitution while, on the other hand, God in His grace blesses those whose lives are far from being exemplary.

God's blessings are never deserved. They are always given by grace. Whoever puts His trust in God will not be subject to the vicissitudes of life. He will reign in life by virtue of the Messiah's strength and accomplishments. Such a person's joy, peace of mind and confidence will not depend on circumstances but on God, in whom there is not a shadow of change. That being the case, such a person's life will be characterized by a stability in the presence of great difficulties. So, let's put our trust in God's faithful grace and reject any teaching that encourages us to rely on ourselves. This might sound like a contradiction, but it is only by such trust in Him and distrust in ourselves that we have real abilities, the fruit of His working in us.

How long is a child subject to his guardian? Up to the time that the father determined in advance. It is on this basis that Paul will ground what he has to say next: But when the fullness of time arrived, God sent his Son, who came into the world through a woman and was subject to law, in order to redeem those who are subject to law so that we would be adopted as sons.

But, contrary to the situation that pertained up to that moment, when the fullness of time arrived. The fullness of time is the time that the father determined in advance. It is up to the father to determine when his sons enjoy the inheritance prepared for them, and it is God who determines the time for any event in history and in the lives of those chosen by His grace.

When the fullness of time arrived, God sent his Son. The task the Father gave the Son is a task of immense importance to the Father: it is the purpose for which the universe was created and toward which history is being guided. For that reason, it was not entrusted even to the greatest of heaven's angels, but to the Son and to Him alone.

Almost incidentally, Paul describes the relations within the Godhead: God (the Father) sent his Son. That is exactly how the Messiah put it. He came as the messenger of the Father (John 5:23, 30, 37, 6:29 and others), to do the Father's will (John 5:30, 36). He always did what was pleasing to the Father (Matthew 3:17, John 5:30), doing what the Father does and speaking the words the Father gave Him to speak (John 12:49, 50, 14:10, 24).

The Father initiates, the Son fulfills the will of the Father, and He does so by the Spirit (Luke 1:30–35, Hebrew 9:14). The Son came in accordance with the Father's command. He is the one who came into the world through a woman and was subject to law. The truth expressed in these words is nothing short of breath-taking. First, we are told that God the Son came into the world through a woman. Although eternally divine, equal to the father in deity, He was conceived (by the power of the Spirit) in a woman's womb and was born as was every human being since creation. He took on real humanity, identical in every respect to that of all men, apart from sin. Unlike the gods of Greek and Roman myths, He did not appear in human form but actually took on human nature. Without ceasing to be Himself, He became man.

People wonder how man can be God. They have things backward. It is more correct to wonder how God can become man and, having wondered, we must admit we do not know. All we do know is that God the Son did exactly that, and that He did so in order to redeem those who are subject to law so that we would be adopted as sons. We therefore worship, awed and grateful, surprised and humbled as we contemplate such flabbergasting grace. We cannot explain, we can only adore.

Second, the Son was subject to law. The divine Law-Giver subjected Himself to the same laws that obliged His creatures. The Creator of all things bound Himself with prohibitions and imposed on Himself duties. The One purer than all purity was forbidden to commit adultery, steal or lie. The One who is the very epitome of righteousness was forbidden to covet his neighbor's donkey or anything that belonged to His neighbor. The One exalted above all was required to honor His father and mother, and to remember the Sabbath day and sanctify it, as if He would no longer be Himself unless He carefully observed these requirements. Not only so but He was to celebrate Passover, live in a booth during the Feats of Booths and thrice a year make his way up to Jerusalem and offer sacrifice! Such was the unimaginable humility that God the Son displayed, and to what end? So that we would be adopted as sons. There is a picture of God's grace in the Messiah!

The Son came into the world to redeem those who are subject to law, because all mankind is subject to God and therefore to His law. That law rules that the soul that sins shall die, that only those who observe God's law perfectly will live. We were all—Jews and non-Jews—subject to the basic things of the world and therefore to a bondage from which we could not redeem ourselves. Nor was there any who could redeem us until God intervened and sent His Son for that purpose.

God indeed intervened by sending His Son. The Son came, atoned for us by His sacrifice and transformed us by His Spirit. We have been born again and are no longer slaves but sons. Think for a moment of the change the Apostle is describing: no longer oppressed slaves but the very sons of God! No longer dependent on our performance but blessed by grace! No longer obliged to labor and to strive for life, repeatedly failing, but reigning in life through the Messiah! Such is our salvation. Those are the privileges we have been accorded by the Son of God, who came to redeem us.

> And because you are sons, God has sent the Spirit of his Son into our hearts, crying, "Abba! Father!," so that you are no longer a slave but a son, and if a son then, through God, an heir.

The first and most important blessing we receive as sons, which blessing testifies to all the others and assures us of the others, is the receipt of the Holy Spirit and His comforting, enlivening activity in our lives. That is the way by which God presently fulfills the promise "I will be with you" (Genesis 26:3, Deuteronomy 31:8, Isaiah 43:2). The Messiah has become our Immanuel by His Spirit who resides in us and who accompanies us in all our ways. This is what the Messiah promised in John 14:18, 20, 26–28:

> I will not leave you as orphans; I will come to you ... In that day you will know that I am in my Father, and you in me, and I in you ... the Helper, the Holy Spirit, whom the Father will send in my name, he will teach you all things and bring to your remembrance all that I have said to you. Peace I leave with you; my peace I give to you. Not as the world gives do I give to you. Let not your hearts be troubled, neither let them be afraid. You heard me say to you, 'I am going away, and I will come to you'.

Where the Son is to be found, there is also the Son and the Spirit. The Messiah comes to us by His Holy Spirit. God is with us by His Holy Spirit. Because we are sons, God has sent the Spirit of his Son into our hearts, crying, "Abba! Father!" These all are aspects of one wonderful reality, an aspect of the salvation purchased for us by the Messiah through His death, secured by His resurrection and ascent to the right hand of the Father.

The Christian Faith is far more than a perspective on life. The new birth is more than a certain understanding, even an understanding of our nothingness and our impurity in the sight of God, and a sincere turning from ourselves to Him. The Christian Faith is nothing less than the presence of God and His activity in our hearts—His activity, not ours. The new birth is not something we do for ourselves but something God does for and in us—it would even be right to say, that He does to us—and the Christian life issues out of what He does. The new birth is from above, from the Spirit.

There is no spiritual life apart from the Spirit, and there is no truly Christian activity apart from the Spirit of God. No one has the Spirit unless God the Father sends Him to him, and God does not send the Spirit to any but those whom He has made to be His sons by the merits of the obedience and sacrifice of the Messiah. The Spirit works in the world and in the hearts of individuals, driving them (more often than not, unconsciously) to accomplish God's purposes, but the Spirit does not reside in them; He influences them.

Here Paul is speaking of a very particular activity of the Holy Spirit, one restricted to those whose sins have been forgiven and who have been made new in the Messiah. The Spirit, he says, cries out in our hearts, "Abba! Father!" That is to say, he witnesses with our spirits that we are the children of God (Romans 8:15–16). Paul is again arguing against the false teaching that the Galatians were inclined to embrace. He is making use of the Galatians' experience of grace to show they ought not accept that teaching. The testimony of the Spirit is in their hearts. It is part of their everyday experience. They know they are children of God, by virtue of which they also know they are inheritors according to the promise. That being the case, why would they attempt to obtain by effort what is already theirs by grace because they are sons? They have in the Messiah all they need. He did it all.

The Apostle reminds them of the sweetness of that moment when they were born again, when the love of God was first poured out in their hearts and they knew they belonged to God and were loved by Him in spite of their sins and failures. He reminds them of the sweetness of their ongoing experience, when they turn to God in prayer, thanksgiving and praise, when they pour their hearts out before Him and seek His felt presence, how He draws near to them, embraces them in His love and reaffirms His faithful fatherhood.

Anyone who endeavors to obtain blessing by exerting himself in any way knows nothing of such sweet realities, although he may deceive himself into thinking he does. The only way we can claim to have done enough to deserve anything from God is by detracting from His awful yet wonderful holiness. We can never be confident of our relations with Him by any other means. Only those who rely on the grace of God can rest in confidence, knowing he is a child of God even when he errs, sins and strays. He knows God is a loving Father, even when he is angry with his erring children. Because you are sons, God has sent the Spirit of his Son into our hearts, crying, "Abba! Father. Hallelujah!

We should again note that the Apostle has moved from you to we. You refers to the Galatians, mostly non-Jews. We refers to Jews and non-Jews alike. From the moment the Galatians became children of God by faith like the faith of Abraham, they and Jewish believers share this wonderful reality of the presence and activity of the Spirit of God in their hearts. There is no difference between them. We also includes Paul because there is no difference between him—the Jew, an Apostle of the Messiah, a faithful messenger of God—and them—non-Jews who but recently heard the Gospel and were saved by it. Paul has no more of the Spirit than do they. He and they share as equals in the wonderful grace of God.

> Because you are sons, God has sent the Spirit of his Son into our hearts, crying, "Abba! Father!," so that you are no longer a slave but a son, and if a son then an heir through God.

Paul laid hold of a certain truth. It is more correct to say that a certain truth laid hold of Paul and changed his life. His world view underwent a revolution. This letter is being penned with the purpose of bringing about a similar revolution in the Galatians' world view and, consequently, in the way they conduct themselves.

They had been granted the greatest of all God's blessing: they became His children. As a testimony to that fact, God sent His Spirit into their hearts, crying "Abba, Father." Having become children of God by grace they also became inheritors by grace. God's blessing on them did not depend on their performance but on the perfection of what God did for them in the Messiah, by whose merits that became children. They no longer needed to exert themselves for fear they might lose or not obtain the promise. You are no longer a slave but a son, and if a son then an heir through God.

In the Roman world, the status of slaves—their very lives—hung on a thread. If their masters wished, they would live. If their masters wanted otherwise, they would die. If their masters wanted, they were sent to work in the fields or the pasture, to clean the house or educate the children. They had no choice. They could not wed but for their master's permission, and their children were often separated from them and sold to other masters. Slave owners had arbitrary power over their slaves over which there was no appeal. Consequently, slaves were almost always insecure. They invested tremendous efforts in winning and then retaining their masters' favor, so as not to be mistreated or have their fate sealed.

But, says Paul to the Galatians, you are no longer slaves. You are children. Your status is secure. Your inheritance is assured and that through God, a God who does not change. He is faithful even when you are not. You should not come under the yoke of any bondage in an effort to earn His favor and obtain blessing. Essentially, "you are no longer slaves, so why are you living as though you were?"

God's grace is a wonderful thing. It creates a reality to which nothing else can compare. We can strive to improve on our conduct and to cultivate our spiritual and moral standards, knowing full well that we shall repeatedly fall on our faces, but also knowing that God is with us, lovingly. We are kept by grace in spite of our failures. We cannot lose what we could not gain, and by the grace of God we will undoubtedly obtain what cannot be had by any other means. In the Messiah, God has secured for us a complete salvation which, when the moment comes, will become fully ours through God. The central characteristic of our lives is that we now exert ourselves as an expression of our gratitude to God, not in an effort to secure what the Messiah has already secured for us. We should trust Him.

In the past, when you did not know God, you served those who by nature are not gods. Most of the Galatians were, as we saw, non-Jews, but some of what is here said of them was not true only of them. It was also true of Jews. Both did not know God. Both believed that God, or the gods, condition His or their love on human effort, and that He or they are likely to turn away from them in anger if they do not obey, do not provide the sacrifices required of them or do not follow the prescribed rituals. The pagans believed in many gods whereas the Jews knew there is but one God. But there the gods of the Gentiles and the God in whom the Jews believed both conditioned their blessing on the performance of their adherents.

The people of Israel should never have thought of God in such terms, after all, they had received His inscripturated self-revelation. That revelation taught that all that exists came into being at God's initiative, for no reason but that which could be found in God. He had no need and there was, nor there be, any compulsion. That revelation further taught that God called Abram to Himself for no given reason but His will, that He led the people of Israel out of Egypt although they had not sought His help and could not even remember His name. The prophets likewise taught that God is faithful to His people even when He disciplines them for their unfaithfulness. But the people of Israel preferred to imagine a different god, one subject to human manipulation, moved by their sacrifices and prayers, motivated by their deeds.

Not only so, but all members of mankind have sworn allegiance to another idol, commonly worshipped to this very day: themselves. We place ourselves in the center of our universe. Our efforts are geared to promote our selfish interests, avoid pain and suffering, increase our wealth and happiness (as if the two are necessarily related) and ensure the fulfillment of our dreams. We are used to slogans such as "every man for himself," "human rights," "a woman has a right over her own body" (as if the child she bears is an extension of her body), "I am free to love whom I want," and so on. People dare believe they have the right to end the life with which they were entrusted by God, that suffering is inherently only evil, that they can ignore their God-given gender, that anything done in the name of love is permitted and that "the most important thing is that you're happy."

These are all lies. We must put our Creator and Lord at the center of our lives. All we do must be directed at forwarding His interests. There are some things for which it is worth suffering, and none more so than the glory of God. Our happiness, let alone our wealth, are not worthy goals; our calling is to live to the glory of God and according to His will. No man is master of his life. The most important thing is not that we are happy but that we do the right thing. No man has rights in the presence of God—we all have duties before Him and one to another. No woman has the right over her body—that right is reserved for God, and the image a woman bears in her womb is created in the image of God. We have no right to love whom we wish; we do not have the right to end our lives in an effort to avoid suffering, nor to change our gender, nor to think that whatever is done in the name of love is justified. We live in God's world, and in this world of His everything must be directed by His will and done for His glory.

That is why Paul says to the Galatians, In the past, when you did not know God, you served those who by nature are not gods. Now you must serve God, and such service begins by putting your trust in Him, not in yourself or anything you can do. But now, when you know God, or rather, now that you are known by God, how is it that you are turning again to the fundamental, weak and empty basics, instead of serving God as He deserves to be served? Is it to these that you want to be enslaved again?

Paul reminds the Galatians of their past because he wants to restrain them from returning to that past. What is surprising is that the Apostle draws a direct line between the time when they worshipped idols (you served those who by nature are not gods) and the present, when they contemplate coming under the authority of the Mosaic Law and of Jewish tradition, which he here describes in terms of the fundamental, weak and empty basics. He spells it out: you take note of days and months and seasons and years, in other words, you commemorate the biblical feasts, the seven-year calendar and the year of Jubilee. He makes it painfully clear that coming under such a yoke is to revert back to those days of pagan misconceptions.

How may such a comparison be justified? By understanding it. We've noted that the guiding assumption underlying idolatry was that, by way of his sacrifices, prayers and rituals, man purchases the goodwill of the gods. His standing in the eyes of the gods is contingent on those performances. We further noted that such exactly was the assumption the Galatians are now considering, this time in relation to the God of Israel: if they would do such and such, practice this tradition, wear this skull cap, celebrate this festival, they will be all the more spiritual, closer to perfection.

Their motives—at least those of many among them—are worthy: they hunger for the felt presence of God. They want to understand the Word of God more fully and to conduct themselves more exactly according to His will. The problem is that worthy motives and the best of intentions are incapable of justifying our actions of those actions are wrong. The Galatians were turning away from a fundamental principle of the Gospel, namely, that all we have from God is by grace.

That being the case, in spite of their good intentions and in spite of the fact that their efforts are directed at the God of Israel, they are departing from his way. As they did in the past, were worshipping a god who does not exist, whose favors they believed they could purchase and whose presence they could secure by human effort.

Paul reminds the Galatians that such a view constitutes a reversion to the fundamental, weak and empty basics of the world.

The people of Israel, like all people, were of course required to conduct themselves as God commanded. This is a first-truth, a fundamental principle in the order of the universe. But obedience does not accord people spiritual privileges before God. Nothing we do can put God in our debt or oblige Him in any way. Human abilities and human efforts, however sincere, however devout are far too weak to change man's heart, purge him of sin and make him acceptable to God. The Messiah having come, the futility of such efforts is all the clearer. The writer to the Hebrew reminds us that the mere fact that sacrifices need to be endlessly repeated indicated that, until Messiah came and made that one and perfect sacrifice, the way of salvation had not been fully opened.

That is why Paul says to the Galatians, I'm afraid for you, lest I exerted myself among you for nothing. I fear that my preaching the Gospel among you was to no end, that your faith was not truly saving faith, that your repentance was not sincere; that you, in fact, were not born again and that the Holy Spirit is not residing in your hearts. If that is the case, you are still in your sins.

Paul's statement is shocking. It is meant to shock. Paul is expressing a deep concern. His words constitute a dire a warning by which he hopes to awaken the Galatians to the implications of their ways and cause them to turn back.

A helpful detail we ought to take into account is the way Paul describes the Galatian's turning from themselves and their efforts to God in response to the Gospel: But now, when you know God, or rather, now that you are known by God. In the past they did not know God, but now they know him. They know that He is a God of grace, too holy to be bound my human action and too generous for there to be any need to bind Him. That being so, why would they turn their back to Him and return to their old ways? More importantly, not only do they know God, but they are known, acknowledged and loved, by Him. Nothing more is needed. They have become children of God because they have become children of Abraham. They therefore inherit by grace according to the promise. God acknowledges them as His children and will therefore undoubtedly accord them the inheritance He set aside for them. It is only right that they find happiness in that, and nowhere else.

Finally, the terms days and months and seasons and years require no further explanation. We should draw the necessary conclusions. Jewish Christians are free to celebrate their national feasts and customs, but none of these, nor all of them put together, can add one iota to anyone's walk with God. For that reason, the Messianic Movement, the Hebrew Roots Movement, much of Evangelical Fundamentalism and every other form of works religion is mistaken. We are saved by grace, blessed by grace and shall be glorified by grace. We cannot and need not do anything to add to our salvation, the Messiah did it all.

Let's Summarize

- Do you evidence stability in your walk through life? If not, why? How can what is taught in this section help you?

- Ever since the Messiah came we are living in the last days. In what practical ways does that truth impact your life?

- Consider the wonder of the Son becoming human and the implications of that amazing act on his part. Try to spell them out, so that they help you worship. Remind yourself that He did that for your redemption.

- Do you experience the presence and activity of the Spirit in your heart in the terms described above? In other words, do you hunger for God? Are you seeking holiness or happiness? If the Spirit did not teach you to despair of yourself and turn to God for salvation, and if He has not confirmed to your heart God's forgiveness, you have not been converted. If your life has not changed in fundamental ways, from self-righteousness to a reliance of God's grace in the Messiah, you have not been converted. Turn to God and plead with Him to redeem you from the bondage of your rebellion and make you His child by grace.

Let's Pray

The universe declares the wonder of Your glory. The Gospel declares the wonder of Your love and wisdom. We bow, dumbfounded in Your presence at the thought that You would stoop so low as to reach us, freeing us from the basic things of the world by sending Your Son to be our Savior. By grace we are now Your sons, no longer bound by the lie that we could be worthy of your kindness. You sent Your Spirit into our hearts whereby we cry out in glad confidence, Abba, Father. No longer slaves but sons and heirs by the power of what You have done for and in us, we exult the knowledge that You will yet have glory through us, and we in You.

Protect us, almighty God, from the arrogant tendency to claim merit in Your presence. Guard our straying hearts in the paths of Your righteousness, so that we attribute all we have to Your generosity, that none of us dare boast in Your presence, but that we attribute all the glory to You, to whom it is due through Jesus the Messiah, Amen.

QUESTIONS FOR DISCUSSION AND STUDY

1. Describe in brief the respective roles of the guardian and the mentor, and the relations between them and the child over whom they have been appointed. Now apply what you have written to yourself and your relationship to the Law of Moses and to law in general.

2. What new insight regarding Israel have you gained from this section? Indicate the important implications.

3. Define the difference between the Spirit's influence and His indwelling. Give Old Testament and New Testament examples of His influence.

4. What is the difference between knowing God and being known by Him? Why is Paul drawing that distinction (how does it serve his argument)?

CHAPTER 12

Love the Truth
(GALATIANS 4:12–20)

[12] Be like me because I am like you, brothers, I plead with you. You have not wronged me in any way. [13] And you know that because of a weakness in the flesh I proclaimed the Gospel to you in the past, [14] and you did not make light of the test to which you were put because of my flesh, nor did you despise me, but you received me as a messenger of God, like Jesus the Messiah. [15] Well then, where has your happiness gone? I testify concerning you that, if it were possible, you would have plucked out your eyes and given them to me— [16] and now, in telling you the truth, have I become your enemy? [17] They are zealous for you, but not for a good purpose. They want to separate you, [18] so that you would be zealous for them. It is always good to be zealous for a good thing, and not only when I am there with you.

[19] My children, for whom I experience the pains of childbirth again until Messiah is formed in you! [20] I want to be with you right now and to speak to you in a different way because I'm confused about you.

Be like me because I am like you, brothers. Some insist that the Apostles continued to observe a way of life subject to the Law and to rabbinical dictum. We already saw in 2:14 that this was not the case. Peter lived like a non-Jew and not like a Jew. We now learn that this was true of Paul.

Paul is appealing to the Galatians not to embrace Jewish custom, not to be circumcised or celebrate the Jewish feasts. Instead, he would have them follow his example. He did not live like a Jew. He no longer considered himself bound to do so. He was now like the Galatians.

To remove all doubt, it is worth considering other statements of the Apostle and to note another instance, described in the book of Acts, which serves some to claim (contrary to the evidence) that the Apostle adhered to the traditions.

In Paul's letter to the Philippians (3:4–11) the Apostle speaks plainly when he says,

> though I myself have reason for confidence in the flesh also. If anyone else thinks he has reason for confidence in the flesh, I have more: circumcised on the eighth day, of the people of Israel, of the tribe of Benjamin, a Hebrew of Hebrews; as to the law, a Pharisee; as to zeal, a persecutor of the church; as to righteousness under the law, blameless. But whatever gain I had, I counted as loss for the sake of Christ.

> Indeed, I count everything as loss because of the surpassing worth of knowing Christ Jesus my Lord. For his sake I have suffered the loss of all things and count them as rubbish, in order that I may gain Christ and be found in him, not having a righteousness of my own that comes from the law, but that which comes through faith in Christ, the righteousness from God that depends on faith—that I may know him and the power of his resurrection, and may share his sufferings, becoming like him in his death, that by any means possible I may attain the resurrection from the dead.

Paul see no advantage in his being Jewish or in keeping the traditions. In comparison to what he has in the Messiah he considered everything that had to do with his former religious devotion and with the fact that he is Jewish as mere "rubbish" (the Greek word is one that is not used in polite company). Of course, in and of themselves, the Law's commandments and some aspects of Jewish tradition have value. But in comparison with the Messiah's achievements and the gifts of God's grace, the Law and the traditions lose all value as to man's standing with God and the way by which man draws near to him.

That is why Paul says in verse 3 of the chapter we just quoted, "we" (as against those adhering to the law and the traditions) "are the circumcision, who worship by the Spirit of God and glory in Christ Jesus and put no confidence in the flesh." Our circumcision is a spiritual one: you have been filled in Him, who is the head of all rule and authority. In Him also you were circumcised with a circumcision made without hands, by putting off the body of the flesh, by the circumcision of Christ (Colossians 2:10–11). Who are those truly circumcised? Those "who worship by the Spirit of God and glory in Christ Jesus and put no confidence in the flesh."

That is why Paul says in his letter to the Colossians (2:16–23),

> therefore let no one pass judgment on you in questions of food and drink, or with regard to a festival or a new moon or a Sabbath. These are a shadow of the things to come, but the substance belongs to Christ. Let no one disqualify you, insisting on asceticism and worship of angels, going on in detail about visions, puffed up without reason by his sensuous mind, and not holding fast to the Head, from whom the whole body, nourished and knit together through its joints and ligaments, grows with a growth that is from God.

> If with Christ you died to the elemental spirits of the world, why, as if you were still alive in the world, do you submit to regulations— "Do not handle, Do not taste, Do not touch" (referring to things that all perish as they are used)—according to human precepts and teachings? These have indeed an appearance of wisdom in promoting self-made religion and asceticism and severity to the body, but they are of no value in stopping the indulgence of the flesh.

That is exactly what Paul says to the Galatians in 4:8–11, in the past, when you did not know God, you served those who by nature are not gods. But now, when you know God, or rather, now that you are known by God, how is it that you are turning again to the fundamental, weak and empty basics? Is it to these that you want to be enslaved again? You take note of days and months and seasons and years! I'm afraid for you, lest I exerted myself among you for nothing.

That is also the logic of what he will write years later in his first letter to the Corinthians (9:20–23):

> To the Jews I became as a Jew, in order to win Jews. To those under the law I became as one under the law (though not being myself under the law) that I might win those under the law. To those outside the law I became as one outside the law (not being outside the law of God

but under the law of Christ) that I might win those outside the law. To the weak I became weak, that I might win the weak. I have become all things to all people, that by all means I might save some. I do it all for the sake of the gospel, that I may share with them in its blessings.

"I became," he says "as one under the law," but I am not longer such. I am no longer obliged by the Law, and when "I became as one under the law," I did so "that I might win" sinners, not because it was my duty to keep law of any kind. "I do it all for the sake of the Gospel."

In spite of these clear words, some use Acts 21 to insist that Paul and the other Apostles kept the Law and the traditions. However, a closer look at that portion of Scripture proves otherwise. True, there were "thousands ... among the Jews of those who have believed ...(were) all zealous for the law" (verse 20). James says a much to Paul when he requests that Paul take part in a religious ceremony conducted in the temple. The question is if those thousands were duty-bound to do so, or if they had not yet comprehended the freedom that the Messiah had purchased for them by His sacrifice.

What is interesting is that James does not say that he and the other Apostles observed the Law, as we would expect him to say in an effort to persuade Paul do act likewise. Nor does he say that Paul should observe the Law or the traditions. He merely asks Paul to take part in the ceremony, and the Apostle was obviously free to refuse. Regardless of whether or not James and the Apostles in Jerusalem conducted themselves, there is no evidence that indicates they believed themselves bound by Israel's traditions. In fact, James language actually indicates that he did not number himself among those thousands of fellow believing Jews, "all zealous for the law." He, like Paul, was zealous for the Gospel.

James explained that those thousands had heard that "you teach all the Jews who are among the Gentiles to forsake Moses, telling them not to circumcise their children or walk according to our customs," as if to say Paul was engaged in a campaign against the Law and the traditions, as if he was engaged in promoting a loss of Jewish national identity. Such accusations were not true. Paul never called on Jewish Christians to forsake their national traditions; he called on them to consider them no longer as spiritual duties. Certain traditions and commandments of the Law inevitably became redundant once the Messiah had come. The first of these were, of course, all the rules that had to do with sacrifices, purifications and the like, that is to say, the heart of the ritual aspects of the Law.

But Paul never opposed Jews celebrating the biblical feasts and other aspects of their national traditions. On the contrary, he wrote to the Corinthians,

> was anyone at the time of his call already circumcised? Let him not seek to remove the marks of circumcision. Was anyone at the time of his call uncircumcised? Let him not seek circumcision. For neither circumcision counts for anything nor uncircumcision but keeping the commandments of God. Each one should remain in the condition in which he was called (1 Corinthians 7:18–20).

That should be our stance.

I plead with you. You have not wronged me in any way. People nowadays are accustomed to view every difference of opinion as a matter pf personal affront. Paul is not as much in love with himself as we are with ourselves. He labored among the Galatians and for them. In the past they had received him with tremendous enthusiasm (as he will say in a moment), but now it seemed they were turning away from him and from his Gospel. This causes him grave concern, but he does not view their behavior as a personal affront. He is sincerely concerned for the glory of God in the Messiah and for the Galatian's spiritual welfare.

Paul considers it important to make it clear to the Galatians that, on his part, there is no sense of insult, nor was he engaged in a personal struggle. He was not taken up with creating a movement that surrounded him and his personality but with the kingdom of God and with God's glory. Some years later he rebuked the Corinthian Christians when they displayed a tendency to exalt one teacher of the Gospel or another:

> it has been reported to me by Chloe's people that there is quarreling among you, my brothers. What I mean is that each one of you says, "I follow Paul," or "I follow Apollos," or "I follow Cephas," or "I follow Christ." Is Christ divided? Was Paul crucified for you? Or were you baptized in the name of Paul? I thank God that I baptized none of you except Crispus and Gaius, so that no one may say that you were baptized in my name. (I did baptize also the household of Stephanas. Beyond that, I do not know whether I baptized anyone else.) For Christ did not send me to baptize but to preach the gospel, and not with words of eloquent wisdom ...

> But I, brothers, could not address you as spiritual people, but as people of the flesh, as infants in Christ. I fed you with milk, not solid food, for

you were not ready for it. And even now you are not yet ready, for you are still of the flesh. For while there is jealousy and strife among you, are you not of the flesh and behaving only in a human way? For when one says, "I follow Paul," and another, "I follow Apollos," are you not being merely human?

What then is Apollos? What is Paul? Servants through whom you believed, as the Lord assigned to each. I planted, Apollos watered, but God gave the growth. So neither he who plants nor he who waters is anything, but only God who gives the growth. He who plants and he who waters are one, and each will receive his wages according to his labor. For we are God's fellow workers. You are God's field, God's building" (1 Corinthians 1:11–17, 3:1–9).

We err if we do not do as did Paul. We err if we are busy promoting our status, broadening the borders of our kingdom or defending our honor rather than promoting the glory of God and His kingdom—and the one always—but always! —comes at the expense of the other. All the more do we err if we use the Gospel for personal interests.

People should be able to disagree with us without becoming our enemies. People may and should stand their ground, even if they are mistaken, until they see things differently. Disagreements should be conducted honorably. Discussions should be to the point, without personal recriminations and without becoming a struggle between personalities. Congregants, congregations and family members may disagree with one other without promoting the self-love that lurks in all of our hearts. We would eliminate a great deal of pain in the world if we were but willing to lend a listening ear and an open heart to other people's views, weigh them courageously and adopt or reject them on fair, objective grounds, without being dragged into personal conflict. For that to happen we need to cultivate sincere humility, but that is exactly what the Gospel calls upon us to cultivate.

And you know that because of a weakness in the flesh I proclaimed the Gospel to you in the past. We are unacquainted with the circumstances to which the Apostle is referring by these words. Many offer various conjectures, some of them quite reasonable. But, for lack of definitive evidence, we do best not to conjecture. Ultimately, even if we chance on the right explanation, it would not affect our understanding of the point Paul is making, and that is what is important. The point is this: Paul arrived in Galatia due to some physical ailment and, in spite of his condition, he made use of the time he was there to proclaim the Gospel. He did not focus on himself or on his health but on the Messiah. He therefore was engaged with the Gospel, even under circumstances in which one would expect him to do otherwise. Paul took every advantage that came his way to serve God. By so doing he set us an example we should emulate.

In a culture that worshipped strength, health, power, wealth and status Paul declared the Gospel at a time when he displayed obvious physical weakness, and Paul describes the Galatian's response as, and you did not make like of the test to which you were put because of my flesh, nor did you despise me, but you received me as a messenger of God, like Jesus the Messiah.

The power of God was evident through the Apostle's weakness, so the Galatians did not take Pauls' weakness into account; they were taken by the power of the Gospel he proclaimed. By the mere fact that Paul did not arrive in Galatia as a conquering general, with a royal retinue or in the company of armed guards, a lictor preceding him to announce the arrival of this important personage, the Apostle exemplified the Gospel by his conduct while proclaiming it verbally. He arrived in bodily weakness, visible to all. He differed radically from those who pretend to proclaim the Gospel and who display their power to heal, work miracles and bring their adherents health, wealth and happiness. Paul could not even cure himself of whatever it was from which he was suffering, let alone run healing campaigns for others.

That is what Paul describes as the test to which you were put: would they prefer health to truth, immediate happiness to God, or would they turn from themselves to God? Would they continue to worship gods in the form of mankind, who are jealous one of another, who compete with one another and offend each other, in hope to obtain from such false gods the satisfaction of their desires, or would they forsake idolatry and turn to the living God?

The Galatians stood the test. They did not despise Paul in spite of his weakness. They did not make light of his message and did not reject the Gospel he proclaimed. Rather, they welcomed him as a messenger of God who brought them God's Word, like Jesus the Messiah Himself, who came to save them. By so doing they evidenced the sincerity and purity of their faith. They proved by their actions that they had not turned from their idols to the Messiah in hope of gaining anything in this word. They did not turn to obtain happiness, meaning in life, the resolution of their problems, healing or wealth. They turned to God because that was the right thing to do. They turned because they understood that the essence of sin is self-love—that very love that causes people to focus on health, wealth and happiness instead of on God.

In so doing the Galatians were, as was their teacher, true to the Gospel. The question we face today—and no question is more important—is, are we are faithful as were the Galatians when they first heard the Gospel? Have we truly turned away from ourselves to God? Have we ceased trying to use God to get what we want or—God forbid—are we still in our sins although we've persuaded ourselves that we are Christians?

> Well then, where has your happiness gone? I testify concerning you that, if it were possible, you would have plucked out your eyes and given them to me—and now, telling you the truth, I have become your enemy?

Paul reminded the Galatians of the enthusiasm with which they received the Gospel he preached because their present conduct contradicts that enthusiasm. At that time the Gospel had been presented to them under circumstances in which the Apostle 's weakness was plain for all to see. Still, it was received. But now, the Gospel the Galatians are inclined to embrace stands in direct contrast to the one they heard from Paul. This supposed gospel speaks of human ability, whereas the Gospel of the Messiah speaks of the absence of such ability. The Galatians are now acting in a way that denies the true Gospel.

Previously, they had received Paul with much affection. Now their attitude toward him has changed. In the past, having been forgiven by grace and accepted by God, they were delighted. Joy filled their hearts and they received the messenger of the Gospel in the same spirit of happiness. Now Paul asks, Well then, where has your happiness gone? I testify concerning you that, if it were possible, you would have plucked out your eyes and given them to me—and now, telling you the truth, I have become your enemy?

It is as sad as it is shocking to see how quickly and for what reasons friends, even Christian friends, can become enemies. So long as someone serves our purposes, he or she is liked and respected. We offset their faults with their qualities. But if they dare challenge us, disagree with us and cease to be useful, we have no difficulty believing the worst about them or attributing to them unworthy motives. Suddenly, their faults loom large and their qualities shrink in our eyes.

That is the price many who serve churches are called upon to pay. That is the price the Galatians required of Paul because he persists in insisting on the principles of the Gospel, which meant him denying they had the ability to ensure God's blessing by their efforts: now, telling you the truth, I have become your enemy, he asks, and not without pain.

Paul refused to take personal offense when the Galatians turned from his Gospel (You have not wronged me in any way, verse 12), but they chose to transform a discussion of Gospel principle into a personal conflict and to view Paul as an enemy because he challenged them. The weakening of their spiritual understanding led, as it inevitably does, to a weakening of their moral commitment. The result is that, instead of preferring truth over a lie, they preferred the false glory that goes with attributing to human beings abilities reserved for God alone.

Without doubt, it is often easier to attack a person's character than to prove the validity of our view, all the more so when everyone suffers from weaknesses that we can easily exploit to discredit the view he espouses.

We would do well to learn from the Apostle's words here. We would do well to honor those who teach us God's Word faithfully, even when the truths declared are inconvenient. We would do well to honor those who serve us in the Lord, even when they are no longer able to serve, and to cherish God's Word even when it denies us the right to boast in professed abilities and calls us to turn away from teachings that encourage our pride and to trust in ourselves rather than in the grace of God. Obviously, there is a great deal that we have yet to learn.

They are zealous for you, but not for a good purpose. They want to separate you, so that you would be zealous for them. The false teachers presented themselves as those who sincerely care for the believers in Galatia, and who therefore seek to promote their spiritual lives. They claimed to have pure motives, that they were showing the Galatians the way to a higher level in God's kingdom, how to ensure more of His presence. But their motives were not pure, nor was their professed love sincere, even if they did not recognize this to be the case. "Who can discern their own errors? Forgive my hidden faults" (Psalm 19:12, NIV).

What they really sought was to enhance their own position by increasing the number of their adherents (that you would be zealous for them). They loved themselves at the expense of the Galatians. What is worse, they loved themselves as the expense of the God they professed to serve. Anything they did for the Galatians was ultimately an effort to serve themselves. To that end they needed to separate the Galatians from the rest of the believers (They want to separate you), and the best way to do that is to persuade them that, if they hitch themselves to the false teachers wagon, they will excel compared to others in the Messiah.

Many make use of professed love to bind others to themselves. Those who do so are likely to display ardent concern for their followers, especially to those they are seeking to include among their followers. They will hasten to respond to needs, display a willingness to sacrifice for the sake of others, take care to be approachable and share their success with others. They are affable, generous, patient, gentle and, at the same time, firm under the guise of an overt kindness. Many are attracted to them because of their personality or the apparent advantages they offer. But the price such people exact is an unthinking loyalty that dares not measure their teaching with the Word of God.

When it comes to the Word of God, we must not be influenced by considerations other than the truth. We are not at liberty to prefer someone's view of things because he is affable, or impressive, or to reject another person's teaching because we like him less. Truth is its own standard. It always exceeds the authority of those who represent it, and we are obliged by God to love truth at all cost.

We ought not to be seeking impressive leaders. Instead, we should seek faithful teachers and shepherds. The modern obsession with leadership is contrary to Scripture—God's Word speaks of Pastors, Elders, overseers and teachers. Serving God's people is not an executive position; it is just that: serving.

It is always good to be zealous for a good thing, and not only when I am there with you. In the following chapters Paul will make it clear that, while our efforts cannot save us, nor can they accord us status in God's sight. Rather, as a product of our salvation and due to the transformation salvation implies, we must be engaged in living in ways compatible with the Gospel. We are not saved by what we do, but salvation is meant to cause us to be up and doing. Christians are people in whose inner heart God has brought about a radical revolution: they no longer seek to promote themselves; they are taken up with loving God and pleasing Him. That being so, they acknowledge the truth of the Apostle 's affirmation, namely that It is always good to be zealous for a good thing. Not only so, but they conduct themselves in the light of that principle.

A Christian is an individual with whom God has made a new covenant, in whom, by the working of His Spirit, God has fulfilled what he promised in Jeremiah 31:32: I will put my law within them and write it on their hearts. God has done for that person what he promised in Ezekiel 36:26–27:

> I will give you a new heart, and a new spirit I will put within you. And I will remove the heart of stone from your flesh and give you a heart of flesh. And I will put my Spirit within you and cause you to walk in my statutes and be careful to obey my rules.

The first evidence of the new birth is an acknowledgement of sin, followed by faith in God and repentance. But that is not where God's working in a person's heart ends. The Holy Spirit purifies our hearts, sanctifies us and drives us to exert ourselves for God's glory as a natural response to His grace. As Paul says in Romans 6, we respond to the grace of God by giving ourselves to his service by way of chosen, determined moral conduct that is driven by gratitude.

God moved in the hearts of the Galatians. In consequence, they aspired to the most and the best of His presence. Some people sought to take advantage of that devotion and to profit from it by enlisting it to their service: they sought to persuade these new believers, who had not yet learned to delve deeply into God's Word and had not yet fully digested the broader implications of the Gospel, that if they but embrace the Israel's tradition, if they would be circumcised, keep the Sabbath, observe the dietary laws and celebrate the Jewish feats, they will enjoy more of God's presence and blessing.

The apostle commends the Galatians for being zealous for a good thing and for their desire of more of God's presence, while he firmly rejects the teaching of those who took advantage of the Galatians' ignorance and sought to hitch them to their bandwagon. At the same time, he rebukes the Galatians for allowing themselves to be led off the Gospel path as laid out by himself and Barnabas when they proclaimed the Gospel to them.

The Galatians had been taught that no law-keeping could add to their rights before God or draw them closer to Him. So long as he and Barnabas were in Galatia, the Christians there conducted themselves in accordance with what they had learned from them. But when they left and the false teachers arrived, the Galatians were inclined to revert to their old, idolatrous way of thinking about how one relates to the gods. That is why Paul says, It is always good to be zealous for a good thing, and not only when I am there with you. In other words, you should have persisted in the path you took while I was present rather than be influenced to the contrary when I am absent.

It is regrettably true that, for lack of oversight by faithful teachers, we are inclined to stray. For lack of a teacher who knows to insist on the truth and serve us as a gracious overseer, a wise encourager, a loving critic and an example worth emulating, we tend to forget what we have learned, grow lax in spiritual matters and revert—even if unconsciously—to our old habits. That Is exactly why we need the church and why the church has Pastor-Teachers and Elders. We need them to help us persist in God's ways.

And yet, it is important for us to remember that It is always good to be zealous for a good thing, not only when someone is watching us. We ought to be sincerely zealous, not just for appearances. To that end it is worth remembering that, even if no one else sees what we are doing, or what is in our hearts, God does, and He sees things as they truly are.

> My children, for whom I experience again the pains of childbirth until Messiah is formed in you! I want to be with you right now and to speak to you in a different way, because I'm confused about you.

The apostle employs every means at his disposal in an effort to bring the Galatians back to the Gospel and the way of life the Gospel implies. He warns. He threatens. He reminds. He argues. He illustrates and explains. He exhorts and does not hesitate to plead.

He is a faithful shepherd. He sincerely loves the flock of God and does not hesitate to form affectionate relations with them. He freely admits his loving pain for them. My children, he calls them. They are his children in the Messiah, and he is their father. He, not the false teachers, birthed them by the Gospel. His love for them is real, and he does not hesitate to say so.

We can learn from this statement that the Scriptures ought not be read in a wooden, thoughtless manner. The Messiah forbade His disciples to address their teachers with the title "father" (Matthew 23:9). But we cannot obey his command unless we understand it. God's Word is to be understood, not just quoted. He was speaking of the title "father" as it was attributed in those days by rabbinical students to their teachers as a way to acknowledge their authority, much as the Roman Catholic priests today are called "father." Paul, on the other hand, is not claiming authority over the Galatian's faith but expressing his love—and that makes all the difference.

My children, for whom I experience again the pains of childbirth until Messiah is formed in you. The apostle is describing his pain in terms of the birth pains a woman experiences, notably the worse any woman experiences, and yet she does so gladly: "When a woman is giving birth, she has sorrow because her hour has come, but when she has delivered the baby, she no longer remembers the anguish, for joy that a human being has been born into the world" (John 16:21). As we noted, Paul arrived in Galatia suffering from ill health, and yet proclaimed the Gospel. His present pain is not physical but emotional. He hurts for the Christians in Galatia. He suffers on their behalf because the purportedly-Christian view of things they are inclined to embrace would drive them further away from God rather than draw them nearer. It threatens their spiritual health.

I want to be with you right now. When we know that a loved one is in danger or sorrowful, we want to be with them, we want to help them, share their sorrow and protect them. Of course, Paul is not ignorant of the fact that God guides all that occurs and that, had he wished it to be so, the Apostle would have been in Galatia. He is, again, expressing his love.

I want to be with you right now and to speak to you in a different way. He would have preferred not to address the Galatians with the strong language he is compelled to employ in this letter. Had he been with them while they were considering the new teaching to which they had been exposed, it is possible that he would have spoken to them otherwise. They might have seen things differently, perhaps not even considered the new-fangled teachings.

No parent takes pleasure in rebuking his children. Paul does not enjoy being forceful, insisting on his authority or rebuking the Galatians. Like any faithful Pastor, like any faithful Christian, he prefers to embrace and commend. He finds it painful to speak sharply, although he is willing to do so if it will do the Galatians any good. Having come to the conclusion that strong language is called for, he fulfilled his duty. We too should be willing to fulfill our duty toward our sisters and brothers in the Messiah, as we must fulfill it as parents and friends, as must our Pastors and Elders sometimes (all too often!) in relation to us. We need such love because we are all inclined to stray.

The Apostle adds a confession: I'm confused about you. He cannot understand the logic of the path the Galatians were inclined to follow. Having tasted of the Lord and seen that he is good, what is the point of turning back to themselves? The course the Galatians are contemplating is so illogical that Paul cannot make sense of it. Who would prefer his abilities to God's? Who would prefer his achievements to the Messiah's? According to what kind of logic can we even think that we should trust ourselves and rely on what we do in the spiritual life, instead of putting our trust in Jesus and relying on what he did for us on the cross, and on what he does in us by his Spirit?

There was, indeed, no logic in the Galatian's inclination. Is there in ours?

Let's Summarize

- Are you offended when your convictions are challenged, or your mistakes exposed? If you do, examine your heart to understand why and, upon discovering the reason, repent.

- Are you prepared to risk losing friendships or social standing if that is the cost of being faithful to the truth? When did you last pay such a price? When and why did you avoid doing so?

- Have you ever been put to the test as were the Galatians according to this section? How did you fare? What could you have been done better?

Let's Pray

Your grace is beyond!

Questions for Discussion and Study

1. Drawing from Scripture, state three reasons why Paul did not consider himself bound by the Mosaic Law or by Jewish tradition.

2. Discuss: why is relying on any form of law-keeping for spirituality equal to putting one's confidence in the flesh? What kind of observance of Christian traditional customs would come under the proscription of putting one's confidence in the flesh?

3. Think of ways in which the bodily weakness from which Paul suffered when he preached to the Galatians makes us think of the incarnation of the Son of God.

4. Discuss: self-love is often at the heart of doctrinal disputes.

5. Consider Paul's pastoral method in this section of his letter.

CHAPTER 13

We Are Free
(GALATIANS 4:21–31)

[21] Tell me, you who want to be subject to law, don't you listen to the Law? [22] It was written that Abraham had two sons, one was born from the slave woman and the other from the free one. [23] But he who was born from the slave woman was born according to the flesh, and the one who was born from the free, through the promise.

[24] These things are an illustration, because there are two covenants, one from Mount Sinai who gives birth to the enslaved, and who is Hagar, [25] and this Hagar is Mount Sinai, which is in Arabia, equal to the Jerusalem of today because she and her children are enslaved. [26] But the Jerusalem that is above is free, and she is the mother of all of us, [27] because it was written, "rejoice, barren one who did not give birth, break out in songs, you who have not experienced the pains of childbirth, because the children of the desolate woman are more than those of the one who has a husband."

[28] And you, brothers, like Isaac, are children of the promise, [29] and exactly as he who was born according to the flesh persecuted the one who was born according to the Spirit, so too now. [30] And what does the scripture say? "Send this slave woman and her son away, because the son of this slave woman will not take part in the in-

heritance alongside the son of the free woman." [31] For that reason, brothers, we are not from the slave woman but from the free.

In these words Paul is referring to the fourth example he has employed in seeking to clarify to his readers in Galatia the nature and extent of their freedom in the Messiah. He wants them to remember their dependence on God's grace and on what He did for them. He wants them to remember their uselessness of their abilities and of what they are able to do for themselves. The first example was the last will and testament. The next two (the mentor and the guardian) were borrowed form daily life in the Roman world. The next, Paul's fourth example, is taken from Scriptures. It is more of an illustration than an actual example. There is no practical parallel between the Mosaic's place in the life of believers and the event described. Paul is not interpreting Scripture; he is using an event described in Scripture to illustrate his point. He does so by drawing a parallel between the efforts to which the Galatians were being called in the hope of obtaining the promise, and those of Abraham to have a descendent who would inherit the promise; between the status of Hagar's son—a slave, his mother being a slave—and the freedom enjoyed by Isaac, the child of Abraham's wife, in whose body God worked according to the promise.

Abraham tried to lay hold of the promise by his own efforts, according to the flesh. As a result, instead of giving himself an heir, he caused the birth of a slave because in those days, the children of slaves were themselves born to slavery. Only the one who was born from the free was born free, and only those born through the promise are entitled to the inheritance (because God promised Abraham that the child to be born to Abraham would inherit him (Genesis 15:4. See also Genesis 21:12). For that reason, those who want to be subject to law, even if their interest is in the Laws of the Law and the traditions of Israel, must understand that any product of human effort will inevitably fail. That is not the way to obtain anything of spiritual value. Nothing but a gift of grace, nothing but an act of God is capable of grating us blessing, spiritual life, God's nearness, increasing spiritual understanding or any measure of stability in our walk with God.

What the Apostle says here is surprising. He claims that Hagar, the slave woman, is Mount Sinai, which is in Arabia, equal to the Jerusalem of today because she and her children are enslaved. That is to say, the people of Israel, devoted to the Law and to their tradition, and he views these as the means by which they can find favor with God, do not recognize their real situation. They believe themselves to be free, but they are not. They have become so accustomed to the chains of their bondage that they no longer recognize reality for what it is. They have bound themselves over to slavery by transforming the commandments of the Law into a means to obtain spiritual blessing and by adding to these commandments a growing host of traditions, interpretations and halachic and rabbinic dictums.

In contrast to them, the Jerusalem that is above is free, and she is the mother of all of us. Paul is pointing here to a radical contrast between two groups. The first group is made up of the people of Israel, subject to bondage because they do not rely on God's grace. The second group is made up of all of us—Jews and Gentiles together, who believe in the Messiah and who put their whole trust in the grace of God. Paul is here using language that Peter will later use in the course of a discussion that will take place in Jerusalem as to the role of the Law in the Christian life. Peter will describe the Law and Jewish tradition in terms of a yoke ... that neither our fathers nor we have been able to bear (Acts 15:10). Devotees of the Law and of Jewish tradition can promise spiritual gain, but their theory in fact leads to loss in comparison with what God gives by His grace and by the virtues of the Messiah.

The Apostle tells us that, in contrast to the bondage of those who are equal to the Jerusalem of today, those belong to the Jerusalem that is above are free and she—that heavenly Jerusalem—is the mother of all of us whether we are Jewish or Gentile, because it was written, "rejoice, barren one who did not give birth, nor experienced the pains of childbirth, break out in songs, you who have not experienced the pains of childbirth, because the children of the desolate woman are more than those of the one who has a husband." In other words, whoever thinks that reliance on God's grace is barren and greatly mistaken. It is, in fact, that apparently barren woman who has reason to rejoice, because she will give birth by way of a miracle, through God's working' and she will have many, many children. It is she whom nobody wants of the desolate woman and to whom nobody pays attention, who will have more children than the one who has a husband, whom everyone expects to have children.

Well, then, we are the children of the free woman, not of the slave woman. We inherit by the grace of God, and precisely because that is true, our inheritance is secure because God does not depend on what we do—the Messiah has already done for us all that is necessary. He did it all.

And you, brothers, like Isaac, are children of the promise. With this statement Paul is applying the illustration he provided. He tells the Galatians they already have in the Messiah everything they are trying to obtain by keeping laws, commandments and traditions. You, brothers, he tells the Galatians, are like Isaac, are children of the promise just as any of the people of Israel who put their trust in Messiah. You are equal with them in blessing, status and assured future. In Messiah, you belong to God, you are children of God and inheritors according to the promise. You need not do anything to obtain these privileges before God.

This is, really, an unexpected development, just as Isaac's birth was unexpected. True, God had promised Abraham a son (as he had also promised Abraham he would be the father of many nations and that all the families of the earth would be blessed through him)' but Abraham and Sarah were well over the age when one can normally have children. Abraham was 100 years old and Sarah was 90. As Scripture puts it. Their bodies were "dead." But God gives life to the dead and is certainly capable of giving a barren women many children. He, who made everything out of nothing, who commanded the light to shine out of darkness (1 Corinthians 4:6) and a lifeless earth to bring forth life, touched Abraham and Sarah's bodies, and brought Isaac to birth.

Why did God wait for so many years? Why did he not bless Sarah while she was young, at the age when most women give birth? Is there not a message for us in the bare fact that Sarah conceived and gave birth at an age when it was clear to all that this would not be possible? God does not need our abilities—He has plenty of His own. Not only so, but He is not willing to allow anyone to steal even a small part of the glory of His grace. He will wait until it is very clear that Isaac was born by grace, the product of divine and not human ability.

So too, you, are brothers, brothers one to another, my brothers and the brothers of all believers among the people of Israel. You like Isaac, are children of the promise. In you God fulfills His promise to Abraham. In you He demonstrates the greatness of His grace. By the mercies of God, you have become like Isaac, are children of the promise. without reference to human ability, with no dependence on human laws or even the commandments of the Law. All of this is true contrary to the rules commonly accepted by mankind, which insist that man can only receive what he deserves, and that he does not deserve anything for which he has not worked. Rejoice in this truth and continue to put your trust in God. What He obtained for you in Messiah, by Messiah's life, death and resurrection is surely yours and no one can take it from you. Just don't presume to deserve any of it.

This kind of logic is exactly the reason why pride is so contrary to the Christian Faith, and why humility characterizes those who have been born again by grace and who put all of their trust in the Messiah. They understand that it is really quite surprising that they should be children of God. They, who rebelled against God, threw off His rule and refused to obey His commandments, they who loved themselves more than their Creator, who sacrificed many on the altar of their selfishness, became the objects of God's love. If we are among those just described, it is only right that we cherish God's grace, acknowledge His goodness and thank Him all the days of lives and beyond—to all eternity.

And exactly as he who was born according to the flesh persecuted the one who was born according to the Spirit, so too now. As we recall this is the first of Paul's letters. It was written in the short time between his first missionary journey, in the company of Barnabas, and the second such journey, which he conducted without Barnabas. The Apostle encountered opposition already at this early stage because, even at this early stage he understood that there is no difference in Messiah between Jews and Gentiles, that salvation in all its aspects and everything that flows from salvation is only available through grace. Therefore, both Jews and gentiles need not keep any law so as to obtain blessing from God.

This perception was radically the opposite of anything the various religions and faiths of the ancient world ever hold, and that includes the Jewish faith. Such a perception denied human ability and depicted man as corrupted by sin, enslaved to sin and lost for lack of the ability to save himself. In so doing Paul's perception attributed to God a glory it denied man and saw its salvation dependent on God and on Him alone. It insisted that man can never obligate God in any way, that God is not dependent to the slightest extent on man. In such a way, the Gospel Paul preached forbad man the possibility to boast in spiritual achievements or to view himself as spiritually better than any of his fellow-believers.

This kind of Faith was not popular in those days, as it is not nowadays. That being the case, it raised and still raises to this very day much opposition, although then and now such opposition often comes from those who should know better. Many Christians find it difficult to shake off the thought that, although man might not be deserving of anything, he has such high value that God cannot but desire to bless, and that man is capable of doing good for God. Those who think in this way do not understand that even the best of our deeds is stained with the stains of our sinfulness, and that any pleasure God has in what we do is the product of His kindness and grace.

Therefore, in an effort to attribute to themselves something that belongs only to God, there were even among the first believers some who persecuted Paul and opposed what he taught. As he described it: he who was born according to the flesh persecuted the one who was born according to the Spirit, so too now. Not all of his persecutors were Christians, although most of those to whom Paul refers here believed themselves to be such. They did believe that Jesus is the Messiah, but they never turned away from themselves to God, never despaired of the effort to improve their standing with God. They assumed that if they correct this or that detail in their lives, if they will not engage in significant, visible sins, if they add to their efforts at self-improvement some exciting spiritual experiences and the affirmation the Jesus is the Messiah, that would be all that is required. Paul describes such fold as "false brethren." The greatest deception in which they engaged was one of self-deception, insisting they were biblical believers although they had never been born again.

These people persecuted Paul and oppressed those who differed from them, assuming that "since they are not like us, they are inevitably less spiritual. They do not keep the Law nor observe Israel's traditions. Their Faith is therefore sincere but faulty."

Paul reminds his readers that Abraham arranged a feast to celebrate Isaac's weaning, at which Ishmael, the son of the slave woman, mocked the son born according to the promise and as the product of an amazing work of the Creator in Abraham and Sarah's bodies (Abraham was a hundred years old when his son Isaac was born to him. And Sarah said, "God has made laughter for me; everyone who hears will laugh over me." And she said, "Who would have said to Abraham that Sarah would nurse children? Yet I have borne him a son in his old age."And the child grew and was weaned. And Abraham made a great feast on the day that Isaac was weaned. But Sarah saw the son of Hagar the Egyptian, whom she had borne to Abraham, laughing. Genesis 21:5–9, ESV). Ishmael's laughter was one of mockery, of presumption. After all, he was the eldest of Abraham's sons and therefore assumed he would inherit their father. And exactly as he who was born according to the flesh persecuted the one who was born according to the Spirit, so too now. But Ishmael was wrong, as are the devotees of the Mosaic law and of Jewish tradition today. Paul will summarize this with his next reference to the story of the relations between

Isaac and Ishmael. What is clear at this stage is that the struggle between those who rely on the grace of God in everything that has to do with their spiritual life and those who rely on the Law and tradition, or anything else man can do, is a continual struggle.

Is it not high time we left off this useless struggle, that we turn away from our arrogant presumption and that we accord God the honor that he deserves? Jehovah God is our Savior, none but Him.

Now comes the clincher: And what does the Scripture say? "Send this slave woman and her son away, because the son of this slave woman will not take part in the inheritance alongside the son of the free woman." For that reason, brothers, we are not from the slave woman but from the free. Paul continues with the illustration he has borrowed from the lives of Isaac and Ishmael, Isaac representing the fruit of God's initiative and Ishmael the fruit of man's—God's promise and action, both of which would clearly have been impossible but for God's mighty power. Paul summarizes his argument with extremely sharp words: Abraham loved Ishmael but God commanded him, "Send this slave woman and her son away." The reason for this is no less sharp than the commandment, "because the son of this slave woman will not take part in the inheritance alongside the son of the free woman."

The two cannot live under the same roof. Just as Ishmael was not allowed to live with Abraham and alongside Isaac (the son who was to inherit the blessing), so too the Law and tradition have no right to enjoy Christina patronage, have a role in the spiritual lives of God's children and presume to play a part in the inheritance, which inheritance is given by grace and by grace alone.

Paul therefore says that the ceremonial aspects of the Law (not to speak of rabbinic dictum of any kind) have no place in the Christian life. As to spiritual practices, they are to be put out, sent away, set aside, rejected. Of course, Abraham did not find it easy to obey. Ishmael was no stranger in the family. He was a beloved descendent and, since his birth, he had endeared himself to his father. We too might find it difficult to let go of the comforting thought that we have abilities Scripture says we do not. It is not easy to deny hoary Jewish national tradition a spiritual value in addition to its culture weight. But Paul's words are very clear: "Send this slave woman and her son away, because the son of this slave woman will not take part in the inheritance alongside the son of the free woman."

"Send away," God says. The Hebrew and the Greek both imply a determined, firm, painful, necessary kind of action required if we wish to inherit what the Messiah has obtained for us. But there is no other way. Jews in Christ are free to observe their national traditions as a form of national culture, but those traditions have no role in the service of God, in our relations with God or our understanding of the Scriptures. We simply must not place these alongside the Messiah, as if they can play any part in what He has achieved.

Therefore, brethren, Paul draws the inevitable conclusion from the illustration he has brought. In doing so he speaks of the Galatians as brethren, and by so doing places himself—the Jew—and them—Gentiles—on the same level. We, he says, whether we are Jewish or not, all of us together, are not from the slave woman but from the free, and should act accordingly.

Let's Summarize

- We believers—Jews and Gentiles—are equal in the Messiah, brothers and sisters, children of God and inheritors of the promise given to Abraham our father. How do these truths find expression in your private and congregational lives?

- We said that pride is contrary to the Christian faith—in what ways does pride find expression in your lives and what are you going to do about that?

- Are you sure you are not deceiving yourselves when you claim to have put all your trust in the Messiah both for salvation and sanctification? On what grounds are you sure that is the case?

Let's Pray

We cannot know You, O God, except by way of the revelation You have provided us. We groped in darkness until You provided us in the Scriptures with the light of life. May you be pleased, our God, to have Your Holy Spirit work in us so that we would be faithful to You and to Your Word that we will never distort what is written in Your Word in an effort to conform the Scriptures to our desires. Grant us to listen to Your voice in the Scriptures. Change and sanctify us by Your Word so that we truly understand it and it becomes a powerful, living reality in our hearts.

You have by grace freed us from bondage and made us to be children of the promise. We have been born again by the powerful working on

Your Spirit. May we always be given grace to preserve the freedom You granted us, to protect it and to thank You for adopting us, for loving us and for never forsaking us—all by the virtues of our Savior, Jesus the Messiah, Amen.

QUESTIONS FOR DISCUSSION AND STUDY

1. Does the illustration Paul uses, drawn from the Scriptures, fill Paul's intended purposes? What are those purposes? What are the limits of the illustration?

2. What lesson can we learn from this example of Paul's use of the Scriptures?

3. Summarize the biblical principles Paul lays out in this passage.

4. How do God's sovereignty and eternal power find expression in what is said in this passage?

CHAPTER 14

Liberty and How to Use It
(GALATIANS 5:1–15)

[1] In the freedom to which the Messiah freed us stand firm and don't get entangled again in a yoke of slavery. [2] Here, I, Paul, tell you that if you become circumcised, you will gain nothing at all from the Messiah. [3] I testify to every circumcised person that he is obliged to keep the whole of the Law. [4] You, who are justified by law-keeping, have been cut off from the Messiah, you have fallen from grace. [5] We, in spirit, through faith, enthusiastically await the hope of righteousness. [6] Because, in the Messiah Jesus, circumcision affects nothing, nor does uncircumcision, only faith acting through love.

[7] You were running well, who hindered from obeying the truth?

[8] This conviction is not from him who called you.

[9] A little bit of yeast causes the whole lump to rise.

[10] I have confidence with regard to you in the Lord that you will not think differently, and that whoever is bothering you will bear the punishment he deserves, whoever he may be. [11] But I, brothers, if I still proclaim circumcision, why am I persecuted? In such a case the offense of the cross would be abolished. [12] I really wish that those who are unsettling you would cut themselves [off],

¹³ because you were called to freedom, brothers, only not to a freedom that becomes an opportunity for the flesh. Instead, serve one another in love, ¹⁴ because the whole of the Law is summarized in one word: "love the other like you love yourself." ¹⁵ but if you bite and consume each other, be careful that you are not consumed by each other.

In the freedom to which the Messiah freed us stand firm and don't get entangled again in a yoke of slavery. At end of the previous chapter Paul stated with regard to all who believe in the Messiah: we are not from the slave woman but from the free. That is to say, we are not the children of Hagar but of Sarah, we do not put our trust in our abilities but in the Messiah and His achievements, we do not rely on the Law or tradition, or both but on the grace of God. Such is the freedom of which the Apostle now speaks when he speaks of the freedom to which the Messiah freed us.

The Messiah gave us the freedom that belongs exclusively to the children of God, freedom to serve and worship God without fearing we might lose the inheritance appointed for us or that, for one reason or another, we will not reach the goal God set for us. Everything we have in the Messiah, everything we will have, is a gift of grace, fully secured by that same grace.

God's grace is precious both because of its inherent value and because of the awful-wonderful price paid to obtain it: the Son of God assumed humanity and lived among us, subjected Himself to the commandments of the Law and lived in perfect conformity to the Law. He then assumed our guilt and died the death we should have died. He was raised from the dead by God the Father and now sits at His right hand, a full partner in His kingdom. There he serves as our faithful representative, interceding for us, protecting and guiding us by His Word and His Spirit. So stand in that freedom. Insist upon it, Rest in it. Revel in it.

It is our duty to preserve that freedom and, when necessary, defend it. We may not deny the achievements of the Messiah nor make light of His sacrifice by becoming entangled again in a yoke of slavery.

It is worth reminding ourselves again what Paul is speaking of, when he speaks of a yoke of slavery. Paul wrote to the Galatians because some were seeking to persuade them that their faith in the Messiah of Israel obliged them to Israel's Law and religious tradition, and that if they submit to these they will achieve a higher spiritual level. Paul insists in no uncertain terms that such is not the case. To follow that course is to accept a yoke that none who fear God and value the Messiah should accept. The Messiah has freed us—us, the Apostle says, not just the Galatians but all who believe in him for the forgiveness of their sin. The Apostle again employs inclusive language, incorporating both Jews and Gentiles. We have been freed. All of us. We ought not, therefore, act as if we are bound, as if we have not been freed. As Paul puts it in his letter to the Romans, you did not receive the spirit of slavery to fall back into fear, but you have received the Spirit of adoption as sons, by whom we cry, "Abba! Father" (Romans 8:15).

We must stubbornly insist on this freedom because it is a measure of the greatness of the Messiah and the salvation he secured for us. We must insist upon it humbly, kindly and yet unyieldingly, without giving in, not even for an hour, so that the truth of the Gospel will continue to be with us (Galatians 2:5).

That freedom permits us to enjoy all aspects of our respective national cultures as natural expressions of who we are but without overshadowing the most central aspect of our identity: we are first and foremost Christians, and only then Israelis, Palestinians, Koreans or Norwegians. We are first and foremost Christians and only then husbands or wives, employers or employees, painters, industrialists, fathers and mothers. All we are is subject to our identity in the Messiah and therefore meaningfully impacted by our faith in Him. That is the practical meaning of the commandment to love God with all our heart, mind, soul and strength. That is the import of the warning that whoever loves father or mother, or anything else, more than God cannot be a disciple of the Messiah.

Such is the freedom the Messiah granted us, and such is the freedom we must defend. Such is the freedom we are invited to enjoy to the full, with all its amazing implications: under God, we are no longer subject to the commands, expectations or whims of other people. We are free! Free to love God and do what is right, free to honor the Lord in all that we do, free from guilt and condemnation, free to live to the hilt without fear, because God has granted us the status of sons and provided us with many means of holy enjoyment. Free because we know that, although we shall fail often, we shall not be forsaken. God's grace toward us has been secured for us by the Messiah.

On the other hand, Here, I, Paul, tell you that if you become circumcised, you will gain nothing at all from the Messiah. I testify to every circumcised person that he is obliged to keep the whole of the Law. Paul again sharpens the contrast by means of these stark warning, reminding the Galatians just who it is who is writing these words. He identifies himself: I, Paul. Well, who is Paul? He is a messenger of Jesus the Messiah, an apostle, the one who first proclaimed the Gospel to them, also known by the name Saul, a Jew the son of a Jew, My manner of life from my youth, spent from the beginning among my own nation and in Jerusalem, is known by all the Jews. They have known for a long time, if they are willing to testify, that according to the strictest party of our religion I have lived as a Pharisee (Acts 26:4–5).

Though I myself have reason for confidence in the flesh also. If anyone else thinks he has reason for confidence in the flesh, I have more: circumcised on the eighth day, of the people of Israel, of the tribe of Benjamin, a Hebrew of Hebrews; as to the law, a Pharisee; as to zeal, a persecutor of the church; as to righteousness under the law, blameless (Philippians 3:4–6).

I, Paul, tell you that if you become circumcised, you will gain nothing at all from the Messiah. The Apostle is crystal clear, repeating what he said earlier: you are leaving him who called you by the grace of the Messiah to a different gospel (1:6). Whoever acts as if he is obliged to or advantaged by Jewish custom is acting hypocritically (2:13) and contrary to the Gospel (2:14). He is annulling God's grace and acting as if the Messiah's sacrifice served no purpose (2:14).

Those who accept the yoke of the Law and the tradition bring a curse of themselves because those who believe are blessed with Abraham the believer, and those who are keeping a law are subject to a curse because it was written: "whoever does not continue in all the matters written in the scroll of the Law and do them is cursed." (3:9–10). If there was a law that was capable of giving life, then righteousness would indeed come from law. But the scripture imprisoned everything to sin that that, in Jesus the Messiah, the promise by faith would be given to those who believe (3:21–22).

We are no longer subject to a mentor (3:25). When we were little children we were subject to the most basic things of the world, but when the fullness of time arrived, God sent his Son, who came into the world through a woman and was subject to law, in order to redeem those who are subject to law so that we would be adopted as sons. And because you are sons, God has sent the Spirit of his Son into our hearts, crying, "Abba! Father!," so that you are no longer a slave but a son, and if a son then an heir through God (4:3–7).

How is it that you are turning again to the fundamental, weak and empty basics? Is it to these that you want to be enslaved again (4:9)? This Hagar is Mount Sinai, which is in Arabia, equal to the Jerusalem of today because she and her children are enslaved. But the Jerusalem that is above is free, and she is the mother of all of us, because it was written, "rejoice, barren one who did not give birth, break out in songs, you who have not experiences the pains of childbirth, because the children of the desolate woman are more than those of the one who has a husband." And you, brothers, like Isaac, are children of the promise. And as he who was born according to the flesh persecuted the one who was born according to the Spirit, so too now. And what does the scripture say? "Send this slave woman and her son away, because the son of this slave woman will not take part in the inheritance alongside the son of the free woman." For that reason, brothers, we are not from the slave woman but from the free (4:25–31).

These saying should be sufficient for anyone reading this letter with an open mind, eager to hear the voice of God in His Word.

What the Apostle has to say next is no less stringent. He explains why the Messiah is of no avail to those who rely, even to the slightest degree, on law-keeping, in any sphere and for any purpose: I testify to every circumcised person that he is obliged to keep the whole of the Law, and who among us is capable of that?! After all, is it not because we are unable that Messiah came and was sacrificed?

We are not entitled to choose between the commandments of the Law. They are all essential to the whole. We cannot say that we are keeping the Law if our men are not circumcised and do not grow ear locks, or if we do not offer sacrifices, even if they are not sacrifices for sin. We cannot claim to keep the Law if we do not allow our gardens to go fallow every seventh year, or bring the firstfruits of our vegetable gardens to the temple. If we break the law in any aspect, its broken, just as if we had lied, stolen, desecrated the Sabbath or murdered.

We cannot say, I am doing my best," or "I'm honestly trying." Our abilities are limited, whereas what is required is perfect obedience. To do our best is a good thing, but it cannot undo or compensate for our failings. Law-keeping cannot be relied upon in any sphere of our spiritual lives, and we certainly cannot rely on tradition. If you undertake to keep the Law, you are obliged to keep the whole of the Law, without compromise and without excuses (compare James 2:10).

Thank God that He, in His kind grace, sent His Son to be the Savior of the world, and who, by virtue of his Son's life and sacrifice, accepts us in spite of our sins. But you, who are justified by law-keeping, have fallen from grace. We, in spirit, in faith, enthusiastically await the hope of righteousness. Because, in the Messiah Jesus, circumcision affects nothing, nor does uncircumcision, only faith acting through love. There is no middle way. There is no wiggle room. Either salvation—all of it! —is by grace, on the grounds of the merits of the Messiah, or it is (even partially) merited by human effort.

Paul is setting before his readers two contrary paths: we are either justified by law-keeping, or they in spirit, in faith, enthusiastically await the hope of righteousness. Their spiritual lives are characterized either by circumcision, the Law's commandments and Jewish tradition, or by faith acting through love. The difference is so stark that Paul insists on saying of those who follow the first of the two that they have been cut off from the Messiah. They have fallen from the grace the Messiah accords those who trust in Him rather than in themselves. The reason for this is obvious: any claim to spiritual achievement by way of human effort is tantamount to a denial of grace, a refusal to rely upon grace.

It is worth thinking for a moment about the phrases, justified by law-keeping and the hope of righteousness. Paul is writing, of course, to the Christian churches in Galatia. He is, therefore, not speaking of the forgiveness of sins that accompanies the new birth but of righteousness in terms of a developing spirituality, of the felt presence of God and His blessing. That is what we saw him do in 2:17, for example, where he spoke of himself and of Peter. I assume we agree they were both regenerate, forgiven, spirit-dwelt followers of the Messiah. Paul is insisting here that there is no room to rely on the keeping of any kind of law, however good and holy it might be. Even the commandments of the Law of Moses cannot accord us merit before God. All the more is this true of the ceremonial aspects of the Law, of rabbinic dictums, Roman law, civil law of any kind or accepted cultural norms. God's grace is the only source of what is necessary for salvation and blessing. It is only by the grace of the Messiah that we can enjoy God's presence, mercy and blessing. The Messiah did it all. We need not attempt to add to His accomplishments.

That is why Paul places himself and all who rely on God's grace (we) over against those who rely on law-keeping (you, who are justified by law-keeping, have fallen from grace. We, in spirit, in faith, enthusiastically await the hope of righteousness). We, he says, dare not make our boast of anything. Instead, in spirit, in faith, we enthusiastically await the hope of righteousness. The expectation of the redeemed is that righteousness in its ultimate perfection will be granted them, not that they will somehow earn it. Their expectation has to do with the future they eager await, which is why they wait in spirit rather than by a purported display of spiritual muscle.

Their eagerness is the product of the fact that they are confident of its fulfillment for the simple reason that is not up to them but to God and to the Messiah. As we said, what we have not gained by our efforts we cannot lose by our failures. What God gained for us by His power no other power can take from us. Not only so, but the perfect righteousness that is reserved for us in the Messiah is so wonderful, so superlatively amazing that we cannot but think of it with excitement:

God appointed us to bear the image of His Son! He has destined us to be utterly cleansed of sin, freed from guilt, released from the impact of a sinful environment and a sinful heart, to share in the glory of the Messiah! He has decided that we will spend eternity in His sweet and awesome presence, blessed bursting with indescribable joy. Who can even begin to think of such a future without being excited?

Paul closes this part of his argument with a simple but clear statement, the reason we in spirit, in faith, enthusiastically await the hope of righteousness and do not rely on the keeping of any law is because, in the Messiah Jesus, circumcision affects nothing, nor does uncircumcision, only faith acting through love. Keeping the ceremonial aspects of the Law has no significance for those who are in the Messiah. It does not matter if you are Jewish or not, if you are circumcised or uncircumcised.

At the same time, we ought not think for a moment that the moral conduct of our lives does not matter. Salvation means, among other things, that we strive to cease sinning and strive instead for holiness. That is to say, true faith always expresses itself in effort. It is faith acting, acting through love. Paul is going to spell that out. Here we simply remind ourselves that, as James put it, "faith apart from works is dead" (James 2:26). Real faith is always active. In moves people to exert themselves. Their exertions do not have to do with ceremonial and symbolic matters but with truly spiritual matters, and therefore with moral conduct. Anyone whose faith has not wrought in him a spiritual and moral revolution does not have the Faith of the Messiah.

You ran well, who kept you from being persuaded by the truth? Many begin well but never reach the finish line. Of course, it is much easier to begin than to finish. On the other hand, what point is there in beginning at all unless we finish? You ran well, the Apostle says to the Galatians. You started out in the race and traversed a significant part of the track, maintaining good speed. That is not enough. "No one who puts his hand to the plow and looks back is fit for the kingdom of God" (Luke 9:62). Remember Lot's wife. The goal is yet before us. We've not come to the end of the track. We must stay on course.

Before Paul spells out how faith works through love (verse 6), he again calls on the Galatians to examine themselves. This is a good opportunity for us to do likewise: having begun on the Messiah's track, have we continued in it? Did we commence the race by the grace of God or by virtue of our own wisdom or anything we attribute to ourselves? Did we deserve to be forgiven? Did we deserve—and do we now deserve—to be children of God, fellow inheritors with the Messiah? Are we in any sense worthy of eternal life? Is it likely that we will now be able to obtain anything by what we do? We commenced running on the right track, have we deviated to another?

We ought to have continued in the truth by which we were persuaded. This has nothing to do with feelings, or with one or another person's convictions. We are speaking of the truth and of the way it should find expression in the everyday of our lives. We should be persuaded by the truth today as we were yesterday. That is, we should allow the truth to persuade us afresh every day that goes by. There resides in the heart of every one of us the arrogant inclination to think we can manage on our own, so we need to constantly remind ourselves how mistaken such a view is.

True, on the one hand, such an inclination is a reflection of the image of God in which we were created. My four year old granddaughter struggles to tie her own shoelaces while insisting, "I can do it myself!" To a real extent, with reference to matters within our capacity, we can and should do it on our own rather than expect others to do it for us. But when the issue is our standing before God, we ought not attempt to claim abilities that lie exclusively within the domain of divinity. It is sheer gall to say to the Creator, "I can do it myself."

If we allow that truth to persuade us afresh today, tomorrow and the next day, we will also know whence to draw the strength to do what is, in fact, incumbent on us, at the same time recognizing the limits of our abilities and never presuming to do what only God can do. That is why humility is such a vital part of the Christian life. After all, if we can do it ourselves, who needs God?

This conviction is not from him who called you. It once again becomes clear that not every conviction we have valid, which is why it is wrong to think every opinion is as valuable as the other. Our generation denies the existence of objective truth, or our ability to reliably know such truth. Everything is thought to be relative, until it faces the real tests of life. Stick your finger into an electric socket and you will experience objective truth. Water boils at 100 degrees. Deny it until you are blue in the face, but 32 degrees Fahrenheit is colder that 74 degrees, and there are ways in which it would be unwise to drive.

Truth is not democratic; it is a hard-nosed dictator. Some understandings are the fruit of the God's Spirit and of our willingness to submit to His Word; others are of a far less worthy source. On an important and very specific level, no man has a right to his own opinion, and we are certainly not entitled to consider all convictions equally. A conviction that is not from Him who called us by His grace and saved us by the sacrifice of His Son is one that, in spite our best intentions, derives from hell and is meant to distort the truth and divert us from following it.

Yes, exactly so. Christians are liable to stray from the truth. They (we) are liable to err. Satan is capable of diverting us from the truth so that we do not accord God the honor due Him.

The status before God of those thus deceived is not changed (we are saved by grace, remember? Not by works however wonderful and not by theological opinions, however correct), but they are saved by the skin of their teeth. Jude, the brother of our Lord, speaks of such when he says,

> you, beloved, building yourselves up in your most holy faith and praying in the Holy Spirit, keep yourselves in the love of God, waiting for the mercy of our Lord Jesus Christ that leads to eternal life. And have mercy on those who doubt; save others by snatching them out of the fire; to others show mercy with fear, hating even the garment stained by the flesh" (Jude 20–23).

To our joy, he goes on to say,

> now to him who is able to keep you from stumbling and to present you blameless before the presence of his glory with great joy, to the only God, our Savior, through Jesus Christ our Lord, be glory, majesty, dominion, and authority, before all time and now and forever. Amen (Jude 24–25).

To such an assurance we can only respond with a hearty Amen! At the same time we need to remember that Paul's words in this letter to the Galatians were meant to serve as a warning. They were mean to encourage its readers to maintain maximum vigilance and a constant, courageous openness to be corrected. We are all prone to err. Regrettably, we all actually do err—far more often than we are willing to admit.

That is why we should be slow to speak, careful in the forming of our opinions, quick to listen and, having heard something, carefully and courageously examine what we have heard: perhaps the opposite is true? Perhaps we need to tweak our understanding? Perhaps what we have heard can serve to broaden our understanding and further strengthen the relationship between our convictions and the Word of God? Moshe Dayan was right when he said than only jackasses never change their minds. When did you last change your mind? When did you last learn something new? Is it really possible that a conviction you or I have embraced is not from Him who called us by His grace, although we learned it from people we respect?

We prefer to be satisfied with "what this verse says to me" instead of trying to find out what it really says. We find it difficult to believe that not every thought that springs up in our head is the work of the Holy Spirit. How many of us prepare for the weekly Bible study and then share in the discussion following our serious study, rather than throwing into the air whatever thought first comes to our mind? How many of us, who teach in our churches, teach the Scriptures systematically, chapter after chapter, portion after portion, verse after verse?

God is the God of truth (Isaiah 65:16). It is our duty to repeatedly ask of Him, "Lead me in your truth and teach me" (Psalm 25:5). We must prefer God's truth to our opinions—which often masquerade as truth but are poor counterfeits.

A little bit of yeast causes the whole lump to rise. These words of Paul are an excellent example of how context determines the meaning of a text. Out of context we might think that Paul is giving us instructions on how to bake bread. Paul was many things, but he was not a baker. He was a messenger of the Gospel and is here using an illustration much as he did when he referred to Isaac and Ishmael, Hagar and Sarah. What, then is he saying? What does he mean?

This letter is dealing with the practical implications of error in the Christian life, and therefore with the correct principles of the Christian Faith. How we live is a product of the worldview we have adopted, regardless of whether we have done so consciously, cautiously and carefully, or if we have absorbed it without examination.

Not only so, but the opposite is also true: how we conduct ourselves impacts our worldview. There is often a wide gap between what we profess to believe and what we believe in fact. Our conduct reveals the extent to which we really know what we believe and the relationship between what we verbalize and the hidden motives of our heart, influenced by our conduct. The wider the gap, the broader our ignorance of ourselves and the wider our departure from the worldview we profess.

That is why it is so important to think clearly about principles, to explore their implications, consider biblical principles and the best way to express them in our daily lives.

We need to beware of influences that are not subject to examination, regardless of whether they relate to conduct or to principle. As those who lovingly fear God and who cherish His glory, we must live carefully. It is our duty to think, to think deeply. It is our duty to learn how to follow a train of thought and to discover whence it began and where it leads. That exactly was Peter's mistake, as noted in chapter 2 of this letter. When James' emissaries arrived in Antioch, Peter did not examine the implications of his standoffish attitude toward Gentile believers. Paul drew his attention to those implications, and Peter, having recognized them, amended his conduct.

We are exposed to many strong influences that constantly strive to mold our thinking: our families and schools, society, the Government, the media, intellectual and spiritual leaders, and—of course—our churches. It is not without reason that Paul instructs the Corinthians to examine what they hear, even from prophets (1 Corinthians 14:29). Ultimately, not only will we give account of our deeds. We will also give account of our worldview; of the way we chose to understand God's ways. Whoever chose to believe a lie will be punished. Whoever was too lazy to examine a view before adopting it will not be excused. A little bit of yeast causes the whole lump to rise, so let's make sure that the lump of our faith is untainted by falsehoods' however convenient.

The Apostle is saying that it does not take much to render our deeds or our convictions faulty. We should be strict with ourselves in large as well as small matters, all the while showing goodwill toward those who think otherwise, so long as they are not promulgating false ideas on central issues of the Faith.

I'm trusting you in the Lord that you will not think differently, and that whoever is bothering you will bear the punishment he deserves, whoever he may be. Paul considers it important that the Galatians Christians not think lightly of the implications of the false teachers' doctrine. He does not want them to view the invitation to assume Israel's traditions as if it were merely a slight departure from Gospel ways. Peter apparently thought that to be the case and, because he was a brother, earned a stern rebuke from the Apostle. But for those who taught believers can benefit from Israel's traditions, or are obliged to them, Paul reserved the designation "false brethren" because their teachings were far more than a slight departure from the Gospel. They had to do with the core of the Gospel because they reflected on the sufficiency of grace and of the Messiah's sacrifice. They constituted a major departure, so much so that the so-called gospel taught by these teaching promulgators was no Gospel at all. There was no room for concessions in this matter, no room for "understanding" those who think otherwise. Neither is there today.

Paul trusts in the Lord for two things. First, that you will not think differently and, secondly, that whoever is bothering you will bear the punishment he deserves, whoever he may be. His trust is in the Lord that the Galatians will, ultimately, not think differently, but will come around to the Gospel as it is in the Messiah because He knows God does not forsake those who are His. The Apostle knows that God is at work in human hearts, and that He controls the most secret motions of which even those who harbor them are unaware. He will bring His redeemed back to the fold. The Apostle further trusts in the Lord that, regardless who is troubling the Galatians' faith, God will rise in their defense and see to it that the troubler will bear the punishment he deserves. Like Peter, Paul believed that "the Lord knows how to rescue the godly from trials, and to keep the unrighteous under punishment until the day of judgment" (2 Peter 2:9).

I'm trusting you in the Lord that you will not think differently. He is trusting them to think, and not to think contrary to what he taught them. He trusts them to continue relying on grace and to reject those who encouraged them to give credence to their religious efforts. He trusts that, once the Galatians read his letter, they will do what he encouraged them to do, and more. How could he have such confidence in them? Because he knew God loved them, and he know they loved God and God's ways. In the long run, even if they deviate for a period, he was confident they would return to the straight and narrow.

May we likewise be trusted? Is our love for God so sincere, so real and so taken up with God's glory rather than with our honor and satisfaction, that it can be said of us as Paul says of the Galatians, that, in the long run, we will return to the straight and narrow path even if we deviate for a period?

I'm trusting ... that whoever is bothering you will bear the punishment
he deserves, whoever he may be. Paul also trusts the Galatian Christians
to the effect that, once awoken from their stupor, they will put the false
teachers in their place.

We have seen that we shall all have to give account for our opinions.
All the more so will we be called to give account if we promote or, by ne-
glect, allow views that do despite to the Gospel. James warned his readers not to be overly eager to teach because those who teach are subject to
a more stringent standard, which is why their judgement will be harsher
(James 3:1).

Those who teach false doctrine are bothering (troubling) the peace
of those who hear them, and every one of them will bear the punishment
he deserves, whoever he may be because God requires of each of us to be
faithful to the truth rather than serve ourselves.

On the day of judgement, whoever betrays the truth by preferring a
lie will discover, as the Apostle puts it, that he deserves punishment, because God, the judge of all the earth, can only do what is right. It does not
matter who we are or what we have done in the name of God, whether we
are the Pope, the Chief Rabbi, a Minister or a common person. We would
do well, therefore, if we would be slow to teach others, and if we would
be careful in what we teach.

Because our heart is still inclined after honor and satisfaction more
than is appropriate, and because our heart is so capable of deceiving us,
we would do well to be careful before embracing opinions. We examine
our hearts and our opinions time and again in the light of Scripture. God
gave us the Scriptures to direct us in the formation of correct opinions.
The Apostle is challenging the Galatians: will they dare deny themselves,
change a view that serves their pride and cast the whole of their salvation
on the grace of God? In response we may ask, will we dare reject a cherished doctrine if we learn we are mistaken?

But I, brothers, if I still proclaim circumcision, why am I persecuted?
In such a case the offense of the cross would be abolished. The above clear
statement clearly stand over against the claim that Paul and the other
Apostles observed the traditions and considered themselves obligated to
the dietary laws, the festivals and the like. Paul never called upon Gentiles
believers in the Messiah to be circumcised. Had he done so, he would not
be able to write to the Corinthians as he later did, describing circumcision and uncircumcision on the same par by stating that circumcision is
nothing and uncircumcision is nothing. Keeping God's commands is what

counts (1 Corinthians 7:19). That is to say, it does not matter if you are circumcised or not because circumcision is no longer included in God's commandments. Being Jewish or following the Mosaic Law is irrelevant to one's walk with God.

Paul knew that he was no longer obliged to observe the ceremonial aspects of the Law, which is how he could act as he did when he wrote the church in Corinth,

> though I am free and belong to no one, I have made myself a slave to everyone, to win as many as possible. To the Jews I became like a Jew, to win the Jews. To those under the law I became like one under the law (though I myself am not under the law), so as to win those under the law. To those not having the law I became like one not having the law (though I am not free from God's law but am under Christ's law), so as to win those not having the law (1 Corinthians 9:19–21).

In Chapter two of this letter to the Galatians we saw that, until the emissaries from James arrived in Antioch, Peter and Barnabas did not conduct themselves as those obliged to Israel's religious traditions. Rather, they acted as true members of the body of the Messiah: in spite of the extremely strict prohibitions of Jewish tradition, they ate at non-Jewish believers' tables. When they ceased doing so, it was not out of conviction but of fear, which is why Peter was so sternly rebuked by Paul.

Further evidence of the fact that Paul no longer proclaims circumcision is to be found in the fact that he is being persecuted. He is being persecuted by fellow believers who taught that Christians are bound to keep the Law. He was also persecuted by fellow Jews who did not believe in the Gospel of the Messiah and described the Apostle as "the man who teaches everyone everywhere against our people and our law" and the temple, even claiming he defiled the temple by bringing non-Jews into its courts (Acts 21:28).

Paul knows the Messiah obtained for us a complete salvation, beginning with the forgiveness of sins and ultimately ending with us being blessed far beyond anything man is capable of imagining, when we—Jews and non-Jews—will be clothed with the image of the Messiah and stand before God, glorious with His Son's endless glory, adorned by His righteousness, made holy by His blood and happily engaged in the praise, worship and honor of our God for the wonder of His grace. That is what renders circumcision of no value. That is where Paul's hope resides.

But I, brothers, if I still proclaim circumcision, why am I persecuted? In such a case the offense of the cross would be abolished. Once again Paul is pointing out the hidden motivations behind the claim that believers are duty bound to keep the Law and the traditions: the offense of the cross is thereby abolished.

What is he talking about? He is talking about the reason why there were in his day (and regrettably are in ours) those who insist that Christians, or at least Jewish Christians, can reach a higher level or obtain an advantage by adhering to the Law and to the traditions. There were two reasons for their insistence. He will mention the first later on in this letter, but we'll mention it now: those who want to look good in the flesh are the ones who force you to be circumcised, with the sole purpose that they not be persecuted for the sake of the cross of the Messiah Jesus, because the circumcised are not law-keepers but they want you to be circumcised so that would be able to boast in your fleshly circumcision (5:12). They want to be liked. They want to find acceptance among the people, hopefully but not necessarily in order to present the Gospel more easily. But they want to do so in a way that will not involve their paying the price that is inevitably demanded of those who dare challenge tradition and disavow its spiritual validity. Jewish tradition has many lovely aspects. It carries great cultural weight for those of us who are Jewish, but it has no spiritual authority.

So too today. In an effort to remove the offense of the cross, some among us Jewish Christians disavow our fellow believers from among the Gentiles by creating a new brand and a terminology of disassociation: we are not Christians but Messianic Jews. We are not converted but completed. We do not speak of Jesus but of Yeshua. We worship on Friday or Saturday rather than on Sunday.

Some among us even claim that we have little or nothing to learn from our non-Jewish brethren, and all too many of us think we have a great deal to teach the Gentiles merely because we are Jewish. The only thing we are willing to receive from them is money—and the recognition that we can use that money as we see fit. Regretfully, not a few of our Gentile brethren think we're naturally endowed with spiritual gifting, that we inevitably can explain the Bible better than others, and that our traditions have more validity than those created over the course of time in the Christian church. The adoration accorded us by some of our well-meaning brethren is not helpful to our spiritual well-being.

Jewish or otherwise, we want to look good in the flesh more than we want to do actual good in the sight of God. We are unwilling to be persecuted for the sake of the cross of the Messiah Jesus. As a result, even some of our worthy deeds are done out of unworthy motives. They are not acts of sincere love for those around us but self-serving acts of love for ourselves. We want to be liked. We want to be respected. So we present ourselves and the Gospel in ways designed to abolish the offence of the cross.

The second reason we prefer to present the Gospel shown of its offense is that we think that it is a more effective way to proclaim the Gospel. We assume the effect the Gospel will have is up to us rather than to the Holy Spirit, and we measure effectiveness by numbers: how many people have we addressed with the Gospel? How many scalps of professed new believers have we on our belt?

We are more concerned to present the Gospel in a convincing manner than in presenting it truthfully. We seek to remove an offense that is part and parcel of the Gospel's very essence, one every sinner must face and that we must *not ever* remove: the message of the cross humbles man into the dust and thereby exalts God. It depicts man as an unclean sinner, unable to do anything for his salvation altogether dependent on the grace of God.

In the Roman world of Paul's day, as now, such a depiction was almost blasphemous. It stood directly contrary to the commonly accepted assumption. It robbed man of his imaginary glory, although whoever understood it correctly would have discovered man's true glory in the fact that he is loved by God, was graciously created by God, and in that he is the object of amazing acts of redemption.

This is the true Gospel, the Gospel of the cross of the Messiah. This Gospel depicts man as he truly is: subject to God and dependent on His good will. This is the Gospel that exposes the wickedness of man's heart and his rebellion against God, and that does so to indicate God's merciful acts toward sinful man which call on man to turn away from himself, deny the arrogance of self-satisfaction and the thought man can stand before God on his own two feet. This is the Gospel that calls upon man to cast himself on God's mercies and kindness.

To some who were confident of their own righteousness and looked down on everyone else, Jesus told this parable: two men went up to the temple to pray, one a Pharisee and the other a tax collector. The Pharisee stood by himself and prayed: "God, I thank you that I am not like other people—robbers, evildoers, adulterers—or even like this tax collector. I fast twice a week and give a tenth of all I get." But the tax collector stood at a distance. He would not even look up to heaven, but beat his breast and said, "God, have mercy on me, a sinner." I tell you that this man, rather than the other, went home justified before God. For all those who exalt themselves will be humbled, and those who humble themselves will be exalted (Luke 18:9–14).

Jesus said, "For judgment I have come into this world, so that the blind will see and those who see will become blind." Some Pharisees who were with him heard him say this and asked, "What? Are we blind too" Jesus said, "If you were blind, you would not be guilty of sin; but now that you claim you can see, your guilt remains" (John 9:39–41).

I really wish that those who are unsettling you would cut themselves. Understandably, many find these words offensive. They are obviously not expressions of affection or commendation. Paul is not wishing the false teachers blessing, happiness and success. Still, here too we can learn something from the Apostle. Paul is in no way indifferent to these teachers doctrines. Contrary to the view of some today, he does not believe that everyone has a right to express his own opinion in every circumstance. Nor does he believe that every opinion is as valid as another.

These teachers not only hold to mistaken views but seek to promote their views among the churches in Galatia. That is something to which the Apostle cannot not and should not agree. Paul believes, as we ought, that there is a difference between truth and error, between true and false doctrine. Because false doctrine is being promulgated, because that doctrine makes light of the glory of the Messiah and casts doubt on the perfection of His achievements, the Apostle simply cannot but be stirred—even enraged—and set out to challenge them.

As noted, Paul does not view the Galatian's behavior in terms of a personal affront, nor does he view the false teacher's activity in such terms. But that does not mean that he can approach the issue unemotionally. He loves the Messiah. He loves God. He loves Messiah's honor. He loves the Galatians. The affront is far worse than personal; it is an offense against the Messiah, and Paul responds with all the warmth of his heart.

We too are not free to be indifferent to teachings that make light of the glory of the Messiah. On the personal level, none of us owe anyone account for our thoughts. But we all can and must judge each other for our conduct, and if we promulgate a mistaken view, we are accountable to one another and to the church of the Messiah. None may be allowed to teach but those who are judged to teach according to Scripture.

And yet, what is the Apostle saying? We recall that the false teachers were calling upon the Galatian believers to adopt Jewish custom, which included the duty to be circumcised. Paul is saying that he would have these teachers castrate themselves in the process. Such an act would render them incapable of worship according to the Law because castrated persons were forbidden to enter the temple (Deuteronomy 23:1).

Some folk are more delicate than Paul and therefore interpret his words as if the Apostle meant for the false teachers to be "cut off" from among the people (Exodus 12:15, Leviticus 7:27 and many others), that is to say, excommunicated. Others introduce a slight alteration and suggest that Paul is expressing the hope that God will bring about their death. But Paul is speaking of an action that the teachers are to perform on themselves. No one excommunicates himself, and Paul is not expecting them to commit suicide.

The Apostle's language is harsh, but he views the implications of the teachers to be even harsher. We will never understand the validity of Paul's reaction unless we believe as he does in the existence of light and darkness, truth and error, the message of God's Word and false teachings that twist the meaning of God's Word. If truth exists, it stands over us and obliges us all, and Paul is convinced beyond doubt that truth exists. The question we must ask ourselves is, will we choose to be faithful to the truth, or to love ourselves and seek popularity—or do we perhaps disagree with the Apostle and deny truth exists?

Because you were called to freedom, brothers, only not to a freedom that becomes an opportunity for the flesh. Instead, serve one another in love. Immediately after the Apostle used such harsh language, he dares to speak of love! The reason is, again, love was what motivated him to speak in such terms. Love is zealous. Love is jealous (Exodus 34:14, 2 Corinthians 11:12). Paul loves the Messiah and he loves the Galatians. He would have them both true to one another.

Paul use strong language toward the false teachers because their teachings distorted the nature the freedom the Messiah had purchased for the redeemed by limiting its scope. In fact, they threatened to enslave the believers all over again.

Paul referred to this in Chapter Four (verses 7–8) and in verse 1 of Chapter Five, when he said that the Messiah had freed those who put their trust in him and that it is their duty to persist in that freedom rather than assume again the yoke of slavery to which they were previously subject. Here he return to this topic with, as we shall see, a slight difference.

Much to our surprise, Paul has equated the bondage of idolatry to Israel's traditional form of the worship of God. As we saw, the reason for this is that that the framers of that ancient tradition misunderstood the purpose of the Law, They transformed it into a means by which one obtains something from God. They thought of the God of Israel in the same terms that characterized idol worship, as if their rituals and sacrifices accorded them advantages in the sight of the gods. They believed they were capable of impacting the behavior of the gods.

To a disconcerting extent, Israel's traditions distorted the image of God in the minds of the people, so that they too began thinking of Him as dependent on their religious acts. What is more, it was thought that His commandments could not stand on their own; they needed the authoritative interpretation of scribes and Rabbis. Man was attributed with capacities at the expense of almighty God, and instead of every individual standing himself before God, understanding His Word and bearing responsibility for the way he understands and applies it, they were made subject to rabbinical dictum.

God was removed from the throne of His glory, and man was subjected to human religious powers. Instead of the freedom of conscience and the right God-given right to bear responsibility for one's choices and preferences, man's freedom as one created in the image of God was subjected to the authority of spiritual leaders: "it is forbidden to eat this and to drink that, to touch this and do that. You must not walk in the morning more than so many steps before saying your prayers. This you must wear, you must turn in this direction to pray and these are the words you must use," and so on, ad infinitum.

Some Christians think in similar terms. Others don't think at all but expect their spiritual leaders to tell them what to do in the varying circumstances of life (I remember congregants demanding that I preach what they termed "practical sermons" because they did not want to think for themselves). Some think that Christians are best known for what they do not do (curse, lie, commit adultery, etc.) rather than by what they do; by the holiness of their lives, by their love for God and their fellow man, by their humility, their honesty, generosity and self-discipline.

We have been called to a very certain kind of freedom. As the children of God, we are called to lead responsible lives in the presence of our Savior. We ought not think we can subject God to our hopes or desires, nor may we subject our consciences to the purportedly authoritative interpretations of others. We hear our teachers, carefully examine what they teach by examining the Scriptures, and only when we are persuaded that what they taught is true, do we submit to them as to the words of the living God.

We are free to enjoy the pleasures this wonderful creation of God affords us, but we may not become addicted to those pleasures because addiction is a kind of slavery. Living according to the commandments of God involves responsible, independent, mature and informed thinking that will sometimes result in apparently contradictory conduct because of the varying circumstances in which we live: Paul circumcised Timothy but refused to circumcise Titus. Although Paul says Christians are free to eat meat sold in the marketplace (and provided by the temple, where animals were sacrificed), he enjoins believers to avoid doing so if the exercise of that freedom injures the uninformed conscience of a fellow believer. Whoever serves God in such a manner experiences real freedom. As Augustine put it, "make me a captive, Lord, then I shall be free."

The freedom the Messiah purchased for us is not anarchy. It has boundaries. It has goals. It takes on a very specific kind of image and, in the verses that follow, these are clearly described. First, it is not to be a freedom that becomes an opportunity for the flesh. There is no room in the Christian life for selfishness, pride, lust, materialism, indifference to other's sensitivities, cruelty or competitiveness. There is no room for sin or for power broking of any kind.

Most people live for themselves. In most cases, even when they do good, their motives are selfish. They act in a certain way because it feels good or in expectation that others will return the favor. Truth be told, we love only those who love us, and when we do good, we expect to be appreciated. Countries assist each other as part of their foreign relations policy, promoting national interests. Companies contribute to society to project and sell their product. Few good simply because it is the right thing to do.

The freedom that God accords us in the Messiah is one that requires us to be different. We are to serve one another in love. We are to be altruistic, to prefer another person's well-being to our own, often to sacrifice on her behalf.

Serve. That is not a popular word A servant is considered to be on the lower level of society. That was also true when the New Testament was being written. The Christian Faith redeemed that term, just as it redeemed the term "slave." Everything depends on the motive and on whom we serve. If we serve because we have no choice, we will inevitably view what we do as a form of humiliation. On the other hand, if we serve willingly, out of love, our service is an enjoyable calling. People enslaved to other human beings can only consider their bondage in the negative. The slaves of God consider their bondage sweet, invigorating—a privilege.

To serve one another in love is to serve one another willingly, not for gain but for love's sake. It means loving our enemies, blessing those who curse us and doing good to those who abuse us. It means giving the shirt off our backs to someone who demands our coat, giving to whomever asks of us, without expecting anything in return. Motive is the main thing, and a pure motive is how we serve God in the way He desires.

To serve one another in love means that we are not active in the church because we crave attention or want a position in the church. We serve because the love of God drives us to love others whether they deserve it or not, with no regard to any advantage we might derive from them. It means doing good eagerly, happily and willingly, giving others more than our surplus. It means sacrificing for others.

To serve one another in love means doing for others what the Messiah did for us. What can we add to *that*?!

Serve one another in love because the whole of the Law is summarized in one word: "love the other like you love yourself." I admit: from the moment I began writing this commentary on Galatians I looked forward to reaching this verse! The Apostle knew how to present the truth in a way that arouses worship and wonder, while requiring each one of us to think, understand and apply what we have learned.

Paul has spoken in no uncertain terms against any kind of law-keeping, including the Law given at Sinai, rabbinic dictum and Israel's heritage. Time and again he insisted that neither of these, nor all of them together, can accord us even an iota of merit before God. One might conclude therefore that the Apostle believes there is no place for any kind of law in the Christian life, that everyone may conduct himself in Messiah as best he understands—and yet here the Apostle faces us with the Law as a standard for life in the presence of God.

On the one hand, we are free from the Law. On the other hand, we are obliged by it. How is this possible? Simply, put, we are free from the Law as to its ceremonial and civil aspects and as to the way in which the Rabbis understood it (contrary to its true nature), as a means by which we ensure our standing before God or obtain something from Him. But we are duty-bound to keep the Law in its moral aspects. they are eternal. That is why God inscribed these afresh on our hearts when He gave us new birth. He did this because the moral aspects of the Law point the way for man to give expression to God's image, the image in which man was originally created and into which he is being refashioned.

The practical, day to day essence of the Law is love, as the Apostle puts it, the whole of the Law is summarized in one word: "love the other like you love yourself." Paul explains this well in Romans 13:8–10:

> owe no one anything, except to love each other, for the one who loves another has fulfilled the law. For the commandments, 'You shall not commit adultery, You shall not murder, You shall not steal, You shall not covet,' and any other commandment, are summed up in this word: 'You shall love your neighbor as yourself'. Love does no wrong to a neighbor; therefore love is the fulfilling of the law.

That is how we reflect the beautiful glory of God, our Creator and Savior.

Human society, on the other hand, conducts itself, as Paul put it earlier, according to the flesh. Men and women devour one another, even if their attitude is disguised by a show of kindness and generosity. Employers endeavor to pay their employees a minimal wage unless it is worth their while to do otherwise. Employees endeavor to take advantage of their employers, and to give in return the minimum. Those who enjoy a position in society show interest in the weaker members of society in an effort to enlist their support and, having derived the maximum, ignore those who support their sought. Men and women competing in sports drug themselves to win a medal.

We are called upon to be different. We are called upon to fulfill the Law by loving one another in the same way that we love ourselves. That is the duty of all human beings. All the more so is it the duty of those whom God has loved, for whom He sent His Son and to whom He gave His Holy Spirit.

The whole of the Law is summarized in one word: "love the other like you love yourself, but if you bite and consume each other, be careful that you are not consumed by each other. A society that is based on human achievement becomes in the course of time a violent, selfish, abusive society in which competitiveness is characteristic. No one rejoices in another person's success. Everyone is envious of the other and tries to out-do the other, even if doing so implies hurting someone, physically or otherwise (for some strange reason we consider physical damage especially grievous) or doubting the truth of his achievements.

Sometimes the symptoms appear only after a period, but they do ultimately appear. The teachers who arrived in Galatia and taught the believers there that they ought to adhere to Israel's traditions had no intention to create such a society. Of course they did not! But they could not forestall the results of their teaching.

Anyone who thinks of himself better than another will inevitably look down of those who differ from him. He will not hesitate to argue with them, demeaning those with whom he disagrees while presenting what he has chosen to believe as absolutely true. A view that affirms man's ability to earn something from God leads to the kind of arrogance that does not hesitate to use force, manipulate or deceive. That is why Paul found it necessary to warn the Galatians, if you bite and consume each other, be careful that you are not consumed by each other.

We need to learn to conduct our disagreements with a mixture of humility and mutual respect. To that end we must beware of any inclination to think ourselves better than others, and to avoid all teachings that tell us that we are wiser, more spiritual or in any way better than those who disagree with us, or that indirectly cultivate an inclination to think in such terms.

We must avoid controversy for the sake of controversy. We need to relieve ourselves of the need to prove we are right—and this is not to deny there are times when we need to defend the truth. However, the delicate difference between the validity of truth and the validity of our views is more important than we assume. In the first case we will be unwilling to lend a listening ear to someone else's argument. We will not respect him, nor will we weigh what he is saying; we are too busy proving ourselves right, come what may.

If, on the other hand, our sincere interest is in the truth, we will listen to the person arguing against our view, weigh his arguments carefully and, should it turn out that we are mistaken (it does happen sometimes, you know), we will hasten to admit as much and correct our views.

In the first case we are self-serving, loving ourselves. In the second we are serving God and loving Him.

Later on the Apostle will say to the Galatians, let's not be taken up with empty boasting, provoking one another, envying one another. Regrettably, this is a warning we all need to hear and would do well to heed.

So there you have it. Such are the sad results of the doctrines the false teachers brought to Galatia. Instead of a fear of God that leads to peace, harmony and brotherly good-will, it caused conflict, jealousy and anger.

> Who is wise and understanding among you? By his good conduct let him show his works in the meekness of wisdom. But if you have bitter jealousy and selfish ambition in your hearts, do not boast and be false to the truth. This is not the wisdom that comes down from above, but is earthly, unspiritual, demonic. For where jealousy and selfish ambition exist, there will be disorder and every vile practice. But the wisdom from above is first pure, then peaceable, gentle, open to reason, full of mercy and good fruits, impartial and sincere. And a harvest of righteousness is sown in peace by those who make peace (James 3:13–18).

LET'S SUMMARIZE

- How do you use the freedom purchased for you by the Messiah? What steps do you take to protect that freedom?

- Is your present spiritual commitment as real and as encompassing as at the beginning of your spiritual life?

- Think further on the practical implications of verse 9 and what they should mean in your life.

- We all want to "look good in the flesh." How do you combat that sinful tendency in your own life?

LET'S PRAY

Almighty God, ever to be loved, praised and adored, in Your great mercy, You purchased for us a wonderful freedom, secured by the sacrifice of the Messiah. Grant us grace to use that freedom as You would have us use it, to the praise of the glory of Your grace. May we ever await the climax of righteousness that is to be achieved in us by Your kindness, and may our awaiting be accompanied by a sincere enthusiasm that will drive us to love others because we love You.

Keep us faithful to the truth. Preserve us from the wiles of the devil, who always seeks to deceive us. Cause us to live, alert and equipped to recognize any departure from the truth, however small, and eager to serve others for Jesus' sake, in whose name we plead, Amen.

Questions for Discussion and Study

1. What is the fear of which the Apostle speaks, why do we need to be warned against it and how can we protect ourselves from it?

2. Define the various aspects of freedom to which Paul refers in this section.

3. Discuss Paul's use of we/you in this section and try to identify the logic behind that use. What lesson should be learned from it?

4. Discuss the relations between assurance and grace.

CHAPTER 15

The Spirit and the Flesh
(GALATIANS 5:16–21)

[16] And I say: behave according to the Spirit and you will under no circumstance gratify the desires of the flesh [17] because the flesh desires against the Spirit, and the Spirit against the flesh. These two oppose each other so that you are unable to do what you want to do. [18] But if you are guided by the Spirit you are not subject to law.

[19] What the flesh does is obvious: fornication, impurity, lewdness, [20] idolatry, sorcery, hostility, quarrels, jealousies, competitions, divisions, factions, [21] envy, drunken parties, and the like of which I warn you in advance as I warned you before, that those who are doing these kinds of things will not inherit the kingdom of God.

And I say: behave according to the Spirit and you will under no circumstance gratify the desires of the flesh.

What does it mean, to behave according to the Spirit? Paul made that clear in the preceding paragraph and will do so again in what follows. Behaving according to the Spirit is not characterized by extraordinary spiritual revelations or by gentle whispers of the Spirit in one's heart, by which a person knows what to do in various circumstances. It means we conduct ourselves in ways that contrast with biting and devouring one another. It means a determined refusal to satisfy the lusts of the flesh (verse 16) and of fulfilling the commandments of God.

In verses 19–26 Paul spells this out:

> What the flesh does is obvious: fornication, impurity, lewdness, idolatry, sorcery, hostility, quarrels, jealousies, competitions, divisions, factions, envy, drunken parties, and the like of which I warn you in advance as I warned you before, that those who are doing these kinds of things will not inherit the kingdom of God.

> But the fruit of the Spirit is love, joy, peace, patience, generosity, kindness, faithfulness, humility, self-restraint—against such things there is no law, and those who belong to Messiah have crucified their flesh with its desires and lusts. We live by the Spirit, so we should conduct ourselves by the guidance of the Spirit. Let's not be taken up with empty boasting, provoking one another, envying one another.

In other words, behavior according to the Spirit is moral behavior motivated by the fear of God and directed by His commandments as given in His Word.

That is exactly what Paul will say in his letter to the Romans when he will write of "the righteous requirement of the Law" being "fulfilled in us." He explains:

> those who live according to the flesh set their minds on the things of the flesh, but those who live according to the Spirit set their minds on the things of the Spirit. For to set the mind on the flesh is death, but to set the mind on the Spirit is life and peace. For the mind that is set on the flesh is hostile to God, for it does not submit to God's law; indeed, it cannot. Those who are in the flesh cannot please God ... So then, brothers, we are debtors, not to the flesh, to live according to the flesh. For if you live according to the flesh you will die, but if by the Spirit you put to death the deeds of the body, you will live (Romans 8:4–13).

Christian spirituality is not a matter of feelings, mystical experiences and direct, supranatural and personal guidance. Christian spirituality is a matter of devotion to God and the desire to do what is pleasing to Him. It is a matter of obedience to His commands. Since our first father sinned, it also means a stubborn struggle with the desires and habits that motivated us before we were converted.

That is just what the false teachers in Galatia did not understand. They focused on ceremonies, festivals, prohibitions and the like. Others, in Corinth and Colossae, focused on supposedly spiritual experiences.

Paul is teaching the Galatians the true nature of spirituality. Any who purport to lead the flock of God and are characterized by ostentatiousness, who boast of supernatural powers, of healings and other such sensual phenomena as evidence of spirituality, do not understand the Gospel. They are promoting an addiction to sensuality, to materialism and to this world, because it is with such things they are engaged.

> And I say: behave according to the Spirit and you will under no circumstance gratify the desires of the flesh because the flesh desires against the Spirit, and the Spirit against the flesh. These two oppose each other so that you are unable to do what you want to do. But if you are guided by the Spirit you are not subject to law.

It is important to see the logic of Paul's argument here. How can we say that, if we behave according to the Spirit we will under no circumstance gratify the desires of the flesh? The answer is found in recognition of the fact that a conflict raging in our hearts. The flesh and the Spirit are at war the one with the other. Sometimes the conflict is so strenuous that we become morally paralyzed: "I delight in the law of God, in my inner being, but I see in my members another law waging war against the law of my mind and making me captive to the law of sin that dwells in my members" (Romans 7:22–23).

In the new birth, the Spirit frees us from the need to respond to our lusts by freeing us from the bondage to sin that Adam's transgression brought upon us. The lusts are still there, as are the habits of sin we developed, but we are no longer bound to obey them. In fact, if born of the Spirit, we do not want to obey them. Although the body will demand that we satisfy its exaggerated yearnings, we are no longer obliged to do so. We can suffer want, need, hunger, cold, loneliness, loss—even the loss of life—for God's sake. We are free to refuse to satisfy any desire that is contrary to purity, honesty and holiness. We are wonderfully, gloriously enslaved to God, and to Him alone.

Once again there is a parallel with what Paul will write to the Romans years later:

> the law of the Spirit of life has set you free in Christ Jesus from the law of sin and death. For God has done what the law, weakened by the flesh, could not do. By sending his own Son in the likeness of sinful flesh and for sin, he condemned sin in the flesh, in order that the righteous requirement of the law might be fulfilled in us, who walk not according to the flesh but according to the Spirit (Romans 8:2–4).

By the merits of the Messiah and His atoning sacrifice, the sin that is
in our body has been condemned. Its death sentence has been written:
"our old self was crucified with him in order that the body of sin might
be brought to nothing, so that we would no longer be enslaved to sin. For
one who has died has been set free from sin" (Romans 6:6–7).

And again:

> But if Christ is in you, although the body is dead because of sin, the
> Spirit is life because of righteousness. If the Spirit of him who raised
> Jesus from the dead dwells in you, he who raised Christ Jesus from the
> dead will also give life to your mortal bodies through his Spirit who
> dwells in you (Romans 8:10–11).

As we said, a conflict is raging in our hearts: the flesh desires against
the Spirit, and the Spirit against the flesh. These two oppose each other so
that you are unable to do what you want to do, which is why we cry out
as did the Apostle, "Wretched man that I am! Who will deliver me from
this body of death?" (Romans 7: 24), and we immediately reply with the
Apostle , "Thanks be to God through Jesus Christ our Lord!" (Romans 7
25). It is He who will save us, by His Spirit, by the power of the new life
He has given us in the Messiah.

Such are the results of the new birth. The Holy Spirit has taken up
residence in our hearts and is inscribing God's law there. New desires are
being formed in us. We adopt new values, new standards. The Holy Spirit
encourages and strengthens us in the struggle against the habits of sin.

Our standing with God is not, however, contingent on what we do or
do not do: if you are guided by the Spirit you are not subject to law, or, as
Paul will put in in Romans,

> there is therefore now no condemnation for those who are in Christ
> Jesus ... What then shall we say to these things? If God is for us, who can
> be against us? He who did not spare his own Son but gave him up for
> us all, how will he not also with him graciously give us all things? Who
> shall bring any charge against God's elect? It is God who justifies. Who
> is to condemn? Christ Jesus is the one who died—more than that, who
> was raised—who is at the right hand of God, who indeed is interceding
> for us. ... I am sure that neither death nor life, nor angels nor rulers, nor
> things present nor things to come, nor powers, nor height nor depth,
> nor anything else in all creation, will be able to separate us from the
> love of God in Christ Jesus our Lord (Romans 8:1, 31–39).

Therefore, increasingly until we arrive at the full measure of the stature of the Messiah, we will under no circumstance gratify the desires of the flesh because we will refuse to do so.

The Christian life is a life chock-a-block full of exuberant hope and confidence, combined with an ongoing struggle in which the flesh desires against the Spirit, and the Spirit against the flesh and these two oppose each other. As a result, we are sometimes unable to do what we want to do, instead, we do the opposite. But, thanks, praise and worship are due to God, who gives us the victory in the Messiah Jesus!

We've already touched on another important aspect of that victory, expressed in Paul's next statement: If you are guided by the Spirit you are not subject to law. Here too, it is worth taking time to clarify what the Apostle is actually saying. He is not saying that Christians are free of all duties, as if they are obliged to no law. On the contrary, just a few sentences earlier he established God's law as the standard of Christian behavior. What Paul is talking about here has to do with the problem that arose in many of the churches of his time, evident ever since as well. People find it difficult to accept the idea that they do not deserve to enjoy health and wealth, success and status. The children of Adam find it difficult not to aspire to be as gods (Genesis 3:5), free of any obligation but that which they choose to undertake.

That is why, apart from Christianity, all religions assume the universe runs on the grounds on man's ability, and that his fate is ultimately in his hands. If he will do so and so for the gods, they will repay him with this and that. Man must be worthy, and if he is worthy, he is inevitably deserving.

In the nominally Christian world this view is expressed in the way Roman Catholicism and other versions of the Faith distorted the Gospel by turning it into a method by which man earns God's blessings. Sometimes this is expressed in an effort to be spiritual at the expense of trust in the grace of God. John and Charles Wesley formed in Oxford what was described as "the Holy Club." Hoping to increase in holiness, they themselves posited 22 questions, such as:

- Am I consciously or unconsciously creating the impression that I am better than I really am? In other words, am I a hypocrite?

- Am I honest in all my acts and words, or do I exaggerate?

- Am I self-conscious, self-pitying, or self-justifying?

- Am I enjoying prayer?

- When did I last speak to someone else of my faith?

- Do I pray about the money I spend?

- Do I disobey God in anything?

- Do I insist upon doing something about which my conscience is uneasy?

- Am I jealous, impure, critical, irritable, touchy or distrustful?

- Am I proud?

- Is Christ real to me?

No doubt, we ought to examine ourselves, and most of the above questions are appropriate. But, when God's felt presence and His blessings are thought of as something to be obtained by virtue of human effort, we have distorted the Gospel and laid claim to abilities at the expense of God's grace.

Who among us can honestly claim the he never acts in a hypocritical manner; that he is always honest, reliable, free of all dependencies, reads the Scriptures and prays enough? Which of us never allows himself to slip into sin, overcomes in all areas of life, is never jealous, never offended and never unjustifiably critical? Who dares say that he always makes responsible use of his free time and that the nearness of the Messiah is always a reality in his life? Of course, we should strive for these things but, in this life, we will never reach perfection.

Anyone who makes such claims is like the Pharisee of whom the Lord said, "if you were blind, you would have no guilt; but now that you say, 'We see,' your guilt remains" (John 9:41). Or, as the Messiah said to the church in Laodicea,

> you say, "I am rich, I have prospered, and I need nothing," not realizing that you are wretched, pitiable, poor, blind, and naked. I counsel you to buy from me gold refined by fire, so that you may be rich, and white garments so that you may clothe yourself and the shame of your nakedness may not be seen, and salve to anoint your eyes, so that you may see (Revelation 3:17–19).

That is exactly the attitude Paul encountered in many of the churches to which he wrote. The Galatians thought they could get more from God if they adhere to Israel's tradition. The Colossians thought they would excel other Christians if they worship angels, undergo a mystical experience and adopt some of Israel's traditions. The Corinthians thought they were more spiritual than others because they had been granted special experiences. The Jews thought they were better than others because they were Jews, and non-Jews thought themselves better than Jews because they were Gentiles, or that they would become better than others if they acted like Jews.

These all have to do with human achievement, with meeting requirements or obeying a law. People who fail are deemed unworthy. Any who does not lay claim to the same level of perfection claimed by others has one of three options: he must try harder, despair of succeeding or lower the standard and claim a relative achievement. I'll never forget the instance when, in speaking to a brother in the Faith and a fellow laborer in the church, I suggested that he and I should respond to criticism with humility. His eyes opened wide, his back stiffened and he asked me in amazement "What?! are you saying that I am not humble?!"

Of course, we are subject to God's commandments. We have duties in the Messiah from which we may not abscond. But we are not subject to any law insofar as our standing before God is concerned, nor are we ever worthy of His blessing.

> Will any one of you who has a servant plowing or keeping sheep say to him when he has come in from the field, "Come at once and recline at table"? Will he not rather say to him, "Prepare supper for me, and dress properly, and serve me while I eat and drink, and afterward you will eat and drink"? Does he thank the servant because he did what was commanded? So you also, when you have done all that you were commanded, say, "We are unworthy servants; we have only done what was our duty" (Luke 17:7–10).

Whatever we have from God, we have by grace.

What the flesh does is obvious: fornication, impurity, lewdness, idolatry, sorcery, hostility, quarrels, jealousies, competitions, divisions, factions, envy, drunken parties and the like of which I warn you in advance as I warned you before, that those who are doing these kinds of things will not inherit the kingdom of God.

We might think what the Apostle says here contradicts what he said earlier. At first sight is appears as if Paul is making privileges before God contingent on actions, whereas he argued for the opposite up to this point. First sight is deceptive. Paul is not explaining who is worthy of God's blessing. He does not say here, or anywhere else, that only those who are not guilty of this catalogue of evils will inherit the kingdom of God. He is not informing his readers how to climb the ladder of spiritual achievements so as to deserve anything from God. Rather, he is indicating the kinds sins of which we are all guilty and because of which we are unworthy of anything but punishment at the hand of God.

As is true of all the Apostle's lists, the list is not exhaustive. There is no shortage of sins that render individuals unworthy of the kingdom of God. That is why Paul appends the closing words, and the like.

The Apostle presents this embarrassing list of sins, works of the flesh, as he describes them, and contrasts it with the fruit of the Spirit to show us how true spirituality expresses itself, rather than the ways the false teachers suggested. True spirituality does focus on emotions and experiences (although both can be fruits of spirituality) any more than it does on rituals (although they can be expressions of true spirituality), but on moral principles shaped and motivated by a loving fear of God and expressed in daily conduct.

Focusing on rituals, experiences and other external matters diverts our attention from the spiritual and moral conflict in which we must engage. Such a focus promotes pride which leads to self-love that, in turn, leads to competitiveness, conflict and jealousy. Not so, says Paul. Holiness is not a matter of how we feel but of how we live, of preferring the good to the bad, the best to the good, the pure over the impure and the true over what is untrue.

The phrase What the flesh does serves Paul to indicate the natural inclinations of the human heart since the sin of our first father, Adam. Paul speaks of inclinations in such terms because the false teachers placed primary emphasis on what an individual does with his body: the ceremonies he follows, feast and holy days he observes, food he is permitted or forbidden to eat, circumcision and other such visible matters. These are not the product of the work of the Holy Spirit but of man's effort to stand on his own in the presence of God. They are a form of hedonism (the conviction that pleasure is man's highest good) masquerading as piety, an aberration of grace according to which man obtains achieves life in the fullest sense by his efforts.

Paul dares place that kind of adherence to Israel's traditions on par with the list of evils he accorded us. Paul is showing us that true spirituality, does not focus on Jewish tradition but on a sincere, humble fear of God, on purity of heart and kindness in the context of human relationships. Where these are lacking, circumcision becomes uncircumcision. Rather than serving God, we are trampling His courts. Our sacrifices are a stench in His nostrils. They raise His ire, not His pleasure.

What the flesh does is obvious: fornication, impurity, lewdness. The relationship between these and hedonism is clear. They are all forms of self-love, of man turned in on himself. Fornicators—male or female—are busy with themselves. They "make love" without loving anyone but themselves. Sexual relations were designed by God to be an aspect of that very special, blessed, inviolable, and mutual commitment between one man and one woman—a marriage. They were designed to serve as an expression of mutual commitment and of giving oneself, unlimited by nothing but those boundaries imposed by holiness and the fear of God.

It is not only permissible to enjoy sexual relations, it is right to do so, just as it is right to enjoy the presence of a loved one, all the more so of the intimate presence of a spouse with whom you have formed a covenantal relationship in the presence of God. Sex was not designed for momentary satisfaction. The main part of sex is not an organism but sincere, pure, true affection that desires to give more than it desires to receive.

God made us to desire one another. Such a desire is pure and utterly natural when it occurs between a man and a woman in the context of marriage. Sin perverted that desire and turned it into lust which demands satisfaction under any circumstance, by any means and often at any cost. In a generation in which self-satisfaction has become an ultimate virtue, when "so long as you're happy" is an acceptable standard, those who fear God must strive to teach themselves restraint. They need to develop moral muscles. They must know how to refuse lust and direct their desires into pure channels.

Paul speak not only of fornication but of impurity, lewdness, the latter of which is a kind of abandon to sexual desires. All three are aspects of the same kind of perverted hunger, and all three are decried by the Apostle. It does not matter if we are speaking of pornography, consensual foreplay or sex between adults who are not married one to another, or masturbation; they are all perversions. They are all abominations in the sight of God.

We belong to a generation swept up in lust, impurity and addiction to sexual fantasies. We must resist the influence of our environment and dare be different. We must dress differently. We must display different values. We must adopt patterns of conduct that differ from those accepted in the world around us. We must challenge our society.

At the same time, we must remember that Paul is referencing these evils in connection with his argument against the attempt to obtain something in Christ by human effort, specifically by adherence to the Law of Moses and to Jewish tradition. The conclusion we must draw from that connection is that any focus, even on the best of bodily efforts, leads in a direction none of us should wish to go.

> Idolatry, sorcery ... and the like of which I warn you in advance as I warned you before, that those who are doing these kinds of things will not inherit the kingdom of God.

Paul continues to point out some of the ways in which self-love expresses itself in man's effort to stand on his own, govern his life and view pleasure as the goal of life. He now speaks of things the flesh does that professedly have to do with spirituality. People engage in idolatry and in sorcery because they prefer to believe in a deity who is much like themselves, subject to manipulation. They want nothing to do with a terrifyingly holy God who rules over all, who cannot be bribed, whose will cannot be altered and whose action cannot by stymied. They imagine a convenient deity.

The gods of the Gentiles are no more than reflections of their worshippers, their world-views, weaknesses, whims and actions. Idolatry assumes the existence of gods who may be motivated by sacrifices, ceremonies and incantations. The difference between idolatry and sorcery is minimal, so much so that both share the same understanding of the world: man determines the actions of the gods or of the spirits, because the latter are dependent on man's actions. In other words, man is the ultimate master of his fate.

The only other option that man can think of is that he is a prisoner of blind, cruel fate. Man refuses to believe that the world is governed by an all-wise, kind God, holy and merciful, and that the fate of every individual is determined by him. Man wants to rule, at any cost—even if it means he is lost in his effort to take over the world. He prefers to drive the vehicle of his life off a cliff rather than hand the steering wheel over to someone gloriously other than him, greater and better by far.

Our present generation does not differ in this regard from those that preceded. Man is still sinful, rebellious and hostile to God. In our days he employs genetic engineering, challenges the very definition of a family and claims the right to determine or alter his gender. He still irresponsibly abuses the world's resources, impacts the environment without thought for tomorrow and claims the right to do so without having to give account. He dares promote invitro pregnancies that involve the destruction of countless unborn and surrogacy. He avoids giving birth by way of pills, condoms and abortions, and hands unwanted children over for adoption or neglects them in front of a television set while he selfishly pursues his career.

Not only so, but sorcery has not disappeared from the world. Many flock to wonder-workers. Others, who consider themselves an educated elite, believe in stones and fragrances with supra-natural powers, become devotees of gurus, Scientology or of some well-spoken preacher.

Those who are doing these kinds of things will not inherit the kingdom of God. because the kingdom of God is very different from all of this mush. The Faith of the Messiah requires mature, informed thought. It imposes on individuals the responsibility to adopt a moral view that acknowledges God's government of the universe and devotes itself enthusiastically to keeping His commandments because it recognizes than no one is more wonderful, more beautiful, more perfect than He is.

When we properly understand the Christian Faith, we dare not think we can redirect God's will by prayer, or move Him to action by anything we do. We recognize that God's will is better than ours, and we accept His will even when it involves pain, loss and suffering.

By virtue of such an understanding, we also come to know that we are not in the hands of blind faith, the powers of nature or of supra-natural beings. We are called to reign in life by the grace of the Messiah, to rule and subdue the earth to the praise of God, and to conduct our lives with a confidence that derives from the knowledge that the promises of God are utterly reliable: they will undoubtedly be fulfilled to the hilt. That is why we dare go through life aspiring, endeavoring, enjoying, hurting, struggling and overcoming. There will be a time when, by the grace of God, we shall also reap the sweet fruits of our pain and sacrifice, struggles and victories.

Such a person experiences life in its thrilling fullness because he has implanted within him an eternal source of vigor that leads to eternal life. Instead of loving himself, he loves God. On the other hand, a man enslaved to himself has no purpose in life beyond immediate pleasure. His love is distorted, and his joys are like the morning dew which dissipates with the rising of the sun.

> How lovely is your dwelling place, O Lord of hosts! My soul longs, yes, faints for the courts of the Lord; my heart and flesh sing for joy to the living God. Even the sparrow finds a home, and the swallow a nest for herself, where she may lay her young, at your altars, O Lord of hosts, my King and my God. Blessed are those who dwell in your house, ever singing your praise! Selah

> Blessed are those whose strength is in you, in whose heart are the highways to Zion. As they go through the Valley of Baca they make it a place of springs; the early rain also covers it with pools. They go from strength to strength; each one appears before God in Zion.

> O Lord God of hosts, hear my prayer; give ear, O God of Jacob! Selah Behold our shield, O God, look on the face of your anointed, for a day in your courts is better than a thousand elsewhere. I would rather be a doorkeeper in the house of my God than dwell in the tents of wickedness. For the Lord God is a sun and shield; the Lord bestows favor and honor. No good thing does he withhold from those who walk uprightly.

> O Lord of hosts, blessed is the one who trusts in you (Psalm 84).

> What the flesh does is obvious: ... hostility, quarrels, jealousies, competitions, divisions, factions, envy ... and the like.

I believe it is not necessary to show how the afore-mentioned sins are expressions of self-love. We are hostile toward any whom we think threaten us. We quarrel with any who dare rob us of property, honor, status or a sense of security (which is why we become angry with those who dare disagree with us).

Instead of being moderate when moderation is called for and uncompromising when compromise is inappropriate, we become zealots with regard to everything and faithful to very little. We are not thoughtful. We do not weigh possibilities. Not only do we maintain this or that contrary view, but we conduct ourselves with regard to others in a radical manner. We display no kindness, no moral wisdom. We think in terms of all or nothing, and we break away from any who are unwilling to tread the path we map out. We cannot live in peace with any but those who agree with us on every little matter, and the number of those decreases as time goes by.

We compete with other churches, with fellow workers, with the neighbors because we find no peace unless we excel others. That is how quarrels and divisions are created in the family, churches and society. If someone is not Charismatic or Reformed, Republican or Democrat, Baptist or Presbyterian (take your pick), or if he eats with a fork and a knife rather than with chopsticks, if he enjoys a different kind of music, and so on—he is at least, of a lower level. Instead of rejoicing over someone else's blessing, we are jealous of those who have what we want and are never short of a way to fault him (Yes, but …).

These are what the flesh does, the fruit of our self-love, of our longing to be free from any kind of dependence—even dependence on God. Our honor is regarded more than His and our freedom valued more than His. We prefer to try and determine our fate rather than recognize it is in the hands of God, and that all we receive from Him is the product His generosity rather than the reward of our faith and willingness to serve Him. In the same spirit we strive to supersede others, influence them or gain control over them so they fulfill our wishes and accept our leadership.

Paul insists that any engaged in such actions will not inherit the kingdom of God. Why is this so? Because it is a kingdom in which God rules, and He is unwilling to hand control over to any. Salvation is nothing less than being brought into the kingdom of God, submitting to His reign.

The Christian life is shaped by the Christian Faith, and the Faith receives its both content and its form from the perfections of God. To the extent that we understand who God is and what He is like, we are also able to understand the Gospel and to live in greater compatibility to its principles.

It is worth stopping for a moment to survey the list of the things the flesh does as a whole. It begins and ends with the sins of the heart—hostility and jealousy. Hostility is the fruit of hatred, of ill-will toward another human being. Jealousy is a sense of bitter frustration because someone has something we want. In both cases, the issue is one of the heart.

That is why we are told, "Keep your heart with all vigilance, for from it flow the springs of life" (Proverbs 4:23). "Out of the heart come evil thoughts, murder, adultery, sexual immorality, theft, false witness, slander. These are what defile a person" (Matthew 15:19–20). We sometimes think that, so long as we have not translated our thoughts into action, we have not sinned. The Word of God says otherwise: sin begins in the heart. "Each person is tempted when he is lured and enticed by his own desire.

Then desire when it has conceived gives birth to sin, and sin when it is fully grown brings forth death. Do not be deceived, my beloved brothers" (James 1:14–16).

We must never hate. We may want something, but we must not give ourselves over to ill will toward someone because she enjoys what we wish to have.

What is in the heart is what creates conflicts, even among friends. The desire that motivates those who love themselves is like the leech, of which it is said "the leech has two daughters: Give [me] and Give [me]" (Proverbs 30:15)."Sheol and Abaddon are never satisfied, and never satisfied are the eyes of man" (Proverbs 27:20). An individual in love with himself will never find satisfaction. He will never be happy with what he has.

It is this kind of self-love like that leads to jealousy. A jealous person lacks a sense of propriety. He sees everything in black and white. He perceives himself as perfect and the other as blemished. The jealous person quarrels because he ignores matters of justice, grace and generosity. Some emphasize the importance of truth over against that of love. Others deny the importance of truth in comparison to love. They are both mistaken. Their radical, extremist stance leads them in directions that, in the best of their moments, they would not want to go. That is how hostility, quarrels, jealousies, competitions, divisions, factions, envy ... and the like occur, rending families and congregations, and creating national conflicts, each side demanding its own version of perfect justice.

Indeed, what the flesh does is obvious: fornication, impurity, lewdness, idolatry, sorcery, hostility, quarrels, jealousies, competitions, divisions, factions, envy, drunken parties and the like of which I warn you in advance as I warned you before, that those who are doing these kinds of things will not inherit the kingdom of God. Such a selfish perspective is the opposite of the path the Messiah calls us to follow, even when it presents itself in terms of spiritual loyalty. At best, it is zeal unaccompanied by knowledge, unmitigated by wisdom and unchecked by moral norms. It remains an expression of arrogance, the source of which is self-love rather than love for God. We must take extreme care to avoid any such view of ourselves or of others.

The way to do that is, first of all, to understand and internalize the truths of God's Word. The second is to be constantly engaged in self-examination, asking the Holy Spirit for grace to recognize the roots of habitual sin in us. The third is that we maintain openness to criticism from others. Finally, we need to rely on God's grace rather than on our presumed righteousness and practice repentance, turning from error and sin and toward God, on a frequent basis.

> What the flesh does is obvious ... drunken parties and the like of which I warn you in advance as I warned you before, that those who are doing these kinds of things will not inherit the kingdom of God.

We are not forbidden to enjoy ourselves. There is nothing wrong with having a party or with moderate eating and drinking. What is forbidden is immoderate engagement in any form of enjoyment. Drunken parties and the like are a kind of abandon to bodily pleasures, which lead to (and often are an expression of) loss of control and the inability to make moral evaluations.

We must not allow ourselves to become addicted to the pleasures of this world, some of which are forbidden, however sweet. Drunken parties and the like mar the image of God in us by reducing our ability to thoughtfully consider our behavior and prefer the good over the pleasant. We were created in the image of God; we are not beasts, to be driven by physical instincts. Immoderation sweeps aside healthy inhibitions, leading individuals to actions in which, at better times, they would never engage.

Paul's added, and the like refers to all kinds of sins, addictions and substance abuse. The only permitted addiction is the one commanded: to love God and do His will

On the other hand, those who do not know how to enjoy themselves do not know how to live. God promised His people, if they are lovingly true to Him,

> if you faithfully obey the voice of the Lord your God, being careful to do all his commandments that I command you today, the Lord your God will set you high above all the Gentiles, and all these blessings shall come upon you and overtake you, if you obey the voice of the Lord your God. Blessed shall you be in the city, and blessed shall you be in the field. Blessed shall be the fruit of your womb and the fruit of your ground and the fruit of your cattle, the increase of your herds and the young of your flock. Blessed shall be your basket and your kneading bowl. Blessed shall you be when you come in and blessed shall you be when you go out.

The Lord will cause your enemies who rise against you to be defeated before you. They shall come out against you one way and flee before you seven ways. The Lord will command the blessing on you in your barns and in all that you undertake. And he will bless you in the land that the Lord your God is giving you. The Lord will establish you as a people holy to himself, as he has sworn to you, if you keep the commandments of the Lord your God and walk in his ways. And all the peoples of the earth shall see that you are called by the name of the Lord, and they shall be afraid of you.

And the Lord will make you abound in prosperity, in the fruit of your womb and in the fruit of your livestock and in the fruit of your ground, within the land that the Lord swore to your fathers to give you. The Lord will open to you his good treasury, the heavens, to give the rain to your land in its season and to bless all the work of your hands. And you shall lend to many nations, but you shall not borrow. And the Lord will make you the head and not the tail, and you shall only go up and not down (Deuteronomy 28:1–13).

As Paul put it elsewhere, God "richly provides us with everything to enjoy" (1 Timothy 6:17). God does not envy us our pleasures. To the contrary, He commands,

for seven days you shall keep the feast to the Lord your God at the place that the Lord will choose, because the Lord your God will bless you in all your produce and in all the work of your hands, so that you will be altogether joyful (Deuteronomy 16:15).

Not only so, but our future, assured by the Messiah, is described in terms of Him presenting us "blameless before the presence of His glory with great joy" (Jude 24).

In other words, a life lived as God would have us live it is one that is led wisely, in accordance with thoughtfully framed spiritual and moral values. As such, it is a life of holy joy.

That is another way in which we differ from animals. We are subject to God and find true life by living according to His commandments. They have no such option. That is why the blessings to which we referred, described in Deuteronomy, are the undeserved reward for doing what is pleasing to God, as we read: "if you faithfully obey the voice of the Lord your God, being careful to do all his commandments that I command you today."

We are inclined to view light-heartedly some of the sins Paul enumerates. Consequently, many are common among us. In certain cases I dare to say they characterize us. Look at the list again. Hostility, quarrels, jealousies, competitions, divisions, factions, envy. Are these absent from our company? Is the body of the Messiah characterized by goodwill among those who hold to different opinions? Is there no hostility among us? Are there no quarrels, no jealousies, no tendencies to compete, no divisions and factions? I am not asking if there are no differences among us. Of course there are—and that is a good thing! It is (hopefully) evidence of the fact that we're thinking. What I am asking is if none of us is so zealous of his opinions that he looks down on those who think otherwise.

Not every aspect of truth is equal in importance to others. Even when there is disagreement in fundamental matters, disagreement does not necessarily mean that those who hold to a mistaken view are not our brethren. Nor is the existence of a different opinion necessarily evidence that he is mistaken. Before we dare write someone off, we ought to hear him out, humbly present our own understanding and, to whatever extent is justified, consider amending our understanding. If we have not been persuaded by what we have heard, we must explain why, and we are to do so with humility, kindness and clarity, praying for all affected. The Lord may well grant our brother the same understanding He granted us, or show us that we have been mistaken.

We are to withstand those who deny the Trinity or question the deity of the Messiah, who insist on adding to His accomplishments any form of law-keeping, or who question the reliability of the Scriptures. These and a small number other truths are the essence of the Gospel. But we ought not question the salvation of those whose views on baptism, church government, the continuance of the spiritual gifts or other important but secondary matters differ from ours. These do not affect the essence of the Gospel. In every case, we are to relate with respect, humility and kindness to those who differ with us.

We are not at liberty to consider someone who insists on denying a fundamental of the Gospel a brother in the Messiah, nor may we enable him to promote his views. But neither do we have the ability to determine his fate. God is the Lord of us all. He alone determines our fate, he alone knows our heart, and he alone has the right to determine who may or may not enter his kingdom.

On the other hand, we must not transform every disagreement into a matter fundamental principle. There is room for disagreement among

Christians, many of which disagreements are merely differing perspectives, the product of premises other than that from which we view a matter. They can see what we cannot. My Gentile brethren in a predominantly Jewish church in Israel, for example, were able to draw my attention to aspects of truth to which I was oblivious. As a result, we had to alter our ways. But they persisted with us kindly, although firmly, until we were persuaded by Scripture. The Messiah has but one church and it is our duty to avoid hostility, quarrels, jealousies, competitions, divisions, factions, envy, drunken parties and the like. They are all sins because of which, Paul says, I warn you in advance as I warned you before, that those who are doing these kinds of things will not inherit the kingdom of God.

Let's Summarize

- Go through the list of the works of the flesh and examine your life: which of these can be found in you? What are you going to do about them?

- The Galatians' motives were sincere and commendable: they were eager for more of God. But they were seriously mistaken. Ask yourself if you have sincere and commendable motives that protect mistaken understandings or courses of action. If they are, reconsider those understandings. Discuss them with those whose opinion differs from yours.

- Find the common denominator for the sins Paul mentions here and examine yourself: is there any of that denominator in your heart? If there is, turn to God in repentance.

Let's Pray

Most blessed God, beautiful in the purity of Your majesty, worthy of all praise, You know our hearts. You see our innermost thoughts. Nothing can be hidden from You. You have given us Your Spirit, yet we confess with shame and sorrow our weakness and our proneness to sin. A conflict is raging in our hearts against the power of temptation and the habits of sin. We long to glorify You, yet constantly fail. We need Your help. We need Your enabling to live by the Spirit and not to satisfy the lusts of the flesh. We plead with You: preserve us from self-righteousness. Grant us the strength to resist temptation and break the habits of sin. Enable us to live in purity, showing kindness to all, treating them with grace, just as You treat us. Preserve us, O God, in Your ways and lead us to Your everlasting kingdom to the praise of Your grace through Jesus the Messiah, Amen.

QUESTIONS FOR DISCUSSION AND STUDY

1. Discuss the relation between law and the Spirit in this letter and in Romans Chapter 8.

2. Compare the guidance of the Spirit in this section and in Romans 8. To what conclusions does your study lead you?

3. View the Holy Club's 22 questions. What is good about these questions? What is their shared underlying assumption? What is wrong with that assumption? What is missing?

CHAPTER 16

The Fruit of the Spirit
(GALATIANS 5:22–26)

[22] But the fruit of the Spirit is love, joy, peace, patience, generosity, kindness, faithfulness, [23] humility, self-restraint—against such things there is no law, [24] and those who belong to Messiah have crucified their flesh with its desires and lusts. [25] We live by the Spirit, so we should conduct ourselves by the guidance of the Spirit. [26] Let's not be taken up with empty boasting, provoking one another, envying one another.

What the flesh does ... But the fruit of the Spirit ... Paul is presenting us with a contrast between what the flesh does and the fruit the Spirit produces in the lives of the redeemed. That is why verse 22, which begins the section dealing with the fruit of the Spirit, begins with the word but. What the flesh does are actions taken by man on his own, the product of his sinful nature. The fruit of the Spirit is the product of the Spirits working in the heart of man, gradually changing him into the image of his Creator by writing the eternal law of the Creator in man's heart and motivating him to live accordingly.

We might have expected Paul to speak here of law-keeping, or keeping the Law and Jewish tradition. Why does he not do so? —after all, that is the subject of this letter. The reason is that both kinds of activity, the arrogance that dares aspire to obtain something from God by religious actions and these other, more obviously baneful behaviors, derive from the same source. Paul is drawing toward the conclusion of his argument.

It is possible to appear to be keeping the Law and Jewish tradition and yet be defiled by the shameful actions Paul has just described. The reason is simple: any effort to obtain a standing before God by virtue of human action inevitably lacks spiritual life. It is not born of the Spirit. It is the kind of action anyone can take without forsaking his sin. Such actions are not dependent on the Holy Spirit and are not necessarily the product of the Holy Spirits activity in a human heart, however sincerely they are undertaken.

No one needs God's grace to be circumcised, avoid driving on Sabbath, wearing a kippah, fast on the Day of Atonement or eat unleavened bread during Passover. These are all things the flesh does easily.

The fruit of the Spirit, on the other hand, is the consequence of the Spirit's activity. Let's not be mistaken: every good, every worthy action taken by man, be he a Christian or not, is the fruit of the Spirit of God. The Spirit is active in the world and in human hearts, stymieing evil so that it cannot control the world altogether. He is the effective obstruction against the powers of darkness's efforts to engulf God's universe. When He is removed, evil will break out of its bonds to a horrific, nauseating extent. It sometimes appears as if that is already happening, until we learn from history that there were similar dark periods in the past.

The delightful combination the Apostle describes here, of love, happiness, peace, patience, generosity, kindness, faithfulness, humility and self-restraint is inevitably the fruit of the Spirit's activity in a human heart, weaning him off of self-love and motivating him to love his fellow human as he loves himself because he has come to understand that God loves him in spite of his ill desert. As we shall see, these qualities are the true expression of a what is in a man's heart when he is engaged with God, devoted to God, and grateful for God's grace to him. All the more so is this combination is the incarnation of true spiritual life in the Messiah as individuals relate one to another, a reflection of the image of God in them.

A life that is truly spiritual will find expression in our relating differently to ourselves and to one another. The difference issues out of an internalization of the Gospel by the powerful workings of the Holy Spirit in the heart of those who hear the Gospel, understand it, immerse themselves in it and discover to their joy that it sends out ever-deepening roots into their very being.

An individual who undergoes such a process is being transformed from glory to glory by the workings of the Spirit, realizing in man the fruit of the sacrifice and resurrection of the Messiah (2 Corinthians 3:18).

True spirituality is always moral without being moralistic. It does not focus on the visible but on the motives of the heart. It is never a matter of obedience in order to obtain but the response of a grateful heart. It is not utilitarian. All it does is done out of love for God and man, because it is right to love both God and man.

Why is it right? For one simple, overwhelming reason: because that is what pleases God. Nothing is more beautiful nor is anything more right than action undertaken for the glory of God. The Spirit, who is thoroughly acquainted with what pleases God, is active in us both to want and to do accordingly, in this way accomplishing in us the righteousness that the Law demands. This is a righteousness we can only reach by the grace of God. This is what it means to be led by the Spirit: the reshaping of our inner beings and of our conduct so that they become compatible with the will of God; the purification of our motives and the increasing formation of moral qualities that reflect the beauty of our Creator and Savior.

The fruit of the Spirit is nothing less than the image of God in man, and the renewal of the image is nothing less than it being reshaped by grace into the perfectly beautiful image of the Messiah:

> Those whom he foreknew he also predestined to be conformed to the image of his Son in order that he might be the firstborn among many brothers, and those whom he predestined he also called, and those whom he called he also justified, and those whom he justified he also glorified (Romans 8:29-30).

> The fruit of the Spirit is love, happiness, peace, patience, generosity, kindness, faithfulness, humility, self-restraint—against such things there is no law.

All the qualities the Apostle mentions here issue out of the first and are the inevitable, necessary result of the salvation God has granted us on the grounds of what the Messiah did on our behalf. One who loves is content with what he has. He is never envious. His relations with others are characterized by peace and brotherly goodwill. He is not driven by desires or frustration. He expresses his love by the patience with which he deals with others, however firmly at times. He is generous, faithful and kind. He responds to people with sincere humility, does not exalt himself, restrains himself, has command of his emotions and is willing to forgo rights and privileges for the sake of others.

These characteristics are the exact opposite of the those described in the previous section.

The fruit of the Spirit is love. Love for others is the opposite of self-love. One who loves another does not take advantage of the other's weaknesses to satisfy his own desires. He is moderate in relation to others. Even when he insists on a matter, he does not use force—physical, monetary, political or emotional—to obtain what he wants or to prove his point. He is not hostile, he is slow to anger, is never competitive. For that reason, he does not create quarrels but exercises restraint.

> That is why the Messiah could say that the most important commandment in the Law was the demand that we love God with all our being, our abilities and our resources, and that the second commandment ("love your fellow human as you love yourself") inevitably flows out of the first (Matthew 22:36–40). That is also why Paul could write that one who loves fulfills the Law as a whole (Romans 13:8, Galatians 5:14) and to claim that the commandments, "You shall not commit adultery, You shall not murder, You shall not steal, You shall not covet," and any other commandment, are summed up in this word: "You shall love your neighbor as yourself." Love does no wrong to a neighbor; therefore love is the fulfilling of the law (Romans 13:9–10).

God loved and therefore gave His only Son. He continues to love and therefore bears us in spite of our sins, and blesses us although who are undeserving. His love is not contingent. It does not depend on anything but Him, because whoever truly loves is not engaged in introverted self-satisfaction but with doing good to the objects of His love. That is why we are told that

> love is patient and kind; love does not envy or boast; it is not arrogant or rude. It does not insist on its own way; it is not irritable or resentful; it does not rejoice at wrongdoing but rejoices with the truth. Love bears all things, believes all things, hopes all things, endures all things. Love never ends. As for prophecies, they will pass away; as for tongues, they will cease; as for knowledge, it will pass away (1 Corinthians 13: 4–8).

The Holy Spirit produces His fruit (the text uses the singular form, not the plural) in the lives of the redeemed by motivating them to become in many respects (and to the limited extent to which a human is capable) like God the Father. The image of God, increasingly renewed in them, causes them to reflect the beauty and glory of God by reflecting the beauty of His glorious love.

Such is the choice that, ultimately, faces every individual: will he choose to love himself—inevitably, at other's expense—or will he love God and—inevitably—his fellow human as he loves himself? Selfishness lies at the root of all our sins. Self-love is the source of our impurity, our central problem. Only God can cleanse us of that aberration, uproot it and sow in its place love for Him and others. For this we need to be born again, and this is another thing only God can do for us. Job was right when he said, "who can bring a clean thing out of an unclean? There is not one" (Job 14:4). And yet, this is something God promised to do, as the prophets repeatedly indicated (Deuteronomy 30:6, Jeremiah 31:31–31, Ezekiel 36:27 and many other instances, sometimes employing different terminology).

Salvation is a powerful act of God by His Holy Spirit. True salvation comes from above. Whatever comes from man is no more than a pathetic counterfeit. The new birth, from above, by the power of the Spirit, implements a radical transformation, a reformatting of human nature, ridding it of the viruses of sin and reformatting him into the image of Him who created him. From that moment on man is in love with God. By virtue of that love he loves others. That is why love is described the fruit of the Spirit.

It is worth remembering that the reason Paul writes of these characteristics (as of the others in the previous section) is that the teaching brought to the Galatians was actually a form of self-love. Instead of promoting true spirituality, it promoted pride, arrogant self-confidence and a tendency to look down of those who would not embrace that teaching, but who chose to hang everything on the Messiah and on his perfect achievements. The lesson we should derive from this is obvious; we should apply it to ourselves.

The fruit of the Spirit is ... happiness, peace. The Holy Spirit produces in the hearts of the redeemed love of the kind that characterizes the Messiah and that served as the source of all He did on our behalf. Those motivated by love for others rather than self-love experience a pure kind of happiness and a real sense of peace. They are not engaged in struggling with others, trying to run ahead of anyone, or busy defending their status. They are not envious of other's happiness and success. They are delighted with other people's success and happily accept a secondary position without thinking they deserve more. As Spurgeon put it, "it takes more grace than I can tell to play the second fiddle well." Humility and kindness render such happiness and peace more than possible, whereas self-love always hungers for more and can never be satisfied with what it has.

All too many strive to get ahead of the pack, to be seen and heard. They must be believed to be wiser, prettier, stronger, better educated, richer, faster or happier than others. They hasten to speak up, even when they are not asked. They must always express an opinion, offer a diagnosis, contradict others and propose solutions for every situation. Every tidbit of information, however unreliable, to be drawn from the Internet or other superficial sources of data serves to strengthen their sense of self-worth. Any expressed doubt or contrary opinion is viewed as a threat. Even when they appear to be calm and easy-going, a hidden storm is raging in their hearts, sometimes unbeknown to them, driving them to insist on their view of things. FaceBook's popularity has to do with the fact that people can use it to promote themselves, often by projecting the image they wish they had, reversing Tycho Brahe's dictum by preferring to appear to be what they are not (Brahe's aspiration was "to be, not to appear to be").

On the other hand, those who love others are not driven by the desire to establish themselves in the sight of others; their interest is in other people's welfare. The kind of friendships they create may be relatively few, but they are generally characterized by sincere good will, giving more than by receiving, peace rather than the surreptitious conflict created by a desire and of contradictory hopes. That is why they are also characterized by a quiet kind of deep-seated happiness that transforms daily life into a pleasure-full experience of humility, goodness, holiness and the presence of God,

> like the precious ointment upon the head, that ran down upon the beard, *even* Aaron's beard, that went down to the skirts of his garments; as the dew of Hermon, and as the dew that descended upon the mountains of Zion, for there the Lord commanded the blessing, *even* life for evermore (Psalm 133:2–3).

The sweet flavor of eternity accompanies those who partake of a relationship that is edifying, encouraging and invigorating in godly ways.

A husband and wife who know how to give to one another sincere love will experience family life characterized by calm, quiet happiness. Parents engaged in the cultivation of their children rather than in the promotion of their own comfort, careers or riches will be able to conduct themselves in a kind, generous manner with their children without conceding spiritual and moral values. They will love their children wisely rather than spoil them. They will labor to install values rather than impose behavioral patterns. They will make sure their children have ample quality time with them, not only to entertain them but also to educate, train and encourage them. Such children will grow into adults who know how to function in ways than will do others good, and they too will experience happiness and peace of the kind others will never know.

Church life that focuses on the glory of God rather than on that of its Senior Pastor or the satisfaction of its members will inevitably be a loving church. Such a church will also be a cultivating, encouraging, challenging, healthy, happy and peaceful church—and all of the first three are necessary for the latter.

To the extent that members of society carry out the commandment to love one another as they love themselves, that society will be characterized by peace and happiness. An achievement-based society such as the one the false teachers were trying to create in Galatia will inevitably be a demanding, competitive, merciless society from which peace and happiness will be as far as the east is from the west.

It is appropriate that we ask ourselves what kind of relations are we forming? Is the way we relate to others in any way reminiscent of the way Jesus related to others while he was here on earth? Does the way we relate to others reflect His love, His generosity, the peacefulness of His personality? A proud person, in love with himself, is described by Isaiah in the following terms: "the wicked are like the tossing sea for it cannot be quiet, and its waters toss up mire and dirt." The prophet goes on to warn: "There is no peace," says my God, "for the wicked" (Isaiah 57:20–21).

The fruit of the Spirit is ... patience, generosity, kindness. The Holy Spirit produces in those saved by Him patience, generosity and kindness, qualities which characterized the Messiah in all that He did on earth and what characterizes God's attitude toward us every day of our lives. The three are inseparably related. Patience is nothing less than an expression of generosity, and generosity is nothing less than kindness.

Patience is the willingness to bear with others in their weaknesses, errors and sins, until they come to recognize their failure and turn from it, often even when they do not. We need to recognize our own propensity to err: not all we believe to be an error or a sin may necessary be so.

Sometimes it may turn out that what we considered to be an inappropriate action was actually the best course possible at the time. I know from painful personal experience that the opposite is also true: I sinned unawares while acting with an untroubled conscience and insisting on the rightness of my actions. Once God opened my eyes, I was horrified and turned to mend my ways, but it took time for me to come to that realization. Of course, even when a person sins knowingly, willfully, God is able to bring him to repentance.

There is, therefore, need for a great deal of patience in the way we relate one to another. God treats us with tremendous patience in spite of our sins, sometimes even when we insist on continuing in them although we recognize that what we are doing is wrong. He does not leave us in our sin but works with endless, loving kindness, firmly yet gently, to bring us to mend our ways; and when we respond, He receives us with great joy, as the Gospel says, "there is joy before the angels of God over one sinner who repents" (Luke 15:10).

Patience is no more than an expression of generosity toward others in areas that are not necessarily material. As such, it is generosity of the most important kind. We just reminded ourselves that God deals with us with consistently generous patience. He employs harsh measures only when it is necessary and prefers to use a gentle hint, the soft rebuke of the Spirit, the pang of an awakened conscience or the loving exhortation of friend. He is slow to use a heavy hand, and even when He does, the purpose is always clear: He seeks to bring us back to His ways and renew His blessing in our lives.

That is how we must deal with one another, and from the same motives. Even when punishment is due, it should never be an expression of anger or out of a desire for revenge:

> Beloved, never avenge yourselves, but leave it to the wrath of God, for it is written, "Vengeance is mine, I will repay, says the Lord." To the contrary, "if your enemy is hungry, feed him; if he is thirsty, give him something to drink; for by so doing you will heap burning coals on his head." Do not be overcome by evil, but overcome evil with good (Romans 12:19–21).

> Brothers, if anyone is caught in any transgression, you who are spiritual should restore him in a spirit of gentleness. Keep watch on yourself, lest you too be tempted (Galatians 6:1).

At the same time, generosity is not limited to the moral level; it finds material expression as well. God showers us out of His treasure house with all we need, and more. It is our duty to care to the best of our ability for the needs of those around us, whether they are fellow believers or are not.

These two, patience and generosity, are reflections of the kindness of our Lord the Messiah. We ought not care for others in the hope that we will gain by doing so, or because we want to preach the Gospel. We must extend a helping hand because it is a privilege to do so, as well as a duty: we received freely in spite of our sins and we must give freely. We are called to be imitators of God.

The fruit of the Spirit is ... faithfulness, humility, self-restraint. Faithfulness is a form of devoted constancy, in this context, Paul is referring to faithfulness with regard to the truth and therefore one to another. He is speaking of faithfulness in the way we relate one to another. Such an attitude often comes at expense of self-love because it may well require us to make sacrifices. There are circumstances in which we are required to own up to a painfully embarrassing truth, or obliged to be true to an undertaking—a promise we've made, a contract we've signed, a debt we incurred—that involves considerable personal loss.

The Apostle is displaying faithfulness by writing the Galatians as he is doing although he might be considered by them to be enemy, as trying to exalt himself over them by defending his position rather than striving for their welfare. All the more was this true, at such an early stage of his ministry, when his position as a messenger of the Gospel can more easily be called into question.

Still more, faithfulness to His Father is what the Messiah displayed when He went to the cross in spite of the horror involved in dying, bearing the sins of the world. It is what He displayed toward those whom the Father gave Him before the worlds were made when He took on Himself the burden of their guilt, suffered and died in their stead.

Such faithfulness, when displayed by us, is the fruit of a humility that enables us to understand we are no better than anyone else:

> by the grace given to me I say to everyone among you not to think of himself more highly than he ought to think, but to think with sober judgment, each according to the measure of faith that God has assigned (Romans 12:2).

We recognize that we are not entitled to more than anyone else, and that what we have is from the hand of God: "Who sees anything different in you? What do you have that you did not receive? If then you received it, why do you boast as if you did not receive it?" (1 Corinthians 4:7). A sincerely humble person attributes to himself less than others would. In so doing his true value is expressed. A humble person does not cherish his pleasures, comfort, status or riches more than those of others (Romans 12:3). That is why he does not compete with them and certainly does not harm them or the likelihood of their success in the course of his effort to succeed.

Humility enables us to be honest because the basis of humility is the recognition that all our privileges before God are given by grace. Our sinfulness has removed any grounds of privilege. Humility moves us to recognize we are dependent on the ever-flowing kindness of God, and to put all of our trust in the Messiah. This is not self-denigration, it is wisdom, "not to think of [ourselves] more highly than [we] ought to think, but to think with sober judgment, each according to the measure of faith that God has assigned" (Romans 12:3).

Apart from such humility no one can be saved. When General Allenby took Jerusalem from the Turks and first entered the city, he rode up to the gates, dismounted and walked in as an expression of humility before God. No one enters God's kingdom mounted. Whoever is truly saved not only has been convinced that God exists and that Jesus is the Messiah. He has recognized the sinfulness of his heart, despaired of any possibility he could save himself, and understood that God owes him nothing, yet shows mercy to those who turn to Him. Such a person has turned from himself to God. God has worked in his heart to bring him to that point, and beyond it.

That is what it means to be saved. That is the fruit of the Spirit. If a person is not born from above, by the Spirit, he cannot so much as see the kingdom of God, let alone enter it. Salvation is not for the proud, who believe in their own resources (Luke 18:10–14, John 9:41). Salvation is altogether at God's initiative and by God's doing, the fruit of His Spirit's working in a human heart, begetting us anew and thereby granting us faith, repentance and endless comforts. Those in whose hearts God has not worked in this manner and yet consider themselves Christians are mistaken—and I fear there are many such!

Once the Spirit has begotten us anew, He produces in us self-restraint, that is to say, the ability to refuse to satisfy our desires (see verse 24), to rein in our desires and steadily redirect them, cultivating holy, pure and beautiful desires. Such self-restraint differs from that evidenced, for example, among sportsmen, who refuse to indulge themselves in hope of excelling in their sport. Christian self-restraint is not utilitarian. Its motives have to do with the glory of God, its source is love for God, it relies on the Spirit of God and is the product of the Spirit's activity in man's heart, by which God carved His law afresh in man's inward being. Such a person now loves God's law and desires to lead a life compatible with it, not because he wants to gain anything but because he was granted the most stupendous of all gifts: God's loving grace.

As we said, the Messiah displayed such faithfulness to God the Father and therefore to God's truth and law. He was humble, He turned his back to those who beat Him although He could have shaken them off with a flick of His finger. He bore the shame sinners attributed to Him, refused to ask His Father to send angels to His defense, and went willingly to an undeserved death. In this way He displayed unparalleled self-restraint: the one richer than any became poor for our sakes. The one more righteous than all died the death of a sinner in order to save sinners from a well-deserved death.

> So if there is any encouragement in Christ, any comfort from love, any participation in the Spirit, any affection and sympathy, complete my joy by being of the same mind, having the same love, being in full accord and of one mind. Do nothing from selfish ambition or conceit, but in humility count others more significant than yourselves. Let each of you look not only to his own interests, but also to the interests of others.

> Have this mind among yourselves, which is yours in Christ Jesus, who, though he was in the form of God, did not count equality with God a thing to be grasped, but emptied himself, by taking the form of a servant, being born in the likeness of men, and being found in human form, he humbled himself by becoming obedient to the point of death, even death on a cross. Therefore God has highly exalted him and bestowed on him the name that is above every name, so that at the name of Jesus every knee should bow, in heaven and on earth and under the earth, and every tongue confess that Jesus Christ is Lord, to the glory of God the Father (Philippians 2:1–11).

I dare say there is much we all need to change in the way we live.

Against such things there is no law. The tradition to which the Galatians are encouraged to adhere is full of prohibitions (foods and fabrics, various activities at certain times, the access of certain people to certain places, patterns of conduct and the like), so much so that they were better known for what they prohibited than by what they enjoined. Any who transgressed these were punished. At the entrance in Jerusalem which led from the outer court of the Gentiles in the temple complex to the court of Israel there was a sign warning that, should Gentiles dare access the court of Israel, they would be killed.

In contrast to this slew of prohibitions the Apostle has posted a list of qualities that the Spirit of God produces in the lives of the redeemed, all of which are the fruit of what the Messiah did for them and continues to do in them. He now tells us that against such things there is no law. That is to say, not only will no one condemn them for displaying such qualities, but no one in the universe would be able to do so. Such qualities are altogether positive. Hence, those saved by the grace of God ought not be condemned for eating non-kosher foods, not sanctifying the Sabbath in the way that Jews sanctify the day, not wearing prayer shawls or kissing Torah scrolls and the like. They have reason to be confident, without shame or guilt. They have ample reason to refuse to concede to the enticements and special pleadings employed by the false teachers. There is no need to add to the Messiah's achievements, nor is it possible. He did it all.

Those who walk in the Spirit, who display the delightful qualities of the Messiah Paul just described, are no longer subject to human manipulations, nor do they pursue the pleasures of this world. They are free in the fullest sense of the term, free to enjoy this world's pleasures without becoming addicted to them, and free to forgo those pleasures for higher purposes. They know that, regardless of whether they live or die, they are the Lord's, and that is their greatest asset. Such persons enjoy the freedom that Messiah promised ("if the Son sets you free, you will be free indeed," John 8:36) because they are guided by the Spirit, the righteousness of the Law is fulfilled in them and they know, on the strength a of a deep-seated conviction, that they and all the redeemed are children of God and, if children, then co-inheritors with the Messiah.

John Calvin's words on this text explain it well:

> where the Spirit reigns, the law has no longer any dominion. By molding our hearts to his own righteousness, the Lord delivers us from the severity of the law, so that our intercourse with himself is not regulated

by its covenant, nor our consciences bound by its sentence of condemnation. Yet the law continues to teach and exhort, and thus performs its own office; but our subjection to it is withdrawn by the Spirit of adoption. He thus ridicules the false apostles, who, while they enforced subjection to the law, were not less eager to release themselves from its yoke. [from Calvin's Commentary on Galatians]

And those who belong to Messiah have crucified their flesh with its desires and lusts. Paul does not want the Galatians to think that life in the Spirit means that man makes no effort at all. The truth is with both extremes: we cannot, in our own strength, do anything worthy but we can do anything in the strength of the Spirit of God. We cannot, in our own strength, do anything worthy, but we are called upon do exert ourselves worthily and at any cost. We are not obliged to obey the commandments of the Law and Jewish tradition to be saved, or to grow in grace, but our salvation obliges us to keep the commandments of God in a manner and a measure that the Law given at Sinai could have never be able to oblige us.

As to our privileges before God, we are free of all law, including the Law of Moses. But the privileges we have received oblige us to the law of the spirit of life in the Messiah. The Law can no longer condemn us, but it instructs, motivates, encourages and directs us as to our spiritual and moral duties in relation to both God and man.

Sin that entered the world following Adam's disobedience. It impacted the nature of every one of us. In consequence, we incline toward sin and naturally develop habits of sin that, in turn, create spiritual and moral disabilities against which we are required to struggle. That is why, if we are in the Messiah, we are inevitably among those who have crucified their flesh with its desires and lusts.

Note: Paul uses the past tense (have crucified). This is not to say that the redeemed do not need to crucify the desires and lusts of their flesh again and again, or that we will ever, so long as all creation has not been renewed, be free of such an obligation. What it does mean is that, if we are in the Messiah, we did so in the past, when we turned from ourselves to God, refused our pride, confessed our sins and our inability to break their chains and purge ourselves of them. The first step in crucifying the flesh with its desires and lusts was that act of repentance that was the result of God's powerful working in our hearts.

After that first step, what does it mean, to crucify the flesh with its desires and lusts? It means that a person prefers God, His honor and will above all, and therefore refuses to satisfy those desires and lusts. He denies himself. He declines to satisfy desires, even those are legitimate in themselves, the satisfaction of which would come at the expense of the glory of God, obedience to God's commands or that person's spiritual growth.

> Do you not know that in a race all the runners run, but only one receives the prize? So run that you may obtain it. Every athlete exercises self-control in all things. They do it to receive a perishable wreath, but we an imperishable. So I do not run aimlessly; I do not box as one beating the air. But I discipline my body and keep it under control, lest after preaching to others I myself should be disqualified (1 Corinthians 9:24–27).

> No soldier gets entangled in civilian pursuits, since his aim is to please the one who enlisted him. An athlete is not crowned unless he competes according to the rules. It is the hard-working farmer who ought to have the first share of the crops. Think over what I say, for the Lord will give you understanding in everything (2 Timothy 2:4–7).

On the one hand, the death of the Messiah frees us from bondage to sin, to which bondage we were handed over because of the sin of Adam. On the other hand, because of that bondage, we developed sinful habits that we must now break and uproot. To do that, it is not enough to rely on what God has done for us. We must be up and doing for Him: we must crucify the flesh with its desires and lusts. We must refuse to meet their demands. We must love God more than we love ourselves.

Doing so is a process that only begins with our initial repentance. It carries on through the whole course of our lives. It will end only when we awake in his likeness (Psalm 17:14). Until then, it is our duty to be actively engaged in this process on a daily basis. Crucifying the flesh with its desires is nothing less than self-denial, and God-oriented self-denial means that we put God, His will and honor first.

> Now when Jesus saw a crowd around him, he gave orders to go over to the other side. And a scribe came up and said to him, "Teacher, I will follow you wherever you go." And Jesus said to him, "Foxes have holes, and birds of the air have nests, but the Son of Man has nowhere to lay his head." Another of the disciples said to him, "Lord, let me first go and bury my father." And Jesus said to him, "Follow me, and leave the dead to bury their own dead" (Matthew 8:18–22, compare Luke 9:23–25).

Have *you* crucified your flesh, with its desires and lusts? No question can be more important than this. Examine your hearts and respond in the presence of God. I promise you: you will not be the loser.

> Those who belong to Messiah have crucified their flesh with its desires and lusts. We live by the Spirit, so we should conduct ourselves by the guidance of the Spirit.

Once again Paul returns to the work of the Holy Spirit and to the central role He plays in the lives of the redeemed. Just as no one is redeemed without receiving the Holy Spirit—after all, redemption means that one is born again by the Spirits power—so too does it mean that the redeemed must conduct themselves by the guidance of the Spirit.

What does it mean for one's conduct to be guided by the Spirit? Some would think that it means they should be passive, awaiting supernatural nudges. They speak in terms of "let go and let God." They are mistaken on a number of grounds. First, God is never subject to man in any sense. We can't "let" Him do anything, nor can we keep Him from doing all He wills. Second, being guided by the Spirit has nothing to do with passivity; it is constant, determined action, often involving tremendous effort while relying on the sacrifice of the Messiah and the empowerment of the Spirit. We stated a moment ago that the crucifixion of the flesh is a process that begins with our initial repentance, and that It carries on through the whole course of our lives. In other words, it means actively crucifying the flesh with its desires and lusts on a day-to-day basis, relying on the merits the Messiah purchased for us rather than any we foolishly claim for ourselves, relying on strength that comes from the Spirit rather than any ability we might think we have.

Life under the guidance of the Spirit involves conduct shaped by the commandments of the Spirit—which commandments are to be found in God's written Word (note the connection between the law of God and the activity of the Spirit as described in Romans 8. Recall what we said about that when we discussed verses 19–21 in chapter 5).

The Spirit guides us by inclining our hearts in a specific direction. He does so by way of moving us toward a proper understanding of the Scriptures, to which end we must delve into the Scriptures, study them carefully and internalize the principles they enunciate. The law written by the Spirit in our hearts is that reiterated in the law of Scripture. That is how we recognize the voice of the Spirit, who guides us by reminding us of the principles by which we frame specific decisions in the varying circumstances of life while we decline to obey our desires and lusts because we prefer God's ways. He then strengthens our hearts and hands to do what we have decided.

We live by the Spirit. It was He who stirred our consciences by reminding us of God's terrible, beautiful holiness and driving us to examine ourselves in its light. It was he who caused us to be ashamed of our sins, turn to God and plead with Him to forgive us because of the merits of the Messiah. It was the Spirt who persuaded us that we were forgiven and who, ever since, rebukes, encourages and strengthens us in our weakness and comforts us by God's gracious promises, so amply described in Scripture. We have life because the Messiah purchased it for us, and the Spirit applied it to us at the commandment of the Father.

We live by the Spirit, so we should conduct ourselves by the guidance of the Spirit. We should dedicate ourselves to God and conduct our lives to His glory, ever relying on the work of the Spirit in our hearts. That is the sum of the Christian life.

One still might think that a life guided by the Spirit is a series of exciting spiritual experiences. Not quite. The Apostle hastens to set our feet solidly on earth. How do we lead a life guided by the Spirit? Paul makes it clear: Let's not be taken up with empty boasting, provoking one another, envying one another. Recall all we said earlier about humility.

False doctrines can never produce the fruit of the Spirit. The farther our understanding of the Gospel is from the truth, the farther will the shape of our lives be from reflecting the image of the Messiah. True understanding yields true fruit. That is why it is important to understand the Gospel thoroughly, to dive into its wonderful depths and internalize its truth. We need for those truths to seep into the fabric of our being, affecting us intimately so that we no longer have merely intellectual comprehensions; Gospel truths will have become a power shaping us into the image of the Messiah by altering our perspectives, molding the motives of our hearts, framing values and aspirations that derive from Him.

The false doctrine presented to the Galatian believers produced the very opposite. In teaching the Galatians that they are able to merit God's blessings by way of their abilities, the false teachers encouraged the Galatians to think they are able to obligate God. After all, merit on their part implied duty on God's. Such an ability was purportedly the way to a heightened spirituality, whereas it actually focused on matters of the body and of this world: circumcision, dietary laws, days and months and festivals. In so doing it reduced concern for matters of true spirituality:

the fear of God, love, joy, peace, patience, generosity, kindness, faithfulness, humility, self-restraint, moral purity, honesty and the like.

Instead, it encouraged pride, arrogance, jealousy, competitiveness,
sectarianism, boasting and everything that the law of God forbids. Instead of encouraging unity it promoted divisions. Instead of putting God
and the Messiah in the center of attention, attention was diverted to rituals and symbols. Instead of adoring God for His grace, the focus was on
man's purported ability. That is not conduct guided by the Spirit. That is
empty pride that takes the place of conduct guided by the Spirit. Wherever the Spirit resides, He produces humility, the focus therefore is not
on what man can do but on the Messiah, who did it all.

Jesus said that the Holy Spirit will direct attention to Him rather
than to Himself (John 15:26), that He will cause followers of the Messiah
to focus on things that have to do with the Messiah (John 16:15, compare verse 13). So, wherever the Spirit—or anything else—is the center
of attention, we can be sure the Holy Spirit is absent. Wherever man's
efforts are the focus rather than what God did for man, the Messiah is absent. Wherever teaching the Scriptures does not produce the fruit of the
Spirit, the Holy Spirit is not active, and the Father is not pleased. Among
people who do not love one another, there is no love for God.

Instead, pride causes people to be provoking one another, insulting
one another and to trying to climb on the backs of one another, in direct
contrast to brotherly love born of the Spirit, which is the evidence of His
presence and sanctifying activity. Can you think of someone who is constantly provoking others, criticizing them, unable to maintain long term
relations of any significance? That man is given to empty pride rather
than to the Spirit of God. The Messiah is not at the center of his life. He
has placed himself there.

LET'S SUMMARIZE

- Is the fruit of the Spirit evident in your life to any meaningful extent? If not, why? If it is, where do you need to improve and how
  will you improve?

- Note the implied and stated indicatives (what God has done) and
  the imperatives (what you must do) in this section. What conclusions are you to draw from what you have learned?

LET'S PRAY

By your mercy and wisdom You have called us to reflect the beauty of Your Son our Savior. We tremble at the weight of that calling and acknowledge our inability to meet it without sustaining grace. We thrill at the wonder of that calling and long to glorify You, so that Your will might be done on earth as it is in heaven. Move us, empower us, lead us, enable us to live by the Spirit and, with His aid, crucify the flesh with its desires and lusts. Preserve us from competition and envy. May we have grace to show grace and to love our brethren as You love them. May we all love You in true fellowship. Forgive us when we fail and enable us to strive to the praise of the glory of Your grace, for Jesus' sake, Amen.

QUESTIONS FOR DISCUSSION AND STUDY

1. What is the common denominator for all aspects of the fruit of the Spirit? In what ways is that denominator an essential aspect of salvation? How can it be shown that these are the fruit of the Spirit rather than the product of mere morality?

2. Think of ways in which God is presented in the Old Testament as exemplifying each of the aspects of the fruit of the Spirit. In the light of Matthew 5:48, what does this mean?

3. Think of specific instances in the life of the Messiah when He exemplified each of the aspects of the fruit of the Spirit. In the light of 1 Corinthians 11:1, Philippians 2:5, what does this mean?

4. Consider: how do the twin experiences of salvation and sanctification relate to one another?

Chapter 17

Practice Love
(Galatians 6:1–10)

[1] Brothers, if someone is caught in some trespass, you, the spiritual ones, restore him while looking humbly at yourselves, and be careful so that you are not tempted. [2] Each of you, carry the burdens of the other and in this way fulfill the Law of the Messiah, [3] because if someone thinks he is really something while he is nothing, he is deceiving himself.

[4] Everyone should examine his own actions, and then he would be able to boast, he and no one else, in what he has done. [5] Each will carry his own load.

[6] Those who are taught the message should share all good things with whoever is teaching him. [7] Don't be fooled: God must not be mocked, because whatever a person sows, that is what he will also reap. [8] He who sows to his flesh, from the flesh will reap rot, but he who sows to the Spirit, from the Spirit will reap eternal life. So, let's not become tired of doing good [9] because, when the moment comes, we will reap if we do not tire. [10] For that reason, so long as we have opportunity, let's do good to all, and especially to those who belong to the household of faith.

Brothers, if someone is caught in some trespass, you, the spiritual ones, restore him while looking humbly at yourselves, and be careful so that you are not tempted. We have seen that the teachings promoted by the false teachers in Galatian fostered pride, controversies and competitiveness among believers. They encouraged an arrogant attitude toward others, particularly toward those considered weak or who differed in their understanding of the Faith. This is the inevitable consequence of a view that affirms man's ability to obtain something from God by human effort. Such a view implies that man is in some way independent of God, and that God is dependent on man, that man has innate spiritual abilities that do not depend on God—as if to say that the world created itself and exists by its own virtue.

This is directly contrary to what God's Word says. It directly contradicts the Gospel. The Scriptures teach that man is dependent on God, that every heartbeat of man is a gift of God. They teach that man is thoroughly infected by sin and that he will never have grounds to expect good things from God but by the grace of the Messiah. Because of man's sin, rather than being endowed with spiritual abilities he suffers from an inherent spiritual disability. Instead of strength, he is subject to weakness. Instead of purity, he is tainted. Instead of blessing, he must expect eternal damnation unless God intervenes by grace and saves man from himself.

People who recognize these truths do not suffer from empty pride. They do not provoke anyone, nor do they compete with anyone, and when they see someone stumble, they hasten to extend a helping hand.

Because of the consequences of the false teaching in Galatia, Paul believes it necessary to remind the Galatians of their duties one to another. Duties?! Yes, duties. Instead of the Law and Jewish tradition, God requires of those who are in the Messiah to obey the law of the Messiah, which is nothing else but the eternal moral law, which reflects the image of God. That law was promulgated at Sinai, but mankind was subject to it from the day of his creation. All mankind is required by the force of God's command to reflect His glory. All are bound by His law, and salvation is nothing less than the carving afresh of that law in man's heart and the Spirit's motivating him to obey it enthusiastically, with devotion and humility. Salvation finds expression in the lives of the redeemed in the fulfillment of that eternal law, that is, in the renewal of the image of God in man.

The false teaching in Galatia encouraged selfish pride that did not hesitate to take advantage of other people's failures. Paul is calling the Galatians to act in the opposite direction. He is calling them to relate to others, especially to the weak among them, and those who stumbled, with patient, kind generosity. Rather than rejoicing in their failure or arrogantly rejecting them, he calls on the Galatians to work for their restoration and encouragement. At the same time, they are to recognize their own weaknesses: if someone is caught in some trespass, you, the spiritual ones, restore him while looking humbly at yourselves, and be careful so that you are not tempted.

To that end he calls them brothers, reminding them that they belong one to another, that they are members of the one family of God, and that they have duties the one to the other. Family members owe one another love, forgiveness, kindness and good-will simply because they belong to the same family, apart from any desert.

If someone is caught in some trespass. The word "if" does not express doubt; it implies contingency. There is no doubt that each of us will from time to time (hopefully, with increasing infrequency) be caught in some trespass, because none of us are perfect. We will never achieve spiritual or moral perfection until the Messiah comes and completes the application of the fruits of His sacrifice on our behalf. Then we will be fully transformed and once again bear the image of our Creator. In spite of what the false teachers promised the Galatians, we shall always be dependent on grace. So long as we are on earth, we shall always need forgiveness and help.

The term caught indicates that Paul is not speaking of a life devoted to sin but to a situation in which one has fallen into a trap laid by the enemy of our souls, God's sworn opponent. He aims to capture us, to enslave us again. Sin enslaves. If we do not admit its existence, if we try to deny it exists, if we try to hide it, we shall find ourselves drawn into a situation in which we sin yet more and more. Instead of humility we will be characterized by hypocrisy; instead of purity, by impurity. The first step to rid ourselves of sin is to recognize and admit its existence.

You, the spiritual ones, restore him. Rather than rejoicing over his failure, you should share his pain and shame, love him, help him free himself from the sin by which he was caught. Support him—not his sin. Love him. "Show mercy with fear, hating even the garment stained by the flesh" (Jude 23). Where necessary, use church discipline but, whatever you do, do it with a view to restoring your brother, not stomping over him or ridding yourselves of a nuisance. The Messiah gave Himself for the salvation of sinners, and ours is the duty and the privilege to work for the restoration of our brothers and sisters.

We must fulfill that duty while looking humbly at yourselves and be careful so that you are not tempted. We must labor for our erring, sinful brethren while conscious of the fact that we are no better than them, taking every precaution so that we ourselves are not tempted. We are not to exalt ourselves above them. We are to be kind, soft-hearted, generous and patient, acknowledging to ourselves if not to them that we are as likely to fail as they did should we face the temptation with which they had to deal.

That acknowledgement must accompany us all the days of our lives. We must never be taken by any teaching that promises immunity. Being dependent on the grace of God, we must treat our brethren with grace. That is how we render the Gospel tangible; that is how we preach it with our lives; that is how we fulfill the law of the Messiah, and that is the test of true spirituality: a humility that evidences itself in grace because it relies on grace, rather than pride that hastens to make light of others because of an overweening confidence in one's spiritual and moral prowess.

Each of you carry the burdens of the other and in this way fulfill the Law of the Messiah. True spirituality expresses itself in the fruit of the Spirit, which, as we saw, is love, happiness, peace, patience, generosity, kindness, faithfulness, humility, self-restraint. The grace which the Apostle demands of the Galatians, to which we too are bound, is expressed in our not focusing on ourselves but on other people's well-being so that, when we see a brother or a sister struggling, we rush to their aid.

The burdens of which Paul is speaking are include those imposed by our attitude to the challenges of life, which often lead to the temptation to respond inappropriately. He is speaking of the temptation created by social, material, physical or financial challenges, which may lead us to focus on ourselves rather than on loving God. He is speaking of the kind of burdens we all experience, every one of which is a test (after all, that is what "trial" means), every one of which is an opportunity to deepen our devotion to God, or weaken it by responding in ways that neither honor him nor do good to others.

Each of you, carry the burdens of the other, the Apostle says. No one is exempt. All who belong to the body of the Messiah must lovingly care for the others. We ought never be too busy to note other people's struggles and needs. Every one of us must go through life premeditatedly conscious of the needs of others. A Christian is a person who cares about others. He is not a hermit who removes himself from society and encloses himself in a monastery or a solitary island. He is a vibrant, energetic person, conscious of those around him, who knows how to assist and be assisted, who is not turned in on himself, his happiness or pain, but on God.

It is impossible to have a truly spiritual life apart from binding relationships with others, that is to say, as members of human society, a church, a family. A Christian who does not meaningfully belong to a church does not understand the essence of the Christian life. Family is the fundamental and most efficient framework within which we relate to others on the basis of grace. It is our duty to cultivate relations in all these contexts, and to do so with care, grace and consistent kindness. Rather than shying away from commitment, we should gladly undertake such an obligation and live it out in the day-to-day of our lives.

Carry the burdens of the other. An active, practical awareness of one another is an important aspect of a life lived as God would have it lived. Good-will, eagerness to assist, to exert oneself for another, to sacrifice one for another—that is how we maintain healthy families, churches and societies in which a pure kind of happiness is experienced at the highest level. That is what the Messiah calls us to implement. In John 15 Jesus tells His disciples that He has loved them as the Father loved Him (imagine!), and then instructs them to love one another as He loves them (verses 9, 12). That is the way we bear much fruit, and that is how we honor the Father (John 15:8). That is how we carry each other's burdens.

Each of you, carry the burdens of the other and in this way fulfill the Law of the Messiah, because if someone thinks he is really something while he is nothing, he is deceiving himself. This is what true humility looks like. It is not an affectation; it is how we view ourselves and others, and how we relate to them. This is the other side of the coin of which Paul writes in Romans 12:3, "by the grace given to me I say to everyone among you not to think of himself more highly than he ought to think, but to think with sober judgment, each according to the measure of faith that God has assigned." We ought not lay claim to what God in His loving wisdom has not granted us any more than we should deny what He has granted. We are to be honestly realistic. We must recognize the limitations of our abilities and of our successes no less than we must dare make use of whatever abilities God has given us, building on successes He has allowed, because our limitations and our abilities were both given by God and are meant for His glory.

Individuals who think of themselves more highly than they ought tend to look down on those who differ from them, especially on those whose views differ from theirs. We have each been granted abilities, discernments and tendencies. Paul's words to the Corinthians are relevant on this matter:

> There are varieties of gifts, but the same Spirit; and there are varieties of service, but the same Lord; and there are varieties of activities, but it is the same God who empowers them all in everyone. To each is given the manifestation of the Spirit for the common good ... All these are empowered by one and the same Spirit, who apportions to each one individually as he wills. For just as the body is one and has many members, and all the members of the body, though many, are one body, so it is with Christ. For in one Spirit we were all baptized into one body— Jews or Greeks, slaves or free—and all were made to drink of one Spirit.

> The eye cannot say to the hand, "I have no need of you," nor again the head to the feet, "I have no need of you." On the contrary, ... God has so composed the body, giving greater honor to the part that lacked it, that there may be no division in the body, but that the members may have the same care for one another. If one member suffers, all suffer together; if one member is honored, all rejoice together (1 Corinthians 12:4–26).

Teachings which attribute God's blessing to human merit inflate pride and lead to despising others, to provocations and competitiveness. Our Lord rebuked the disciples for such an attitude when they forbade children to approach Him. The kingdom of God is meant for those who, by the grace of God, view themselves as no more privileged than children were viewed in those days. It is meant for those who say of themselves "I was brought forth in iniquity, and in sin did my mother conceive me" (Psalm 51:5), "I am a worm and not a man" (Psalm 22:5). It is meant for those who dare not lift their eyes to heaven, who beat on their breasts and plead, "God, be merciful to me, a sinner" (Luke 18:13). Those are the people whom God blesses. Anyone who thinks otherwise is deceiving himself.

Everyone should look into his own actions, and then he would be able to boast, he and no one else, in what he has done. Each will carry his own load. In contrast to the pride referred to in the previous verse, Paul now calls the Galatians to be realistic, to examine their lives honestly and to avoid comparing themselves with others. Such comparisons are never useful. We can always manage to find someone in comparison to whom we look come out looking better.

We enjoy prying into other peoples' lives and motives. We are quick to attribute to others what we would be unwilling to attribute to ourselves. We all tend to be busybodies and gossipers. In Peter's first letter, 4:15, the Apostle warns his readers against being the kind of people who poke their nose into other people's business. In 1 Timothy 5:13 Paul speaks of "idlers, going about from house to house, and not only idlers, but also gossips and busybodies, saying what they should not."

Since fearing God and conducting ourselves by the Spirit of God implies avoiding competitiveness, what is the point of comparing ourselves with others? We ought, rather, to be engaged in self-examination: are my motives today purer than they were yesterday? Have I managed to break that bad habit that caused me to fail on Wednesday? Do I now understand that portion of Scripture with which I had difficulty yesterday? Has my attitude toward others improved? Do I love God more?

If we examine ourselves honestly in the light of God's Word, we will be far less inclined to boast. And if, after such self-examination, our consciences are clear, we will know whom to thank. Paul wrote the Corinthians, saying, "our boast is this, the testimony of our conscience, that we behaved in the world with simplicity and godly sincerity, not by earthly wisdom but by the grace of God, and supremely so toward you" (2 Corinthians 1:12). In other words, I behaved in that way because I was motivated by the grace of God rather than by considerations that characterize a person who has no love for nor fear of God.

On the other hand, if we do as the Apostle instructed the Corinthians to do as they approach the Lord's table (1 Corinthians 11:28), and examine ourselves, we shall discover time and again that, due to what we have done and to what we have left undone, we are not worthy to partake, because each will carry his own load, recognize his own sin and have to deal with it and so, because of what the Messiah has done, eat of the bread and drink of the cup.

That is the kind of "boasting" no one can take from us. Neither can anyone perform such self-examination in our stead. Everyone should look into his own actions, and then he would be able to boast, he and no one else, in what he has done.

Those who are taught the message should share all good things with whoever is teaching him. Most commentators understand Paul to be speaking here of the duty to care for the material needs of those who serve churches in the Gospel. There seems to be room for little doubt that such a duty is incorporated in the reference to all good things. Of course, it is only right that those whose main task is to teach God's Word would be appropriately cared for by the churches they serve.

Paul wrote to Timothy, instructing him,

> Let the elders who rule well be considered worthy of double honor, especially those who labor in preaching and teaching, for the Scripture says, "You shall not muzzle an ox when it treads out the grain", and, "The laborer deserves his wages" (1 Timothy 5:17–18).

The term translated "double honor" may also be translated as "double wages," and the context seems to indicate just that. As Jamieson, Fausset and Brown put it, "that is, the honor which is expressed by gifts (1Ti 5:3, 18) and otherwise. If a presbyter as such, in virtue of his office, is already worthy of honor, he who rules well is doubly so [Wiesinger] (1Co 9:14; Ga 6:6; 1Th 5:12)." [from *Commentary Critical and Explanatory on the Whole Bible*]

Later Paul wrote,

> what you have heard from me in the presence of many witnesses entrust to faithful men, who will be able to teach others also. Share in suffering as a good soldier of Christ Jesus. No soldier gets entangled in civilian pursuits, since his aim is to please the one who enlisted him. An athlete is not crowned unless he competes according to the rules. It is the hard-working farmer who ought to have the first share of the crops. Think over what I say, for the Lord will give you understanding in everything (2 Timothy 2:2–7).

Churches should take these words to heart and be sure to honor those who serve them well by according them the double honor of ample wages and social benefits, including such matters as medical insurance, an annual vacation, a pension and the possibility for reasonable savings.

Having said as much, I suggest that the context does little to indicate that what Paul has in mind is primarily material remuneration. His primary concern is the respect that faithful teachers of God's Word deserve. From what the Apostle has written so far we've learned that the false doctrines taught in the province of Galatia gave rise to controversies, competitiveness and sectarianism. The natural consequence of that would be that the Elders serving the Galatian churches would become a focus of attention because they would be obliged to oppose those doctrines. The primary means by which Elders lead the church is through the teaching and application of God's Word. That would immediately subject them to criticism by those who were committed to the promulgation of the new doctrines.

The verb share and the commandment to share all good things indicate more than just material support (see also verse 8). In Romans 15:27, 1 Timothy 5:22 and 2 John 11, where the same verb appears, it refers to moral rather than to material support.

In other words, Paul is calling on the Galatians to identify with and support those of their teachers who are faithful to the Word of God by according them all good things. I can tell you from many years of pastoral experience: serving the church as a Pastor or an Elder, as with all positions in which leadership is involved, is one of the loneliest callings imaginable. Anyone bearing that holy, cherished burden will often experience a vivid sense of loneliness in the struggles of the ministry. Such a person is both in need and deserving of the affection, encouragement and support of congregants.

It is easy to criticize those serving us—only those who do nothing have no fault (apart from their blamable indolence). Pastors and Elders are as painfully human as any of us. They err, they stumble and—yes, they sin. There are no supermen in God's kingdom. None are void of defect. That is why we should pray for those who serve us faithfully, support and follow them when they are right. That is why we should lovingly challenge them when they err and heartily forgive them when they recognize their error. That is why we should always rejoice when they are blessed.

Those who attend church to have something to criticize are wrong. Those who take advantage of the mistakes and failures of their Pastors and Elders sin. Such selfish self-promotion is the opposite of life shaped by the Gospel:

> Brothers, if someone is caught in some trespass, you, the spiritual ones, restore him while looking humbly at yourselves, and be careful so that you are not tempted. Each of you, carry each the burdens of the other and in this way fulfill the Law of the Messiah, because if someone thinks he is really something while he is nothing, he is deceiving himself ...

> Those who are taught the message should share all good things with whoever is teaching him. Don't be fooled: God must not be mocked, because whatever a person sows, that is what he will also reap. He who sows to his flesh, from the flesh will reap rot, but he who sows to the Spirit, from the Spirit will reap eternal life. So,

let's not become tired of doing good because, when the moment comes, we will reap if we do not tire. For that reason, so long as we have opportunity, let's do good to all, and especially to those who belong to the household of Faith.

Obey your leaders and submit to them, for they are keeping watch over your souls, as those who will have to give an account. Let them do this with joy and not with groaning, for that would be of no advantage to you" (Hebrews 13:17).

That is our duty before God to those who serve us faithfully.

Don't be fooled: God must not be mocked, because whatever a person sows, that is what he will also reap. As always, the context is necessary. Without it we cannot discover the intended meaning of what is said. It is common to use this verse to enunciate the general principle that God ensures that everything we do had its inevitable consequence. As a general principle, that is obviously true. But the context indicates that Paul is making specific reference to the way congregants treat those who serve them. Paul is applying a general principle to a specific circumstance. Ultimately he is saying that we shall have to give account to God for the way we treated our Pastors and Elders.

After all, it was God who equipped and called them to serve us. He provided them with the capacity to understand and teach the Scriptures. We as a church recognized that call and appointed them. Faithful teachers of God's Word are God's messengers for the welfare of the churches they serve. Hence the duty incumbent on the church in relation to those who teach her. Hence the seriousness with which the church should approach the appointment of anyone to this awesome task. It is not enough to be talented or to have what are described nowadays as "leadership abilities." Candidates must be characterized by additional qualifications: a humble fear of God, transparent integrity, sincere devotion to the God and affection for people, spiritual maturity, emotional stability, uncompromising honesty and a willingness to sacrifice without advertising it.

Once a person has been appointed, we as congregants are obliged to support him in any way within our means. If we do not, we will reap from the hand of God what we sow. A church that relieves itself of the duty to function in a responsible manner in relation to its pastoral oversight does despite to its health.

True, no one is to lord it over us. None but God has the right to govern our consciences or judge our thoughts. Those who serve us in the Gospel must do so humbly, considering themselves, lest they too be tempted. Obedience driven by fear is not Christian obedience. Spiritual growth is measured by the spiritual and moral lives of the congregants, by their ever-increasing understanding of God's Word and their expanding application of what they understand. It is expressed in the holiness of the congregants' lives, in their ability to think for themselves, in their humility, love and ability to express their understandings in ways conducive to the life of the church.

But if we tire our teachers with incessant criticism, if we decline to encourage and support them, to advise, challenge and forgive them when appropriate, our churches will inevitably reap what we have sown. They will become spiritually and morally weak, even if they appear to be growing numerically. Not only so but, if we do not accord those who serve us the affectionate support of which the Apostle speaks, which enables them to lead us toward scriptural goals, God will take personal umbrage, because those who make light of those He commissioned, make light of Him.

Of course, much depends on the way those who teach and lead in the church fulfill their duties. But we will have to leave discussion for a later time because that is not the subject of this portion of God's Word.

Paul spoke of the deeds of the flesh and of the duty to crucify the flesh with its desires and lusts. Over against the deeds of the flesh he presented the fruit of the Spirit, which fosters brotherly love, forbearance and generosity.

Paul is calling the Galatian Christians not to embrace the false teachings that were being presented to them and to be more cautious as to their relations one with another. He reminds them that the issue is not merely between themselves; God is involved. If they oppose faithful teachers of God's Word they are opposing Him. In so doing they are sowing what they do not want to reap. On the other hand, if they remain true to God and His Word, by God's grace they will be sowing blessings greater than any human can imagine, and the harvest is sure. He who sows to his flesh, from the flesh will reap rot, but he who sows to the Spirit, from the Spirit will reap eternal life.

We are responsible for what we do. Our actions have consequences. It is wrong to think that God's sovereign grace negates human responsibility or releases man from the consequences of his actions. Those who persist in sin will perish in sin—and it is a sin to pervert God's Word by claiming that, because all we have from God is by sovereign grace, man bears no responsibility.

No one is able to explain how the sovereignty of God and man's responsibility dovetail, but the two principles are undeniably in Scripture. We must not, therefore, make light of either of the two. We understand that God's gifts to us are not the wages of our efforts, and yet they do not normally come apart from such efforts. God graciously receives our faulty strivings so long as they are the fruit of sincere devotion to Him and in obedience to His Word. But he rejects the very the best of our strivings when we engage in them with a view to earning merit in His eyes. The place preserved for us in eternal feast that God prepared for those who love Him is reserved for us by grace, by grace alone.

Note the tremendous distinction the Apostle makes: rottenness contrasted with eternal life, not only in the world to come but also here and now. Reliance on our abilities robs us of much blessing in the present, whereas those who put their trust in the Messiah have already "passed from death to life" (John 5:24). They already enjoy the firstfruits of the future eternal blessing: "If anyone loves me, he will keep my word, and my Father will love him, and we will come to him and make our home with him. Whoever does not love me does not keep my words" (John 14:23–24). THAT is a wonderful firstfruit, a harbinger of what is to come.

"Therefore let no one pass judgment on you in questions of food and drink, or with regard to a festival or a new moon or a Sabbath," rather than encouraging you to trust in the Messiah's finished work. Why? Because

> these are a shadow of the things to come, but the substance belongs to Christ. Let no one disqualify you, insisting on asceticism and worship of angels, going on in detail about visions, puffed up without reason by his sensuous mind, and not holding fast to the Head, from whom the whole body, nourished and knit together through its joints and ligaments, grows with a growth that is from God … If then you have been raised with Christ, seek the things that are above, where Christ is, seated at the right hand of God. Set your minds on things that are above, not on things that are on earth (Colossians 2:16–19, 3:1–2).

In the Messiah, is does not matter where or not we are circumcised. What matters is faith active in loving God and others. For that reason, so long as we have opportunity, let's do good to all, and especially to those who belong to the household of faith.

It is right to do "good works," and ever better to persist in doing them. It is easy to begin well. The real test is to be found in our reaching the goal.

> Which of you, desiring to build a tower, does not first sit down and count the cost, whether he has enough to complete it? Otherwise, when he has laid a foundation and is not able to finish, all who see it begin to mock him, saying, "This man began to build and was not able to finish" (Luke 14:28–30).

God by His grace rewards us when we do well, but not necessarily at once. Sometimes the reward come much later. So, let's not become tired of doing good because, when the moment comes, we will reap if we do not tire.

And who will determine when the time has come? The Master of the universe, He who governs all events and all processes, in whose hand are all times and seasons. "There is a time for everything," and God is the one who determines what time is for which event. One thing is clear: the judge of all the earth always—but always—does what is right. He is true to His Word. He has promised that we will reap if we do not tire, and there is no room for doubt that such will be the case.

Wearying of doing good because of doubt is a vote of no confidence in God. It is an expression of a lack of trust. We are to persist. We are to act in certain ways because it is right, and, by the grace of God, when the moment comes, we will reap. (Paul uses a term that implies a moment in time. In the next verse he uses a different term that implies a course of time, a period). We will reap in spite of all that is missing, all that is faulty in our efforts. This is eschatology, the doctrine of the last things, and this is the way eschatology is meant to shape our lives. God teaches us what is to be in the future so we will know what we are to be in the present. Any other use of that doctrine is mistaken.

We must endeavor to do what is right now because we are already in the last days and because, when the moment comes, we will reap—and even then what we reap will be the fruit of The Messiah's grace rather than of our efforts. Even after we have done everything in our power, we are no more than unprofitable servants who did less their due. Everything they did is stained with the stains of their sinfulness. What we will then reap is the climax of God's amazing grace.

This is an important aspect of the Gospel. Eschatology (the doctrine of the last things) is nothing less than the climactic fulfillment of soteriology (the doctrine of salvation), and the moment is nothing less than the accomplishment of the creation's purpose. That is precisely why the false teachings in Galatia were a perversion of the Gospel in its most fundamental nature. That is why Paul accused Peter of acting in such a manner that denied the necessity of the Messiah's death and annulled the grace of God.

Let's persist in doing what is right because we love God and because we know that it is our duty. Let's act out of love for God rather than for profit. If we do, God promises us that, by grace, when the moment comes, we will reap.

Just what does doing good mean? At the very least it means what the verses 1–11 of this chapter indicate.

For that reason, so long as we have opportunity, let's do good to all, and especially to those who belong to the household of faith. Paul says, so long as we have opportunity. Paul speaks of the last days and of the moment that is to come for the purpose of motivating his readers to make the most of the time yet one hand. It is not for us to know the times. God the Father has reserved that knowledge for Himself. What we do know is that the last days are now upon us (1 Corinthians 10:11), our Lord is at the door and it is incumbent on us to live our lives carefully, in the fear of God and with warm-hearted faithfulness.

Paul has spoken in stark terms about efforts to obtain anything from God, but he in no way opposes efforts to do good so long as the motive behind them is appropriate. Many years later he will write to Titus, saying that the Messiah "gave himself for us to redeem us from all lawlessness and to purify for himself a people for his own possession who are zealous for good works" (Titus 2:14. See also Ephesians 2:10). He therefore insisted that "the saying is trustworthy, and I want you to insist on these things, so that those who have believed in God may be careful to devote themselves to good works. These things are excellent and profitable for people" (Titus 3:8).

As we can learn from the sermon on the mount, the fundamental question is not what we do (although that, too, is important) but why. If we strive to do good because we love God, because we understand that God is love and because we know that it is our duty to love others as we love ourselves, we are acting out of right motives. But if we do good to get something out of it from God or from man—so we can preach the Gospel to them or any other ulterior motive—our good deeds are spoiled by unworthy motives. We are, in reality, serving ourselves, and our deeds are expressions of the self-love that motivates us. They are, in fact, not good but evil in the sight of God.

Let's do good to all, says Paul, be they friends or enemies, whether they do or do not believe, whether they are members of our nation or foreigners who oppose us, from whatever race or culture. If we took this commandment to heart, there would be no more wars, no more controversies and no divisions in the church, no divorces, no taking advantage of employees or employers, the wolf would lie down with the lamb and the lion with the fattened calf. We would all be busy doing good to one another.

How many of our decisions are framed to do good to others? Are we considerate of our neighbors? Of the driver in the other lane? Of our spouse? Our children? To what extent do we frame our expectations of church life with the purpose of doing good to others? To what extent do we think of others in the context of society? A host of relevant questions may be posed, all of which would expose the level of our selfishness or of our consideration of others. Let's mend our ways and, so long as we have opportunity, let's do good to all.

The good that we should do includes emotional, social, physical and material good. It means supporting single-parent families, solitary widows, the homeless and the jobless, combatting abortions and reaching out to the addicted. It includes hosting people in our homes, enlisting to assist those who have undergone natural disasters, praying for our enemies and a determined daily effort to avoid selfishness in the smaller moments of life. It includes our seeking to do good to others when we sign contracts, sell cars, engage a craftsman or make a purchase.

When he will write to the Philippians, he will set before them the supreme example of generous selflessness and humility, busy with the good of others rather than with personal interests:

> Let each of you look not only to his own interests, but also to the interests of others. Have this mind among yourselves, which is yours in Christ Jesus, who, though he was in the form of God, did not count equality with God a thing to be grasped, but emptied himself, by taking the form of a servant, being born in the likeness of men. And being found in human form, he humbled himself by becoming obedient to the point of death, even death on a cross" (Philippians 2:4–8).

So long as we have opportunity, let's do good to all, and especially to those who belong to the household of faith. Why especially to them? I believe the reason is that we, who are saved by grace and to whom all we have has been given by grace tend to forget grace when it comes to those who belong to the household of faith. We rightly expect more of them, but are less willing to bear with their weaknesses and failings. We expect of them a perfection we ourselves have not achieved. Evidence of that may be found in the simple fact that the Apostles' letters were addressed to believers, and yet he needed to write to the about issues such as the importance of humility, forgiveness, kindness, avoiding competition, and so on.

Let's Summarize

- We tend to look at others more than ourselves. Why? How does focusing on other's failures help us avoid examining ourselves? How does condemning others help us justify ourselves? How does that deepen sin's hold on us?

- Are you living out your duties to society, church and family? Indicate ways relative to each of the spheres just mentioned. How can you improve?

- Do you support those who serve you in the Gospel to the full extent of your abilities? How can you improve?

Let's Pray

Eternal God, You are righteous and merciful, terrible in Your majesty, astounding in the liberality of Your grace. You command us to treat our brethren as You have treated us, endeavoring to restore rather than condemn them. But we are quick to condemn. May Your Holy Spirit carve the law of the Messiah in our souls, so that we willingly carry each other's burdens and endeavor not to burden them with ours.

We thank You for those with whom you have gifted us who teach us the Gospel by the example they set before us and by their labors as teachers of Your Word. We undertake to love and encourage them, to provide for them and for the cultivation of their spiritual lives. We will lovingly challenge them if we think they err. Rebuke and restore us when we fail, that we might serve You by serving one another. May we make the most of opportunities to do good to all, especially to those who belong to the household of faith, through Jesus, our glorious Savior, Amen.

Questions for Discussion and Study

1. What does spirituality have to do with the way we treat our brethren?

2. How is church discipline and act of love? How should it be conducted so as to be seen as such by all involved?

3. Discuss the importance and practical value of self-examination.

4. Why do we tire of doing good and what are the remedies for those reasons?

5. Discuss the statement: "Eschatology is nothing less than the climactic fulfillment of soteriology." Indicate the implications of such a statement.

CHAPTER 18

Closing Words
(GALATIANS 6:11–18)

[11] You see how I have written you with large letters by my own hand. [12] Those who want to look good in the flesh are the ones who force you to be circumcised, with the sole purpose that they not be persecuted for the sake of the cross of the Messiah Jesus, [13] because the circumcised are not law-keepers but they want you to be circumcised so that they would be able to boast in your fleshly circumcision. [14] But so far as I am concerned, it will never be that I would boast in anything but the cross of our Lord Jesus the Messiah, by which the world is dead so far as I am concerned, and I am dead so far as the world is concerned, [15] because circumcision and uncircumcision amount to nothing. The only important thing is a new creation. [16] Peace and grace to all who live according to this principle, and to God's Israel.

[17] And now, no one is to cause me trouble because I bear the scars of Jesus on my body. [18] May the grace of our Lord Jesus the Messiah be with your spirits, brothers, Amen.

You see how I have written you with large letters by my own hand. It is not altogether clear if Paul is referring here to the letter as a whole, to the last few sentences, or to this sentence alone. It was customary in those days for people to correspond with the aid of a professional scribe because the actual writing on a papyrus or a scroll was complicated and required knowledge that exceeded the mere ability to express oneself clearly. Whatever may be the case, Paul is using this means to assure his readers that the letter is from him, as he explains in 2 Thessalonians 3:17: I, Paul, write this greeting with my own hand. This is the sign of genuineness in every letter of mine; it is the way I write.

In all fairness, those who sought to persuade the Galatians to embrace the views against which Paul has protested in this letter did so because they sincerely believed that the Galatians would be advantaged by adhering to Jewish tradition. No one consciously intends to deceive. No one but Satan asks himself, "what kind of theory can I develop in order to mislead the believers?" Most teachers of false doctrine believe what they teach. Sometimes they are blinded by pride, their hearts are hardened, and they cannot recognize or admit to themselves they are wrong. Sometimes they hold to a doctrine due to ulterior, irrelevant motives, conscious or otherwise. But, if they are open to examine their views, they will discover their error.

In any case, be they captives of their pride or driven by unworthy motives, we must rebuke them humbly and firmly. We must not yield to them, nor view their teachings as one opinion among many, as if to say false doctrine and God's truth can exist side by side and as if one is not obliged to choose between them. The teachers who arrived in Galatia were sincere, but their teachings were false—more so than first met the eye—because they contradicted the Gospel of God's grace. Paul was right to oppose them as he did.

Peter later wrote of those who twist the Scriptures "to their own destruction" (2 Peter 3:16). Paul will write to warn Timothy that the time is coming when people will not endure sound teaching, but having itching ears they will accumulate for themselves teachers to suit their own passions, and will turn away from listening to the truth and wander off into myths (2 Timothy 4:3–4).

We must beware of the first of these and not be like the second because even today there are many counterfeits. Many present their teachings as if they are true to the Scriptures. They purport to prove the validity of their message by quoting verses aplenty, often divorcing them from their context, making them to say what they do not say naturally.

Paul would have the Corinthians examine what they heard: "let two or three prophets speak, and let the others weigh what is said" (1 Corinthians 14:29). To do that we need a well-informed alertness that is not only acquainted with the Scriptures but understands them well. That is why it is so important to study the Scriptures, not just read them.

It is simply not enough to quote verses. What is said must bear the seal of the Lord's Apostles in spirit as well as in word. It must be true to the context. It must arise naturally from what is written, without manipulations. Instead, it must be the result of a carefully logical reading, taking into account the rules of grammar and syntax, true to its style, kind of literature and the historical situation addressed or described. God the Holy Spirit inspired the Scriptures' various authors to write according to those principles, so that all generations will have access to heavenly truth by it being declared in accessible, earthly terms. That is how the Holy Spirit paved the way for us to know the truth of God, and that is the path we must follow.

Those who want to look good in the flesh are the ones who force you to be circumcised, with the sole purpose that they not be persecuted for the sake of the cross of the Messiah Jesus. Paul is turning the tables on the false teachers. They claimed to know the way to a heightened spirituality; Paul responds by showing that they are actually busier with the earthly than with the spiritual. They claimed to be teaching God's ways; Paul responds by insisting that they are actually want to look good in the flesh. Not only so, but the false teachers claimed they were laboring for the good of their disciples; Paul says they are caring for themselves by wanting look good in the flesh and with the sole purpose that they not be persecuted for the sake of the cross of the Messiah Jesus.

Consciously or otherwise, those teachers' motives were selfish. They took advantage of the Galatians' good-will to promote themselves. Woe betide those who serve in the church of God out of such a motive (I fear there are not few)! It is only right that all who serve ask themselves: am I serving our of a pure and sincere love for God or for myself? Am I serving the people of God in order to satisfy myself, or do I truly want to serve the people of God even if they do not acknowledge my devotion and take no notice of my sacrifice, even if I derive no benefit for myself?

The teachers who came to Galatia wanted to look good in the eyes of their people in the hope that they would not be put outside the national camp. They were the pioneers of those who teach today that the way to persuade the Jewish people of the truth of the Gospel is by dressing it up in traditional Jewish garb, or at least clothe it with a prayer shawl and a kippa, say "Yeshua" instead of Jesus, "Messianic" rather than Christian, keep kosher, kiss a Torah scroll and avoid speaking of the Trinity. Let's get them in first, and then we'll tell them where they are. Others assumed Jewish tradition because they believed it would enhance their spirituality and accord them some merit before God.

All of them were mistaken in Paul's day and they are all mistaken now. Not only is it wrong to try and render the Gospel more attractive than it is in and of itself, it is impossible to make it more attractive. The Gospel is the epitome of beauty, although it is a beauty people who love themselves and want to stand on their own merits are unable to recognize.

They, says the Apostle, force you to be circumcised (compare 2:14, where the same word is used). They tried to bring Jews and Gentiles in the Messiah under the yoke of the Law and rabbinic dictum. When performed on an adult, circumcision represented that the person's willingness to commit himself to those authorities. For Christians it was the first public, formal undertaking that caused a person to turn, even if ever so slightly, from the Messiah. The teachers "forced" them to be circumcised by teaching them that it is the only way they can be true to the God of Israel. It was an imposition of the crassest, most despicable sort because it appealed to the purest motives of the new Galatian Christians, who longed to know God better, to please Him more and to know yet more and more of His presence.

And what were those teachers' motives? To look good in the flesh and that they not be persecuted for the sake of the cross of the Messiah Jesus. The cross of the Messiah stands over against any human merit or ability. The cross depicts man in his truest colors: utterly sinful and incapable of pleasing God, unable to do anything for his own salvation, wholly dependent on what God would do for and in him through the Messiah—not only as to man's first steps in the path of faith but for all eternity. That is the kind of Gospel in which the false teachers had no interest, for which they were unwilling to suffer. They knew full well that Israel's views are shaped by the Rabbis, and that the Rabbis taught that God's favor is dependent on man's merits. The teachers wanted to continue to be acceptable in the eyes of their people, and so they chose to shape the Gospel to their people's preference.

Woe betides us if we do as they did!

Because the circumcised are not law-keepers but they want you to be circumcised so that would be able to boast in your fleshly circumcision. Paul is speaking of the people of Israel in general and of the false teachers in particular. He says that they do not faithfully keep all the Jewish traditions. Not only so, but they do not keep the Law of Moses, which is at the heart of those traditions, and they certainly do not keep any other law (except the one they wrote for themselves).

First, they do not faithfully keep the very traditions whose authority they seek to promote, because that tradition relates to every minute of life, and no-one is able to keep all its commandments. All the more is that true in light of the fact that many who claim to keep the traditions do so only when others are watching. When they're alone, they dare deviate.

Second, a good deal of the tradition is geared to enabling its adherents to transgress the heart of what the Law demands while, at the same time, appear to be keeping it. For example, Jewish tradition allows Jews to employ non-Jews on the Sabbath, have him light fire for him and perform other deeds forbidden to Jews. But the Law clearly says,

> remember the Sabbath day, to keep it holy. Six days you shall labor, and do all your work, but the seventh day is a Sabbath to the Lord your God. On it you shall not do any work, you, or your son, or your daughter, your male servant, or your female servant, or your livestock, or the sojourner who is within your gates (Exodus 20:8–10).

As to lighting fires on the Sabbath, Exodus 35:3 says, "you shall kindle no fire in all your dwelling places on the Sabbath day" —not you, nor you by the means of anyone else, be he Jewish or otherwise.

Third, the focus on ceremonies and matters that meet the eye runs contrary to the spirit of the Law, because the Law demands above all that we love God and that we love our fellow human as we love ourselves. A focus on ceremonies diverts our attention from the major to the minor. The prophets castigated those of the people of Israel who were strict in the observance of ceremonies and sacrifices at the expense of spiritually framed moral duties:

> with what shall I come before the Lord and bow myself before God on high? Shall I come before him with burnt offerings, with calves a year old? Will the Lord be pleased with thousands of rams, with ten thousands of rivers of oil? Shall I give my firstborn for my transgression, the fruit of my body for the sin of my soul?" He has told you, O man, what is good and what does the Lord require of you but to do justice, and to love kindness, and to walk humbly with your God? (Micah 6:1–8).

The Messiah has something very similar to say:

> you have heard that it was said, 'You shall not commit adultery.' But I say to you that everyone who looks at a woman with lustful intent has already committed adultery with her in his heart. You tithe mint and dill and cumin, and have neglected the weightier matters of the law: justice and mercy and faithfulness. These you ought to have done, without neglecting the others (Matthew 5:27–27, 23:23).

An emphasis on the visible and ceremonial inevitably comes at the expense of the spiritual and moral. Evidence of that can be seen in the immorality that is rife among those whose religiosity is most overtly proclaimed, and that consists primarily in ceremonies and the purportedly miraculous.

Indeed, the circumcised are not law-keepers. Those who, in fact, are law-keepers are those who dare not claim to be such, who confess their failings and devote themselves to the worship of God in a predominantly spiritual way. They are the ones who are motivated to maintain high moral standards because their main concern has to do with the motions of their hearts. God's law is meant to remake us into His image, and that is a process which takes place from inside out, not the other way around.

A proud person is breaking God's law even if he wears 5 kippot (Jewish skull caps), never travels on the Sabbath and fasts every Monday and Thursday. Lazy and lustful people, liars—all such—transgress the Law even if they are the disciples of the strictest of Israel's Rabbis. A selfish person disobeys the Law even if he puts on phylacteries every morning and evening, because we all fail in each of these points to some extent. We all need to repent and entrust our fate in the hands of the Messiah.

We err by placing too much of an emphasis on externals, on the visible and the superficial while neglecting the core of God's demands. Gossip, love of the world, anger, self-love, an effort to best others—these and other such sins are not absent among us. They ought to be.

Some find no peace unless they are seen to be better than others. Such people are insecure, they lack a solid, mature sense of identity. Of course, to no small degree, we all define ourselves in relation to others. But our essential identity must not be dependent on anything but the knowledge that we were created in the image of God, that we are the objects of His grace and that we have been appointed by Him to live in this world to His glory—each of us in a different way.

In the family and in society, just as in church,

> there are varieties of gifts, but the same Spirit; and there are varieties
> of service, but the same Lord; and there are varieties of activities, but it
> is the same God who empowers them all in everyone. To each is given
> the manifestation of the Spirit for the common good, for to one is given
> through the Spirit the utterance of wisdom, and to another the utter-
> ance of knowledge according to the same Spirit, to another faith by the
> same Spirit, to another gifts of healing by the one Spirit, to another
> the working of miracles, to another prophecy, to another the ability
> to distinguish between spirits, to another various kinds of tongues, to
> another the interpretation of tongues. All these are empowered by one
> and the same Spirit, who apportions to each one individually as he wills
> (1 Corinthians 12:4–11).

Since that awful day when man was overtaken by the arrogant aspiration to be like God, the one who determines what is good and what is
evil, human beings seek their identity by the wrong means, and there are
many such ready at hand: husbands in relation to their wives, parents
in relation to their children, employers in relation to their employees,
employees in relation to their employers, and so on. We strive to rule, to
manage, to control so that we can boast in front of others or at least to
ourselves of the value we've managed to attach to our lives. That is the
root of much of the evil in human society, and that is what motivated the
teachers in Galatia: they want you to be circumcised so that would be able
to boast in your fleshly circumcision.

Why do you want to be better than others—or appear to be such?
Why do you want to control? Why do you compete with one another,
striving to best each other? Why are so many sports events accompanied
by violence and anger? James perceptive diagnosis is still valid: "what
causes quarrels and what causes fights among you? Is it not this, that
your passions are at war within you? You desire and do not have, so you
murder. You covet and cannot obtain, so you fight and quarrel" (James
4:1–2).

On the other hand, the Messiah said that the kingdom of God is assured to the lowly, the poor in spirit, those who refuse to respond to the
desire to excel others and who, instead, are engaged in seeking to excel
themselves.

Paul withstood those who sought to boast in their ability to persuade
Gentile Christians to be circumcised and to embrace Israel's traditions

by means of the declaration: But so far as I am concerned, it will never be that I would boast in anything but the cross of our Lord Jesus the Messiah. In the next verse he will describe the grounds of his boasting: but so far as I am concerned, it will never be that I would boast in anything but the cross of our Lord Jesus the Messiah, by which the world is dead so far as I am concerned, and I am dead so far as the world is concerned.

We ought not establish our self-image on our standing in society. Nor ought we establish it on the extent to which we manage to impose our will or opinions on others. We ought not follow the example of the teachers in Galatia, who adopted a certain view because it served their hidden motives by according them follower. Let's serve God sincerely, and let's serve others out of a pure heart.

> But so far as I am concerned, it will never be that I would boast in anything but the cross of our Lord Jesus the Messiah, by which the world is dead so far as I am concerned, and I am dead so far as the world is concerned.

So far as I am concerned—Paul positions himself over against the false teachers who sought to benefit by bringing others under their wings. He does not claim to be better than them, but he consciously chose not to boast of the same things in which they put their boast. He later will write,

> though I myself have reason for confidence in the flesh also. If anyone else thinks he has reason for confidence in the flesh, I have more: circumcised on the eighth day, of the people of Israel, of the tribe of Benjamin, a Hebrew of Hebrews; as to the law, a Pharisee; as to zeal, a persecutor of the church; as to righteousness under the law, blameless. But whatever gain I had, I counted as loss for the sake of Christ. Indeed, I count everything as loss because of the surpassing worth of knowing Christ Jesus my Lord. For his sake I have suffered the loss of all things and count them as rubbish, in order that I may gain Christ and be found in him, not having a righteousness of my own that comes from the law, but that which comes through faith in Christ, the righteousness from God that depends on faith—that I may know him and the power of his resurrection, and may share his sufferings, becoming like him in his death, that by any means possible I may attain the resurrection from the dead (Philippians 3:4–11).

It will never be, says Paul, that I would boast in anything but the cross of our Lord Jesus the Messiah. The Apostle chose this course because of an inner sense of obligation, the fruit of the activity of the Holy Spirt. The Gospel forbids all boasting but that which focuses on the grace of God.

Paul did not view the message of the Gospel in terms of a theory that merely needed to be understood and affirmed. He viewed it as a truth every individual must apply to himself. That is the sense of Paul's it will never be. It was not the product of some religious prohibition, social norm or his education. It stood in direct opposition to every cultural norm of his time, including the Jewish norms which he was taught from childhood, just as it is today. The Messiah had carved this principle on the Apostle's heart.

It will never be that I would boast in anything but the cross of our Lord Jesus the Messiah because recognition of the necessity of that cross as an atonement for our sins removes all grounds for boasting an any achievements but those of the Messiah. It causes us to recognize that we are empty vessels; and only then fills us to overflowing with God's blessing. It calls us to deny ourselves, forgo our sense of honor, our property, even our sense of personal security, to serve others. It calls us to avoid any effort to excel others or use them for our benefit.

It is in this sense that Paul says, the world is dead so far as I am concerned, and I am dead so far as the world is concerned. He is not saying he could no longer enjoy a good meal, a beautiful landscape or any other kind of earthly pleasure. He did not hesitate to celebrate God's gifts. But he refused to embrace earthly pleasures at the expense of his mission. He refused to be addicted to this world at the expense of the opportunity to labor for others to be blessed through the Messiah. He followed the example of his Lord ("I will give you all the kingdoms of this world if you but worship me" ...) and chose to forgo many of this world's enjoyments so he could serve those to whom he was sent. That is why he later described his sufferings:

> imprisonments, ... countless beatings, and often near death. Five times I received at the hands of the Jews the forty lashes less one. Three times I was beaten with rods. Once I was stoned. Three times I was shipwrecked; a night and a day I was adrift at sea; on frequent journeys, in danger from rivers, danger from robbers, danger from my own people, danger from Gentiles, danger in the city, danger in the wilderness, danger at sea, danger from false brothers; in toil and hardship, through many a sleepless night, in hunger and thirst, often without food, in cold and exposure. And, apart from other things, there is the daily pressure on me of my anxiety for all the churches. Who is weak, and I am

not weak? Who is made to fall, and I am not indignant? (2 Corinthians
11:23–29).

Do we not have the right to eat and drink? Do we not have the right to
take along a believing wife, as do the other apostles and the brothers
of the Lord and Cephas? ... Who serves as a soldier at his own expense?
Who plants a vineyard without eating any of its fruit? Or who tends a
flock without getting some of the milk? Do I say these things on human
authority? Does not the Law say the same? For it is written in the Law
of Moses, "You shall not muzzle an ox when it treads out the grain." Is
it for oxen that God is concerned? Does he not certainly speak for our
sake? ... If we have sown spiritual things among you, is it too much if
we reap material things from you? If others share this rightful claim on
you, do not we even more?

Nevertheless, we have not made use of this right, but we endure anything rather than put an obstacle in the way of the gospel of Christ. Do
you not know that those who are employed in the temple service get
their food from the temple, and those who serve at the altar share in
the sacrificial offerings? In the same way, the Lord commanded that
those who proclaim the gospel should get their living by the gospel. But
I have made no use of any of these rights, nor am I writing these things
to secure any such provision ... What then is my reward? That in my
preaching I may present the gospel free of charge, so as not to make full
use of my right in the gospel" (1 Corinthians 9: 4–18).

Paul carried out that sense of duty to its uttermost: he was executed
for his activity in the service of the Gospel and of the church of the Messiah. Do his words describe *our* view of life in this world? Or do we prefer to boast in the passing earthly gains and pleasures at the expense of
those which are eternal?

Because circumcision and uncircumcision amount to nothing. The
only important thing is a new creation. Paul is explaining yet further what
he means by saying that, so far as he is concerned, he is dead to the world,
and that his boast is in nothing but the cross of the Messiah. He refuses to ground any sense of his value in Jewishness, in his circumcision,
in keeping the traditions or in anything else attributable to himself. He
takes pride in one thing and in one thing only: the cross of the Messiah.
The grounds of his security, the source of his sense of worth are not in
what he achieved but in God and in what God did for him in the Messiah.
The Apostle's view of life was focused on the Messiah and on the amaz-

ing majesty of the Messiah's achievements (of which he will say much when he will write to the Colossians).

Think for a moment on what Paul is saying here: circumcision and uncircumcision amount to nothing. With these few words he has set the Law aside in every respect that has do to with our standing before God. Accordingly, the covenant made with Israel at Sinai is no longer binding and there is no spiritual significance to a person being Jewish or Gentile. That is just another way to say that, in Messiah, there is no difference between a Jew and a Gentile, just as there is none between a man and a woman, a slave or a freeman (Galatians 3:28). It is just another way to say that, in the Messiah Jesus, circumcision affects nothing, nor does uncircumcision, only faith acting through love (Galatians 5:6). That is also just another way to say it will never be that I would boast in anything but the cross of our Lord Jesus the Messiah, by which the world is dead so far as I am concerned, and I am dead so far as the world is concerned.

The emphasis placed in certain circles on Jewish identity and on Jewish custom is directly contrary to these words of the Apostle because Jewish things have no special standing in the sight of God. We are not allowed to attribute to them any such standing. We certainly are not allowed to encourage people to be circumcised, keep kosher, celebrate the Jewish or biblical feasts and adhere to Jewish tradition. Every nation and every race has the right to preserve and celebrate its own tradition. But no tradition can add to our walk with God. In terms of our spiritual life, they count for nothing. The Apostle posits circumcision over against the new creation because one view considers circumcision, Jewishness and Jewish tradition as a grounds for a relationship with God, whereas the other view refuses to accord such a status to anything but the grace of God.

Paul had no interest in this world's values (including Jewish tradition) because circumcision and uncircumcision amount to nothing. The only important thing is a new creation. What counted in his mind is not what man can do but what God did (a new creation), not what man can do for God but what God did for man: because circumcision and uncircumcision amount to nothing. Is that our opinion too?

Of course, the expression new creation refers to the new birth, that activity of God in the course of which God saves us by grace. The term itself indicates much of its meaning. First, it is a creation. An act of God of which He alone is capable. It is a divinely sovereign, unilateral, uncontingent, powerful intervention in human lives. What was has become no longer and what is has as its source God's activity, not in ours or in that of any other created being. No religious activity can accord us new birth. Only God can create. Only He speaks into nothingness and all things become. Only He can command the light to shine out of darkness: we are born again. At the first stage of birth, we are passive. We are acted upon by God. Our activity (faith, repentance and the life that follows) are the fruit of His saving act. He begot us anew according to His will and by His Holy Spirit.

Just as the material world exists for Him, so we too were created anew "for good works, which God prepared beforehand, that we should walk in them" (Ephesians 2:10).

Second, our creation is a new creation. The redeemed are recreated. Their previous existence is no longer. They are renewed, repaired as it were. Their previous existence was broken, perverted, defiled and sinful. The tendencies of their heart were against God. Their assumptions were mistaken. Their preferences were wrong. They called good evil and evil good and believed that they could stand on their own merits, as if there is no God. Now everything has changed. God has wrought this change. He gave them a new heart and placed a new attitude within them. He carved His commandments in their innermost being and thereby utterly changed their assumptions, preferences and values. Old things have passed away; everything has become new.

Third, anyone who has not undergone such a transformation is not a new creation. He is uncircumcised at heart even if he has undergone physical circumcision. His future is not to be determined by grace but by God's righteous anger. He has no part in the world to come. Efforts at self-justification only serve to fortify his guilt and, if he has heard the Gospel to and refused to entrust himself to the grace of God, his guilt is greater.

We would, therefore, do well to examine ourselves: have we become a new creation?

Peace and grace to all who live according to this principle, and to God's Israel. To what rule is the Apostle referring? To the rule he described in the previous verse, which states that circumcision and uncircumcision amount to nothing. The only important thing is a new creation, or, as he stated earlier, in the Messiah Jesus, circumcision affects nothing, nor does uncircumcision, only faith acting through love.

Peace and grace—those are the words with which the Apostle opened this letter (1:3): grace to you and peace from God our Father and the Lord

Jesus the Messiah, and with them he closes. There is no need for us to repeat what we said there, but it is worth noting the difference in the order of Paul's words because I think it is significant. In his opening words Paul spoke first of grace and then of peace because he was at the very beginning of his defense of the Gospel of grace. It is by grace that we have peace with God, we should therefore continue to rely on grace so as to enjoy the peace it brings and because the logic of the Gospel teaches us to continue on the same grounds on which we commenced our walk with God. We were given new life by the Spirit and should carry on with the guidance of the Spirit (5:25).

Now, at the end of the letter, once that important principle has been repeatedly established, Paul inverts the order so as to intimate that ongoing grace is the fruit of the peace between himself and us that God established by the sacrifice of the Messiah. That peace promises eternally ongoing blessings—all the fruit of grace, and for which we need not strive. Some might question the validity of the distinction I have made. I have no quarrel with them.

What is clear, however, is that all who conduct themselves according to the rule the Apostle established—all without exception, be they Jewish or Gentile—are the objects of the blessings of which Paul speaks. There is no difference between any who are in the Messiah as to privileges or duties, obligations or blessings. That is why Paul concludes by speaking of the whole Israel of God.

These last words have given rise to mountains of theories. Some, on the basis of Paul's statement that believers from all nations of the world are children of Abraham (3:7), conclude that God has accorded the church Israel's former place in His purposes. Nowhere in the Apostle 's writings or elsewhere in the New Testament is there indication that adding others to the family of Abraham is to be at the expense of God's faithfulness to His covenant with Israel.

Quite to the contrary, Paul makes it clear in his letter to the Romans that God's gift and callings are not subject to change, replacement or revocation. He is faithful in spite of his people's sin. If this were not so, we would all be lost and the Apostle's message of grace in this letter would be groundless, because none of us is as faithful as we ought to be. Paul is not saying that God revoked His covenant with Israel and replaced the nation with the church. He will fulfill every one of His promises to Abraham, and He will do so by grace rather than due to human merit, individual or communal (after all, the church has been no more faithful than have the people of Israel, nor have any one of us). God is not subject to man, nor are his doings determined by what man does. He is true even though every man is a liar.

I repeat what I said earlier: The Israel of God is the remnant of the people of Israel whom God had preserved for Himself and for whose salvation He acted in the Messiah, among whom is included a countless number of Gentile believers. It is not the visible church (the larger part of which is far from God), nor the evangelical church (that is far from perfect), nor is it the totality of the people of Israel (most of whom do not fear God), but those in the nation of Israel who, alongside many non-Jewish disciples of the Messiah, are by grace members of the body of the Messiah. There is no room in Scripture to replace grace by human merit, or to annul, grace by man's demerit. The Messiah did it all.

Faith in the Messiah is altogether necessary for the salvation of Israel, just as it is for the salvation of anyone. That is an important principle in the life of the redeemed: Everything is in the Messiah. Everything is from the Messiah. Everything is because of the Messiah. Everything is by the merits of the Messiah. All who are in Him are represented by Him and entitled to enjoy the blessings God promised Abraham because they are all His spiritual descendants. We are mistaken if we attribute to Israel eternal blessings without their turning from themselves and their tradition to the Messiah. As for Jews who do not put their trust in the Messiah—their circumcision is equal to uncircumcision. The uncircumcision of non-Jews who put their trust in the Messiah is a true circumcision.

And now, no one is to cause me trouble because I bear the scars of Jesus on my body. We will better understand what the Apostle is saying if we remember that at the time Paul dictated these words, he was at the beginning of his ministry. This letter was composed sometime between his first and second expeditions, apparently after he and Barnabas visited Jerusalem and returned to the church in Antioch, which had commissioned the two.

At this stage of his life we know of the danger that awaited him in Damascus (Acts 9:23–25) and then in Jerusalem (Acts 9:29–30) and in Iconium (Acts 14:5–6). In each of these cases there is no indication that Paul was actually harmed. The first and only time we hear of physical harm to which the Apostle came was in Lystra, where he was stoned, dragged to the outskirts of the city and left for dead (Acts 14:19–20).

Lystra was a city in Galatia—the very area in which the churches addressed in this letter were to be found. Iconium, Lystra and Derbe were close to one another and there is no reason room to doubt that the Christians in these cities would maintain close and frequent contact. They would, therefore, know of the danger in Iconium and of the grievous event in Lystra. Apparently, that is what Paul is referencing when he speaks of the scars of Jesus that he bears.

He is, in fact, appealing to the Galatians' conscience: he had suffered much for them. Would they now turn from him and from the Gospel he taught? What did those teachers who arrived in Galatia suffer for their sakes? Clearly, they were unwilling to suffer. That is why Paul said of them in verse 12, that they want the Galatians to be circumcised, with the sole purpose that they not be persecuted for the sake of the cross of the Messiah Jesus.

True faithfulness is measured by the sacrifices a person is willing to make. Did Paul desist from his efforts for the Gospel after he was stoned and left for dead? Not by a long shot. He and Barnabas went on to Derbe, where they preached the same Gospel again—and that when Paul's wounds would not have even had time to dry and he undoubtedly suffered much pain. That is what he will mean when he will write later to the Colossians and say he is delighted to full up whatever might be lacking in the sufferings of the Messiah on behalf of the church (Colossians 1:24).

Paul speaks here of his bearing the very scars of Jesus. He viewed himself as continuing the sufferings of the Messiah for the founding and confirming of the life of the church. What is more, he was not only willing to suffer to that end but actually bore the scars that proved his willingness. He bore those scars without shame, because he loved the Messiah more than he loved himself, and therefore he loved the church of the Messiah.

Do we love the church as he did? Are we willing to serve the church with such devotion, at the price of such sacrifice—or are we rather taken up with enjoying life? Does the Messiah deserve anything less than such devotion? Paul loved God with all his heart, all his soul and all his strength. Do we? He loved the Messiah and therefore His church—do we separate the two? Or do we think we can love the Messiah without loving the church in spite of her shortcomings?

> May the grace of our Lord Jesus the Messiah be with your spirits, brothers, Amen.

That's it. Paul has come to the end of his letter. He encourages the Galatians to persist relying on the grace of the Messiah, and therefore, once again, for the third time (1:3,6:16) prays that the grace of the Messiah continue with them. Although a large part of the responsibility lays on the shoulders of the Galatian Christians, the final determining factor is our Lord Jesus the Messiah. That is the sum of his argument in this letter: the Messiah did it all. Man's standing before God is not up to man or to what man does. God determines even that by grace. Man's standing is determined by God on the grounds of what the Messiah did for that person. Like everything else in the universe, God is the determining factor, and He is uncontingent, fully independent of anything and of anyone else.

Not only so, but in verses 2–3 of chapter 5 Paul made it clear that grace comes from God our Father and the Lord Jesus the Messiah. From both, equally, in tandem, because God the Father does all things through the Son, whom He sent to be the Messiah of Israel and of the Gentiles. He blesses none but due to the merits of the Messiah. Because He and the Son are equal in deity, glory and their love for sinners, grace from God is always the grace of the Messiah, and the grace of the Messiah is nothing but the grace of God. And grace—as we recall—is the opposite of desert. What is given by grace is not deserved for any reason to be found in the recipient. It is given in spite of the fact that it has been forfeited.

God is described here as *our* Father. This letter was written by Paul, a Jew and the son of a Jew, to a church largely comprised of non-Jews. Still, Paul takes a stand alongside them, as their equal, as a member of the same family at the head of which is God. After all, God has only one family. He is father to the Galatian Christians just as much as he is father to Jewish Christians. Paul, the Jews, is no different from the Galatian believers, nor any better, nor does he have in the Messiah more than they do.

He describes Jesus as the Messiah, the object of Israel's longing, the sum of Israel's hope. The end of time has arrived (1 Corinthians 10:11, Hebrews 1:2). The Messiah has come and did what God promised would be done. The blessings that accrue from what the Messiah accomplished are not meant for Jews alone; the promise given Abraham had reference to all the families of the earth. The one and only Gospel is not meant only for Jews. That is why the Apostle repeatedly addresses the Galatian with the title brothers. By the merits of the Messiah they have been made into one family, they are loved in the context of that one family and are called upon to relate to one another as members of that family, without competing, with mutually kind generosity.

The grace, Paul prays, is to be with their spirits. That is to say, it is to accompany them, guide them, encourage them, comfort them and bless them while shaping their lives and their conduct. It is to be an internal reality flowing from them, because the Holy Spirit dwells in them and, by the Spirit, the Messiah is fulfilling His promise not to leave them as orphans but to come to them and remain with them. Emmanuel—God with us!

Such are the principles according to which the Galatians are to live, and with them all who lay claim to faith in the Messiah. These are the principles that are to motivate and guide us.

> May the grace of our Lord Jesus the Messiah be with your spirits, brothers, Amen.

Let's Summarize

- What compromises are you tempted to make to avoid being persecuted, or embarrassed?

- Is the world dead to you? In what ways? Where can and should you improve? How do you give practical expression to the world's death in respect to you?

- Are you dead to the world? ? In what ways? Where can and should you improve? How do you give practical expression to your death to the world?

- How would the false teachers "look good in the flesh" by having the Galatians submit to circumcision? How does this show that they were not dead to the world, nor the world to them?

Let's Pray

You have chosen to reveal Yourself to us in the Scriptures. We thank You for those who suffered so that we might have the Scriptures today. Grant us to love You as they did, and to be willing to pay the price of faithfulness. May we never compromise to avoid being persecuted for the cross of the Messiah Jesus. May we never boast in anything but what You have done for us in the Messiah, in what He has done for us through His life, death and resurrection, and in what the Spirit has done for us in applying to us the fruits of the Messiah's merits.

Enable us to live as those who are dead to the world, as those on whom the world has no rightful claim. Grant us to put our trust in the sufficiency of the Messiah's work on our behalf, and to live in ways that demonstrate that trust to a watching world. May the grace of our Lord Jesus the Messiah be with us, that we might be forgiven our shortcomings and strengthened to serve You truly through Your Son our glorious Savior, Amen.

QUESTIONS FOR DISCUSSION AND STUDY

1. Compare what is said in verse 13 with similar tendencies today to seek strength and measure success in numbers. What is wrong with such an attitude?

2. How, in practical terms, are we to fulfill what is said in verse 14?

3. Explain the statement in verse 15 in terms of your life. Why is a new creation the only thing that matters?

4. Why is the desire to look good in the flesh contrary to the Gospel and to the cross of the Messiah?

SUMMARY QUESTIONS ON THE BOOK OF GALATIANS

1. Basing your conclusion on concrete statements in the letter, what is the main issue Paul is dealing with—is it law-keeping versus grace accorded to faith, or is it the Mosaic law and Jewish tradition versus the Gospel?

2. Follow the various uses of the term law in the letter to the Galatians, systematize and summarize your findings.

3. Summarize the stated and implied motivations of the false teachers, Peter, and Paul as depicted in this letter.

4. Summarize the role of the Spirit in the book of Galatians.

5. Create a summary of Paul's argument and an outline of his letter to the Galatians.

From A Treatise of the Law and the Gospel

BY JOHN COLQUOHOUN

Soli Deo Gloria, reprint, Morgan, PA no date. pp. 136–137, 196–197, 236–260

Moreover, it appears from what has been said that when our apostle asserts, in his epistles to the Romans and Galatians, that no man can be justified before God by the works of the law, he does not mean the law merely as promulgated from Sinai, or the law of Moses as such; for those churches consisted chiefly of Gentile converts who had no concern with the law of Moses merely as such.

Before their conversion they were heathens; they were under the law not as delivered from Sinai, but as the law of nature and as a covenant of works made with Adam, and with them in him. As therefore no Jews can be justified by the works of the moral law as a covenant displayed on Mount Sinai, so no Gentiles can be justified by the works of the moral law as a covenant made with Adam. They among the Gentiles who have been redeemed are said to have been redeemed from the curse of the law (Galatians 3:13), that is, of the moral law in its covenant form as given to Adam.

...

The Believer's Privilege of Being Dead to the Law as a Covenant of Works, with a Highly Important Consequence of It

The Apostle Paul, when speaking in his epistle to the Romans of this important privilege, expresses himself thus: "Wherefore, my brethren, ye also are become dead to the law by the body of Christ ... But now we are delivered from the law, that being dead wherein we were held" (Romans 7:4, 6). By "the law," in these passages, our apostle evidently means not so much the ceremonial as the moral law under the form of a covenant of works. For it is the same law that says that a man should not steal, and should not commit adultery (Romans 2:21–22).

It is also the law which "says to them who are under it, what things soever it says; that every mouth may be stopped, and all the world may become guilty before God." It is also the law by which "is the knowledge of sin," and which is not "made void through faith," but on the contrary "is established" (Romans 3:19–20, 31).

It is the law, likewise, which "entereth that the offence might abound" (Romans 5:20), and of which the apostle speaks thus: "When we were in the flesh, the motions of sins, which were by the law, did work in our members, to bring forth fruit unto death ... I had not known sin but by the law: for I had not known lust except the law had said, Thou shalt not covet. ... I was alive without the law once; but when the commandment came, sin revived, and I died ... The commandment which was ordained to life, I found to be unto death ... The law is holy, and the commandment holy, and just, and good ... Sin by the commandment, became exceeding sinful ... We know that the law is spiritual ... I consent unto the law that it is good ... I delight in the law of God after the inward man ... With the mind, I myself serve the law of God" (Romans 7:5–25).

The law in question is that the law, the work of which "the Gentiles show to be written in their hearts" (Romans 2:15); that law by the transgression of which "Jews and Gentiles are all under sin" (Romans 3:9); that law against which "all have sinned and come short of the glory of God" (Romans 3:23); and that law without which "there is no transgression" (Romans 4:15).

It is also the law to which, as their first husband, the believers in Rome were, in their unregenerate state, espoused, and by which "they were held" (Romans 7:4–6). But most, if not all, of those believers were Gentiles (Romans 1:13 and 11:13) who were never held by the ceremonial law of the Jews, and therefore could not be said to have been delivered from it.

In a word, it is that law the righteousness of which was fulfilled in those believers (Romans 8:4). Now, in most, if not all, of those passages the things asserted by our apostle are peculiar to the moral law. This, then, is the law which he had in view when he affirmed to those believers

that they had become dead to, or were delivered from, the law, and that
the law in which they had been held was dead to them.

...

Of the Necessity of a Believer's Being Dead, to the Law as a Covenant in Order to His Living unto God

As the believer's living unto God, according to the law as a rule of life
in the hand of the Mediator, is the necessary consequence or fruit of his
having become dead to the law as a covenant of works, so his being dead
to the law is necessary to his living unto God; so absolutely necessary
that were he not dead to the law as a covenant, it would be utterly impossible for him to live unto God in conformity to the law as a rule.

This will be evident to the devout reader if he considers the following
particulars:

1. The man who is under the power of the law as a broken covenant
is under the power of sin; for the law under that form "is the strength of
sin" (1 Corinthians 15:56). Hence our apostle said to the saints in Rome,
"Sin shall not have dominion over you; for ye are not under the law, but
under grace" (Romans 6:14), intimating to them that if they had been still
under the law as a covenant, sin would have had dominion over them.
The believer's deliverance, then, from the dominion of sin, so as to be
rendered capable of living to God, necessarily depends upon his having
become dead to the law in its covenant form.

2. The sinner who is under the law as a covenant is without strength;
and therefore he cannot serve God in a holy and acceptable manner (Romans 5:6). And the law, being "weak through the flesh," is as unable to
sanctify him as it is to justify him. The works of the law cannot sanctify
him, seeing they are evil and not good works. They can render him more
and more unholy, but they cannot make him holy. He must be created
unto good works before he can perform them. But the new as well as the
old creation is the work of God alone.

Therefore, while a man is under the law as a covenant of works, and
is unregenerate, he cannot perform a single holy or good work. He may
do many things that are materially good, but he can do nothing that is
formally good. All his works are dead works, the works of a man who is
dead in sin and dead to God; and therefore it is as impossible for them to
make him alive to God as it is to merit for him eternal life.

3. He who is under the law as a covenant is without Christ, in whom

only quickening and sanctifying grace is to be found. They who live unto God "are sanctified in Christ Jesus" (1 Corinthians 1:2) and are saints in Him (Philippians 1:1). Their implantation in Christ, instead of being from the law or works of the law, is wholly from grace; and their sanctification, while it is wholly from grace, is only in Christ "who loved the Church and gave Himself for it, that He might sanctify and cleanse it with the washing of water by the Word" (Ephesians 5:25–26).

4. The man who is under the law as a covenant of works has no principle of holiness in him. The grand principle of evangelical holiness, or of living unto God, is the holy, sanctifying Spirit of Christ dwelling in the heart. Now a man receives the Spirit of sanctification "not by the works of the law, but by the hearing of faith" (Galatians 3:2). He becomes a partaker of the Holy Spirit not by obedience to the law of works, but by means of hearing and embracing the doctrine of faith.

It is the new testament or covenant, and not the law or legal covenant that is "the ministration of the Spirit" (2 Corinthians 3:6–8). It is the glorious gospel in which the new covenant is offered and the Spirit promised that, through grace, calls a sinner effectually to a life of sanctification (2 Thessalonians 2:13–14). When the sinner is effectually called, he "receives the promise of the Spirit through faith" (Galatians 3:14). This is through the faith of the gospel, not by the works of the law. As long, then, as a man is under the law of works, and is of the works of the law, he is destitute of the Spirit of Christ, the main principle of living to God.

5. Once more, the sinner who is under the law as a covenant has no promise of sanctification by that law. The law in its federal form promises life to him only on condition of perfect obedience to be performed by himself, and performed in that strength which was given him in the first Adam; but it promises him no quickening or sanctifying influences to enable him to obey. On the contrary, by its awful curse it bars effectually all sanctifying influence from his soul, and shuts it up under the dominion of sin. Indeed, if true holiness or ability to live unto God were to be found in the man under the covenant of works, the promises of the covenant of grace, with reverence it is said, might be altered, and that of sanctification be expunged from it.

We might erase from that well- ordered covenant especially these promises: "I shall put My Spirit in you, and ye shall live" (Ezekiel 37:14). "A new heart also will I give you, and a new spirit will I put within you. I will put My Spirit within you, and cause you to walk in My statutes, and ye shall keep My judgments, and do them" (Ezekiel 36:26–27).

Were it possible for a sinner, while he continues under the law as a covenant and, consequently, under the dominion and strength of sin to possess, notwithstanding, true holiness or ability to live unto God, there would be no need of these and similar promises. But suppose we had no other proof of it; the very existence of those absolute promises in the covenant of grace proves, with the highest degree of certainty, that no man, while he continues under the law as a covenant of works, is capable of living to God.

Thus it is evident that a man must be dead to the law as a covenant, in point of justification, and must be dying daily to it, in point of temper and practice, in order to his living unto God, in reference to sanctification. The former is indispensably requisite to the latter; and the latter is not only the consequence, but the necessary consequence, of the former.

It is absolutely necessary that a sinner be dead to the law in its federal form, with respect to his state before God, and also that he be dying to it, in respect of his inclination and practice, in order to his being capable of living a holy life. But to evince still more clearly the necessity of a man's becoming dead to the law, in order to his living unto God, I shall take a different view of this fundamental subject and inquire what causality or influence his having become dead to the law as a covenant has upon his living unto God.

In the first place, a man's being dead to the law has a physical, or rather a spiritual influence upon his sanctification, or his living unto God. They who are become dead to the law are married to another, even to Him who is raised from the dead. And so they cannot but live or bring forth fruit unto God. In union and communion with Christ Jesus, they have life, spiritual and eternal life. While they were under the law as a covenant, they were spiritually as well as legally dead, "dead in trespasses and sins"; but now in Christ, their Head of righteousness and life, they have life, and have it more abundantly.

Because He lives, they shall live also. "He that hath the Son hath life." Now that they have been divorced from the law of works, their first husband, and are united to Christ, they live and act spiritually. In Christ, their Head of influences, they have light as well as life. As long as a man is under the law as a covenant he dwells in darkness, and cannot see to work the works of holiness or be spiritually active in living unto God. He is blinded with ignorance, prejudice, and self-conceit; and as he cannot see the vanity of his legal works, so neither can he discern the way of evangelical holiness.

But no sooner is he united to Christ, who is "a Light to lighten the Gentiles," than he receives "the spirit of wisdom and revelation in the knowledge of Christ"; and by this spiritual light, shining on the Word of Christ, he sees distinctly how to live to God. He discerns the beauty and amiableness, as well as the manner, of true holiness. In the Lord Jesus, they who are dead to the law have strength likewise.

Sinners who are joined to the law as their husband cannot live to God; for they have no strength for acceptable obedience, and the law cannot afford them any. But believers have in Christ, their spiritual Husband, strength to enable them to perform spiritual obedience. He affords them, from His overflowing fullness, sufficient and continual supplies of grace and strength. His grace is sufficient for them; for His strength is made perfect in weakness (2 Corinthians 12:9).

The consequence is that all things are possible to them who believe. When, by trusting in Him at all times, they are "strong in the Lord, and in the power of His might" (Ephesians 6:10), they can do all things through Christ who strengthens them (Philippians 4:13). In union with Christ, their Covenant Head, they also have liberty, the glorious liberty of the children of God. While they were under the law as a covenant which genders to bondage, they were in bondage, severe bondage to the command of perfect obedience on pain of eternal death; and were also in bondage to the curse of the law and the fear of eternal wrath.

In this miserable condition it was impossible for them to live unto God; they could not have either a heart or a hand to serve Him. But in union and communion with the Lord Jesus, believers have liberty. If the Son shall make you free, you shall be free indeed—free to serve God in spiritual and acceptable manner. "Where the Spirit of the Lord is, there is liberty."

Partaking of the Spirit of the Lord Jesus, they walk at liberty, yea, they run the way of God's commandments; for He enlarges their hearts. Now that they are delivered from the hands of their enemies, they serve the Lord without fear, in holiness and righteousness before Him, all the days of their life. They serve Him willingly, affectionately, and cheerfully. They are now at liberty to serve Him in hope, knowing that their labor shall not be in vain. They are at liberty to serve Him spiritually and acceptably; for as they are so joined to the Lord Jesus, as to be one Spirit, so they are made accepted in the Beloved.

Christ, their Representative and Surety, satisfied all the demands of the law as a covenant for them; they are therefore accounted in law as having answered them all in Him, and so are accepted in Him. In union with Him, their persons are accepted as righteous and their performances as sincere. Oh, how grateful, how cheering is this liberty to the exercised believer! And what a delightful and powerful inducement is it to that holy and acceptable obedience, which is a living unto God!

In the last place, a man's being dead to the law as a covenant has not only a physical, but a moral influence upon his sanctification or living unto God. The love of Christ, manifested in delivering believers from the law as a covenant of works, constrains them to live not unto themselves, but to Him who died for them and rose again (2 Corinthians 5:14–15).

Men's natural way of thinking and speaking is, "We should serve God that He may save us"; but the evangelical way is, "He saves us that we may serve Him. He redeems us from the law as a covenant that we may serve Him, and so live to Him, in obedience to the law as a rule." When our apostle said, "I am dead to the law that I might live unto God," in the next verse he enlarges in these words: "The life which I now live in the flesh, I live by the faith of the Son of God, who loved me, and gave Himself for me" (Galatians 2:19–20).

It is true believers only, who are dead to the law of works and are united to the Son of God, who have a true faith and sense of His immense love to them, and who are powerfully constrained by it to love and live to God. And while redeeming love to them constrains them to love God as their Covenant God, they see that they have every encouragement to live to Him. They see that their adorable Surety has, in wonderful condescension, fulfilled all that righteousness of the law as a covenant for them which they could never have fulfilled for themselves; and when by the eye of faith they perceive this, they are sweetly impelled and encouraged by it to holiness of heart and of life.

If a man has no faith in the love of God in Christ, no hope of His favor as a God of grace, how can that man be pure in heart, and holy in all manner of conversation? Nay, he cannot; it is only the man who has this hope in Him who purifies himself, even as Christ is pure (1 John 3:3). All exercised Christians know by experience that when their souls are most comforted, and their hearts most enlarged with the faith of God's favor in Christ, and with the hope of His salvation, then it is that they are most disposed and encouraged to live to His glory. And, on the contrary, when through the prevalence of unbelief they are most suspicious of God and His love to them, they then find themselves most averse from the exercise of graces and performance of duties.

But that the moral influence which dying to the law as a covenant of works has upon living unto God may be more evident, it will be proper to show how every part of the law itself—having been changed to believers from the form of a covenant of works into that of a rule of life in the hand of the Mediator—constrains them to evangelical obedience. The law in the hand of Christ as a rule of duty, in all the commands, promises, and threats of it, is, as it were, a chariot paved with love for believers. It wears a smiling, inviting, encouraging aspect to them.

1. The commandments of the law in the hand of Christ, having been divested of their old covenant form, discover to believers much of the love and grace of God. The command of the law as a covenant, as was observed above, is "Do and live"; but that of the law as a rule is "Live and do." The precept of the law of works is "Do or you shall die"; but that of the law of Christ is 'You are redeemed from eternal death, therefore do."

The command of the law in its federal form is "Do perfectly that you may be entitled to eternal life," but that of the law in the hand of Christ is "He has merited for you and given you eternal life; therefore do, by His grace, as perfectly as you can until you attain absolute perfection." The command of the law as a rule is materially the same as that of the law as a covenant; and therefore, though as much obedience is required in it as in that of the law of works, yet less is accepted from those who have the perfect obedience of their divine Redeemer imputed to them.

And as the command is materially the same, so the authority which enjoins obedience is originally the same, and yet vastly distinct; for the commandment of the law as a covenant is the command of God out of Christ; but the command of the law as a rule is the precept of God in Christ, of God as a God of grace and love in Him. The sovereign authority of God in commanding obedience is not in the smallest degree lessened in that His law is in the hand of Christ; for He, as the eternal Son of God, is the Most High God and co-essential with the Father and the Holy Spirit.

But while it is not, and cannot be, in the least degree lessened, it is, notwithstanding, rendered so mild, so amiable, and so desirable to believers as powerfully to constrain them to spiritual obedience. For His design in commanding their obedience is not to require from them a righteousness for their justification, but to show them the holiness of His nature, to beautify them with His holy image, to afford them illustrious displays of His glorious grace, to do their soul good in the most effectual manner, and to favor them with daily opportunities to glorify Him, to edify their neighbor, and so to manifest their love and gratitude to Him for having redeemed them from the law as a covenant.

2. The promises of the law in the hand of Christ, having dropped their old covenant form, display to believers much of the love of God, and so constrain them to live to Him. The law in its federal form promises eternal life as a reward of debt for perfect obedience; but the law as a rule in the hand of Christ promises rewards of grace in and after evangelical obedience—especially as this obedience is an evidence of union with Him in whom believers are justified, and in whom all the promises of God are "yea and amen."

The consideration that "in keeping His commandments there is great reward," that in the way of evangelical obedience there is a gracious promise of delightful communion with God and Jesus Christ (1 John 14:21, 23), and that after the course of such obedience in this world is ended there will be an eternal reward powerfully constrains and greatly encourages believers to live unto God.

3. Finally, the threatenings of the law as a rule of life are also divested of their old covenant form, and are changed into paternal threats issuing from redeeming love which powerfully incite true Christians to live unto God. There is now no such threatening to the believer as: "If you do not do this, you shall die." Now that he is dead to the law of works and delivered from condemnation, the believer has no more cause to fear its threatening of eternal death than a woman has to fear the threats of a dead husband (Romans 8:1). Believers, because they are not under the law as a covenant, but under grace, are under no threatening of eternal wrath, no sentence of condemnation to eternal punishment.

The law in the hand of Christ has indeed threats of chastisement, but they are fatherly and all from love. "If his children forsake My law, and walk not in My judgments; if they break My statutes, and keep not My commandment; then will I visit their transgressions with the rod, and their iniquity with stripes" (Psalm 89:30–35). It is as if Jehovah had said, "Although I will not send them to hell, nor deprive them of heaven, any more than I will break My covenant, or violate My oath to My eternal Son; yet, as a father, I will chasten them. I will not only visit them with the rod of external affliction, but I will hide My face from their souls. I will deny them that sensible communion with Me which they have sometime enjoyed; and I will fill them with trouble instead of comfort, with bitterness instead of sweetness, and with terror instead of hope."

A filial fear of these paternal chastisements will do far more to influence the believer to holy obedience than all the despondent fears of eternal punishment can do. Accordingly, when he has gone aside, it is commonly such a reflection as this that through grace makes him return to the Lord: "Oh! How am I now deprived of those delightful interviews with my gracious God and Savior, which I formerly enjoyed!" Therefore, "I will go and return to my first Husband; for then it was better with me than now" (Hosea 2:7).

And when he is enabled to see that he is delivered from the threatenings of eternal wrath, and that he is only under threats of fatherly correction, this breaks and melts his heart more than all the fire of hell could do. The slavish dread of avenging wrath disquiets and discourages him, weakens his hands in spiritual obedience, and disposes him to flee from God; whereas the filial fear of God's fatherly anger, which is kindly, is a motive of love that excites and urges him to holy living. The former works upon his remaining enmity and rouses it; but the latter acts upon his love and enflames it.

But here the attentive reader may be ready to ask, "Ought not the believer to live unto God without respect to the threats of paternal chastisement?" I answer, as long as he is in this world a body of sin dwells in him; and therefore he needs to be incited to his duty by threats of fatherly correction. He ought indeed to serve the Lord, as the redeemed in heaven do, merely from love to the command itself, and because it is his God and Savior who commands him.

Still, however, as on the one hand he is perfect in Christ, his federal Head and Representative, he needs not have respect to what the law in its covenant form either promises or threatens (It is not here meant, that believers need not regard with holy admiration and gratitude, the grace manifested in the promise of the covenant of works; nor, that they need not regard with holy awe, the terrible wrath revealed in the threatening of that broken covenant, but only that they need not, and should not, have respect to them, or take them into their view as motives to live unto God or obey the law as a rule of life) so, on the other, as he is imperfect in himself while here, it is his duty to have, in his obedience, regard to what the law as a rule in the hand of Christ promises and threatens—which indeed is a holy and affectionate regard tending to promote holiness in his heart and life.

Thus it is manifest that the whole form of the law as a covenant of works, having been dissolved to believers, the law as a rule of life in the hand of Christ, is all love, all grace; and so it influences and constrains them to advance, with increasing ardour, in evangelical holiness. Instead of affording them the smallest encouragement to commit sin, it not only requires, but like a cord of love it draws them to, the love and practice of universal holiness.

For the greater part of what has been advanced in the last two sections, I have been indebted to the substance of four excellent sermons by Mr. Ralph Erskine. If the reader chooses to receive further information respecting the highly important subject of this chapter, he may peruse Abraham Booth's treatise entitled The Death of Legal Hope the Life of Evangelical Obedience, Robert Hall's sermon on Galatians 2:19, and Thomas Boston's sermon on Romans 6:14.

So much for the influence, that a believer's being dead to the law as a covenant, has upon his living unto God. A few reflections from what has been said will conclude this chapter.

Is it the privilege of true believers only to be dead to the law as a covenant of works? Then the law in its covenant form is, to every unregenerate sinner, as much in force as ever it was. It retains all the authority and dominion over unconverted sinners that ever it had. As it is dead to believers, and they dead to it, so sinners in their unregenerate state are alive to it, and it is alive to them. Retaining all its original authority over them, it continues to demand from them perfect obedience as the condition of life and complete satisfaction for sin.

This is clearly taught us not only by the Lord Jesus, but also by the Apostle Paul (Luke 10: 25–28; Galatians 3:10); and all who continue to reject the second Adam and His consummate righteousness, shall, to their everlasting confusion, find it so. Oh, that secure sinners would believe this and flee for refuge to the great Redeemer before it is too late!

Does the law as a covenant require of every descendant of Adam personal as well as perfect obedience? Then it inevitably follows that the obedience of two or more cannot form a justifying righteousness. Righteousness for justification must be the obedience of one only. It must be the obedience either of the sinner himself alone or Christ alone. The Lord Jesus will either save sinners Himself alone or not save them at all (Acts 4:12).

If a man would be justified before God, he must exhibit to the law either a perfect righteousness of his own, and have no dependence on that of Christ, or the perfect righteousness of Christ, in the hand of faith, and place no reliance on his own (Philippians 3:9). The righteousness of Jesus Christ, imputed to believers for their justification, is a righteousness without works; a righteousness wholly unconnected with works of any kind, performed by themselves. These two cannot stand together in the affair of justification. "I will make mention of Thy righteousness," says the holy Psalmist, "even of Thine only" (Psalm 71:16).

Oh, let my reader take heed that in the affair of justification he does not connect his own obedience with that of Christ, nor Christ's obedience with his own; that he never presumes to make up a justifying righteousness for himself, partly of his own works and partly of those of Christ. Let him be zealous for good works and perform them as fruits and evidences of justification, but never as grounds of right to it. For it will be impossible for him to live unto God till he begins to die to all hope of justification and salvation, either in whole or in part, by his own performances.

Is it through the law that a man becomes dead to the law? It is obvious, then, that ignorance in unregenerate sinners is a principal cause of their self-righteous temper (Romans 10:3). Their ignorance of the infinite holiness, justice, and faithfulness of God; of the precept and penalty of His righteous law; of the covenant, promise, and design of His gospel; of the person, righteousness, fullness, and glory of Christ; and of their own extreme need of Christ—this willful, pharisaic ignorance is a special cause of their desire to be under the law of works (John 3:19; Galatians 3:1).

Oh, that they would no longer condemn the counsel which the exalted Redeemer offers to each of them! "I counsel thee to buy of Me gold tried in the fire, that thou mayest be rich; and white raiment, that thou mayest be clothed, and that the shame of thy nakedness do not appear; and anoint thine eyes with eye-salve, that thou mayest see" (Revelation 3:18).

Ah, secure sinner, how gross, how reproachful is your ignorance when you expect to become righteous in the sight of an omniscient and holy God by your own partial and polluted obedience! How blind are the eyes of your understanding when you can presume to hope that the holy and righteous law will accept your amendment and sincere obedience, your penitence and tears, instead of perfect obedience and perfect satisfaction for your innumerable sins!

Alas! You do not know that the violated law demands, and cannot but demand from you, perfect obedience, and, at the same time, complete satisfaction for all your aggravated crimes; and that it will not absolve you till all its high demands are fully satisfied. Oh, continue no longer ignorant of the exceeding sinfulness of sin of your inexpressible misery and danger under the law as a covenant, and of your extreme need of the righteousness and grace of the second Adam.

Is a man's being dead to the law as a covenant the reason why he lives unto God? Then it must be admitted that the reason, or at least one reason, why unbelievers and formalists live not to God, but to sin and self and the world, is that they are not dead to the law in that form. The very reason why sin reigns in the sinner is because he is under the dominion of the law; which stands as a bar to prevent sanctifying influences from flowing into his heart. The law, especially in its condemning and irritating power, "is the strength of sin" (1 Corinthians 15:56).

Every man, therefore, who is under the dominion of the law as a covenant is, and cannot but be, under the dominion and strength of sin (Romans 6:14). It is impossible for that man who continues alive to the law to be a holy or a godly man. He may have the form, but he cannot experience the power of godliness. He may take his encouragement from the law as a covenant, and delight in the works of it; but he cannot delight in the holiness and spirituality of the law as a rule. He may advance to a high degree of counterfeit virtue, but he remains an entire stranger to true holiness.

Reader, the only way in which it is possible for you to attain true or evangelical holiness is to be so convinced of sin and righteousness as to part with your legal righteousness. You cannot trust cordially in the Lord Jesus for righteousness and strength till you begin utterly to despair of being able to work out for yourself such a righteousness as the law requires. You cannot desire the great salvation offered to you in the gospel, until you despair utterly of salvation by the works of the law. Nor is it possible for you to live unto God till you die to all hope of redemption from the curse of the broken law, and from the justice of an offended God, by any righteousness of your own. Be assured that you must be dead to the law as a covenant in order to be either able or willing to yield the smallest degree of acceptable obedience to the law as a rule.

How inexpressibly miserable are they who are alive to the law as a covenant of works! They may have a name to live, but they are dead. They are dead to God—to the favor, image, service, and enjoyment of God. They are legally dead, for they are under the tremendous curse of the violated law, and are liable every moment to the intolerable and eternal wrath of Almighty God. They are morally dead, likewise, for they are destitute of spiritual life; and they have no inclination or ability to live unto God.

Such persons know not what it is to live a life either of justification, sanctification, or consolation. The righteous law condemns them because they have transgressed it; and its awful sentence not only shuts them up under the dominion of spiritual death, but binds them over to all the horrors of death eternal.

Oh, secure sinner, the state in which you are is that of a criminal condemned to temporal, spiritual, and eternal! Do not say, "I hope that is not my state," for you are of the works of the law; you are depending on your own works for a title to the favor of God and the happiness of heaven. And this renders it certain that you are under the curse or condemning sentence of the law: for thus said the Spirit of inspiration, "As many as are of the works of the law are under the curse" (Galatians 3:10).

Oh, renounce, and that without delay, all dependence on your own works. Believe that the Lord Jesus, with His righteousness and salvation, is freely, wholly, and particularly, offered to you. And relying on His consummate righteousness alone for all your right to justification and salvation, trust in Him not only for deliverance from the curse of the law, but for complete salvation. So shall you become dead to the law of works and, in union with the second Adam, be instated into the covenant of grace.

All believers have, in the eye of the law as a covenant of works, obeyed, suffered and satisfied fully in Jesus Christ, their federal Representative and Surety. As all mankind has sinned and become subject to death in the first Adam, so all true believers have obeyed, died, and so satisfied the law and justice of God in the first Adam. Thus they have answered and completely satisfied all the demands of the law as a covenant. The consequence is that the law in that form, having received all that it had to demand from them, absolves them from guilt and declares them righteous.

Hence they become dead to the law, and the law to them. The Representative and the represented, the Surety and the principal debtor, are, in legal estimation, but one person. They therefore are accounted in law to have done and suffered all that Christ, their Representative and Surety, did and suffered for them. Accordingly, they are said in Scripture to be crucified with Christ (Galatians 2:20), to be dead and buried with Him (Romans 6:4, 8), and to be raised up together in Him (Ephesians 2:6). They have obeyed and suffered, and so satisfied every demand of the law as a covenant not in their own persons, but in the person of Christ.

Although the sins which believers commit after the commencement of their vital union with Christ are not formally transgressions of the law as a covenant of works, yet they are all, by legal interpretation, sins against it. In the justification of believers, in which they have become dead to the law as a covenant, all their future sins, considered as transgressions of the law in that form, are forgiven. As sins against the law as a covenant, in the act of justification they are so pardoned that a non-imputation of them to believers is inviolably secured. "Blessed is the man," says the Apostle Paul, "to whom the Lord will not impute sin" (Romans 4:8).

All the sins of believers after, as well as before, their vital union with Christ were charged and punished on Him as transgressions of the law in its federal form, and as such are, in their justification, freely and wholly pardoned. The Lord Jesus, their divine Surety, has satisfied the justice of God for all their sins committed after as well as before the act of their justification— and that by enduring in their stead the punishment threatened in the covenant of works.

Though, therefore, their sins after union with Christ are directly and formally committed against the law as a rule of duty, yet, by legal interpretation, they are transgressions likewise of the law as a covenant of works.

Are believers wholly delivered from the condemning power of the law as a covenant? The guilt of sin, then, in reference to them is twofold: the guilt of eternal wrath and the guilt of paternal anger. The guilt of eternal wrath is a sinner's obligation or liableness to the avenging and eternal wrath of God as the just punishment of his sin. The guilt of fatherly displeasure, on the other hand, is a believer's obnoxiousness to the awful effects of God's paternal anger as chastisements for his disobedience. Accordingly, the pardon of sin is twofold: namely a removal of the guilt of eternal wrath from him in the act of his justification, and an absolving of him from the guilt of paternal displeasure in the progress of his sanctification.

The former is called "legal pardon," the latter "gospel pardon." The one is the instantaneous and perfect removal of all that guilt which was contracted by transgressing the law as a covenant; the other is the gradual removal of that guilt which is contracted daily by disobeying the law as a rule. That is afforded completely and at once to a converted sinner upon his first acting of faith, when he becomes dead to the law as a covenant: this is vouchsafed to a believer repeatedly upon his renewed exercise of faith and repentance.

When therefore a true Christian—who is in some happy measure assured of his justification prays with understanding for the pardon of his iniquities— he prays that the Lord may preserve and increase in him his assurance of the pardon which was given him in his justification (Larger Catechism, question 194), and also that he may graciously remove from him the guilt of fatherly displeasure which he is daily contracting (Psalm 51:8–12). And when he asks divine acceptance, he prays that the Lord may preserve and increase in him his assurance of the acceptance of his person in the Beloved; and that He may favor him daily with the acceptance of his performances.

Are believers dead to the law as a covenant, and is it dead to them? Then it cannot either promise eternal life or threaten eternal death to them. "What things soever the law saith," either in its promise of life or its threatening of death, "it saith to them who are under the law" (Romans 3:19). But believers are not under the law, but under grace (Romans 6:14); and therefore the law in its federal form can say nothing to them. In their justification by faith they are delivered from condemnation to eternal death, and are accounted so righteous as to be fully entitled to eternal life (John 3:16). They are already redeemed from eternal death, and they have already the begun possession of life eternal. How, then, can the law either promise eternal life or threaten eternal death to those who, by their communion with Christ in His righteousness and fulness, have already attained the one and escaped the other?

Though believers ought always to regard the threatenings of the law as a covenant with holy awe, as a glass in which they may contemplate the dreadful demerit of their sins, and their infinite obligations to redeeming grace; yet they ought not to consider those threatenings as directed to them or as denunciations of evil against them. They should regard them at all times with filial awe, but never with slavish dread.

Is every man who is justified before God, and so dead to the law as a covenant, taught to believe that his own works of obedience form no part at all of a justifying righteousness for him? It would surely be very unreasonable and unjust to infer from this that he needs not perform good works. He is indeed delivered, and wholly delivered, from the law as a covenant of works; but he is still under the infinite and eternal obligation of it as a rule of duty. To infer, then, from a believer's being directed and exhorted to place no confidence in his good works for a title to justification and eternal life, that it is not necessary for him to perform and maintain good works; would be as absurd as if a man should conclude that, because it is the ear only that hears, there is no need of the foot or the hand (Romans 3:8; Jude 4).

Once more, are true believers delivered from the commanding, condemning, and irritating power of the law as a covenant? Let them, then, amidst all their trials, and all their conflicts with spiritual enemies, be of good comfort. Oh, let them rejoice exceedingly in that almighty, compassionate, dear Redeemer who, in His love and pity, has redeemed them from the dominion and curse of the broken law (Galatians 3:13).

You, O believer, have become dead to the law by the body of Christ, and are married to another husband, even to Him who is raised from the dead, that you may bring forth fruit unto God (Romans 7:4). You are dead to the law of works; nevertheless you live. You live to God as your own God, your covenant God, and you serve Him in newness of spirit. In union with your living Redeemer, who loved you and gave Himself for you, you live a life of justification—and consequently it is your privilege as well as your duty to live a life of sanctification and consolation.

Being justified by faith, you have peace with God through our Lord Jesus Christ, and, in some measure, peace of conscience. If then the law as a covenant of works should at any time enter your conscience again, and require perfect obedience from you as the ground of your title to eternal life, saying "This do, and you shall live," present to it, in the hand of faith, the perfect obedience of your divine Surety in answer to that demand.

And as often as the law in your conscience repeats the high demand, renew your application of His consummate obedience, and trust firmly that it was performed for you in order to entitle you to eternal life. The righteous law, magnified and made honorable by that meritorious obedience, will, in proportion as you do so, cease to disturb the peace of your conscience. The spotless obedience of the second Adam is, as was observed above, the only obedience which you ought to exhibit to it as a rule of life.

And should the law as a covenant ever be permitted to rise again as from the dead, and to attempt exercising its condemning power over your conscience by demanding from you satisfaction for your innumerable transgressions of it; present to it, in the hand of an appropriating faith, the infinite satisfaction for sin given by your adorable Surety in answer to that demand.

Trust anew that your living Head, your heavenly Husband, has given complete satisfaction for all your sins; and so, referring the law to Him, plead that if it has any charge to exhibit against you the action must lie between it and Him. Never say to the law, in answer to any of its demands, "Have patience with me and I will pay you all"; but without delay present it with full payment. In answer to its demand of perfect obedience as the condition of life, present in the hand of faith to it the perfect obedience of the second Adam; and in answer to its demand of complete satisfaction for sin, exhibit to it His infinite atonement for the sins of all who believe in Him. That is the way to honor it and, at the same time, recover and maintain peace of conscience.

The High Obligation under which Believers Lie to Yield Even Perfect Obedience to the Law as a Rule of Life

All who are united to Christ, and justified for His righteousness imputed to them, are dead to the law as a covenant; not that they may be without law to God, but that they may be under the law to Christ; not that they may continue in disobedience, but that they may be inclined and enabled to perform sincere obedience in time, and perfect obedience through eternity, to the law as a rule of life.

One design of their being delivered from the obligation of the law in its federal form is that they may be brought under the eternal obligation of it as a rule of duty in the hand of the adorable Mediator. Divested of the form of a covenant of works to believers, and invested with that of the covenant of grace, it stands under the covenant of grace as the law of Christ, and as the instrument of government in its spiritual kingdom, enforced by all its original and immutable authority. It loses nothing of its original authority by its being conveyed to believers in such a blessed channel as the hand of Christ since He Himself is God over all, and since the majesty, sovereignty, and authority of the Father, the Son, and the Holy Spirit are in Him as Mediator (Exodus 23:21).

Indeed, it behooved the law of the Ten Command-merits, inasmuch as it is the substance of the law of nature, a delineation of God's moral image, and a transcript of His unspotted holiness, to be a perpetual and unalterable rule of conduct to mankind in all the possible states and circumstances in which they might be placed. Since God is unchangeable in His moral image, nothing but the entire annihilation of every human creature can divest His holy law of that office. Its being an immutable rule of duty to the human race does not in the least depend on its having become the matter of the covenant of works. Whatever form it might receive, whether that of the covenant of works or that of the covenant of grace, still it could not but continue an authoritative rule of conduct.

No form, no covenant whatever, could at any time lessen its high obligation as a rule of duty on the reasonable creature. As the form of the first covenant was merely accessory to the moral law, so the law continues, and will forever continue under that form as the rule of duty to sinners, even in the place of torment. And as the form of the second covenant is also accessory to it, so it will remain eternally under this form, the rule of life, to saints in the mansions of glory.

The sovereign authority of the divine law continues eternally the same; and it can never be in the least impaired by any of the forms under which that law is promulgated to us. And seeing God the Father has so consulted the necessity of His redeemed, in subordination to His own glory, as to put His law into the hands of His eternal Son as Mediator, from these hands they receive it invested with all the sovereign authority that ever belonged to it, together with all that God the Son as their great Redeemer has added to it. That believers ought not to receive, nay, and cannot receive, the law otherwise than from the hand of the infinitely glorious Mediator, is so far from being injurious to the infinite Majesty of God, the sovereign Creator, or to the high obligation of His holy law, that the infinite honor of His glorious majesty and His holy law is thereby most illustriously displayed. As the law as a covenant of works was honored in an infinite degree by its having been obeyed and satisfied by the eternal Son of God in our nature, so, as a rule of life to believers, it is magnified in no less a degree by its being conveyed to them in His hand.

Their obligation to perform not only sincere, but even perfect obedience to it, is on these accounts confirmed and increased. Now the obligation under which all true believers are to yield such obedience to the law as a rule of life proceeds chiefly from the following sources:

1. It arises from God's being the Lord, or from His being the sovereign, super-eminent, and supremely excellent Jehovah. The obligation under which believers lie to yield obedience to His law arises from His universal supremacy and sovereign authority over them as rational creatures. 'Ye shall, therefore, keep My statutes and My judgments—I am the LORD" (Leviticus 18:5). "Ye shall keep My statutes and do them; I am the LORD which sanctifieth you" (Leviticus 20:8).

Because God is Jehovah, "the eternal, immutable, and almighty God, having His being in and of Himself, and giving being to all His words and works" (Larger Catechism, question 101), all obedience is due to Him. The infinite greatness, excellence, and amiableness of the perfections of Jehovah make it the duty of all men, and especially of all believers, to love Him supremely, to obey Him in all things, and to make His glory the chief end of all their obedience to Him. The infinite supereminence and amiableness of Jehovah lay them under inconceivably high obligations to love Him above themselves, and to live to Him ultimately and not to themselves.

And as His greatness, excellence, and loveliness are infinite, immutable, and eternal, and as the highest possible degree of love and obedience is therefore due to Him, so the obligation under which believers lie to love and obey Him even in a perfect degree is infinite, immutable, and eternal. They are thus bound to love and obey Him with all their hearts because He is the LORD, or because He is what He is. On this account principally, and antecedently to every other consideration of Him, He is inexpressibly amiable; and therefore they are under the firmest obligation to love and obey Him, and that in the highest possible degree.

This obligation, arising from that infinite greatness, excellence, and loveliness of God which result from His natural and moral perfections, is binding upon believers previously to any consideration of rewards or punishments, or even of the revealed will of God; and it is that from which all other ties to duty derive their obligatory force. It is from the infinite excellence and amiableness of the divine nature that every additional obligation under which they lie to perfect love and perfect obedience derives its binding force.

2. The obligation under which believers are to yield perfect obedience to the law as a rule flows also from God's being their Creator and their being His creatures. It is He who made them and not they themselves (Psalm 100:3). They receive life, breath, and all things from His creating hand. His right therefore to them, and to their perfect and perpetual obedience, is not only original, underived, and perfect, but infinite. The power which He employed in creating them was infinite; and therefore He has an infinite right to all that they are, have, and can perform. By right of creation, the Lord has an irreversible and perpetual claim to their supreme love and their cordial and grateful obedience.

The relation subsisting between Him as their Creator and them as His creatures lays them under the firmest bond of subjection and obedience to Him; and the grace of the gospel, instead of diminishing, increases the force of that natural obligation. The sovereign Creator is far from having resigned His right of dominion over His saints by His having afforded them, independent of their own works, a title to eternal life. For as they cease not to be creatures by being made new creatures, so they are bound, and shall eternally continue bound, by the sovereign authority of the triune God as their Creator to yield personal and perfect obedience to His law as a rule of life.

The divine law, as I have already observed, loses nothing of its original obligation by being divested of its covenant form, and conveyed to believers in the hand of Christ; for "by Him were all things created that are in heaven, and that are in earth, visible and invisible" (Colossians 1:16). And the sovereignty, authority, and all other excellencies of the Father, are in the Son; yea, "in Him dwelleth all the fulness of the Godhead bodily" (Colossians 2:9). Indeed, that high obligation cannot cease to retain its original force as long as the immutable and eternal Jehovah cannot cease to be the Creator, and the saints to be His creatures.

3. Their obligation to obey the divine law as a rule of duty arises from God's being their continual Preserver. "In Him," says the Apostle Paul, "we live and move and have our being" (Acts 17:28). And, says the holy Psalmist, "Lord, Thou preservest man and beast" (Psalm 36:6). His eyes are upon all His works, so that even a sparrow cannot fall to the ground without Him. By the word of His power, He upholds all His creatures in their being and operation. Every living creature lives upon His goodness and subsists by His bounty. His infinite power every moment upholds all; His unsearchable wisdom governs all, and His unbounded goodness cares and provides for all.

"He openeth His hand, and satisfieth the desire of every living thing" (Psalm 145:16). But in a special manner "He preserveth the souls of His saints" (Psalm 97:10). "The Lord preserveth all them that love Him" (Psalm 145:20). "The Lord shall preserve thee from all evil; He shall preserve thy soul. The Lord shall preserve thy going out, and thy coming in, from this time forth, and even forevermore" (Psalm 121:7–8).

Since believers, then, are every moment dependent on God for the continuance and comfort both of their natural and spiritual life, they are bound, in obedience to His law as the rule of their life, to love Him supremely, to serve Him constantly, and to glorify Him in their body and spirit, which are His. The necessary relation in which they stand to Him as their constant Preserver obliges them to devote cheerfully all that they are, have, and do to His service and glory. Their being and their welfare are continually upheld and defended by His omnipotent arm; and therefore these ought at all times to be employed for Him. And because His manifested glory is His chief end in preserving His saints, they are bound to make it their chief end also in all that they do (1 Corinthians 10:31).

4. The obligation under which the spiritual seed of Christ lie to perform perfect and perpetual obedience to the law of God flows also from His being their God in covenant.

He is their God in Christ, and in the covenant of grace; and this obliges them to perform universal obedience to His righteous law as it is in the hand of Christ, and as it stands under the covenant of grace.

He is also their God in grant or offer. He offers Christ, the blessed Mediator to them, in common with all the other hearers of the gospel; and He also offers Himself to them, to be, in Christ, their God. In the preface to the Ten Commandments, He says to every hearer of the gospel, "I am the Lord thy God." It is as if He had said, "I am your God in offer." And in the first commandment, as was observed above, He requires everyone to believe the gracious offer with application to himself, saying, "Thou shalt have no other Gods before Me" (Exodus 20:2–3). He commands every man to know and acknowledge Him to be the only true God, and his God, upon the ground of the unlimited offer; and He enables all His own people to believe cordially that He is their God in offer.

He is also their God in choice. In the exercise of their faith, they choose the Lord Jesus to be their Savior and God in Him, to be their covenant God, saying, "What have we to do any more with idols?" (Hosea 14:8). "This God is our God forever and ever" (Psalm 48:14). Each of them is enabled to say to the Lord, as the Psalmist did, "I trusted in Thee, O Lord. I said, 'Thou art my God' " (Psalm 31:14); it is as if he had said, "Thou art my God not only in offer, but in choice (or in preference to every other god); and I, accordingly, have trusted in Thee as my God, and placed all my hope and happiness in Thee."

He is their God also in possession. By believing cordially that He is theirs in offer, and by choosing Him for their God and portion in preference to every other god, as well as by trusting that in Christ He will perform the part of a God to them, they take possession of Him as their God. According to their faith in Him is their possession and enjoyment of Him; and in bestowing Himself on them as their God and portion, He makes over to them all that He is, has, does, and will do to be theirs in time and through eternity (Hosea 13:4; Psalm 84:11; 1 Corinthians 3:21).

Seeing, then, that in amazing condescension He bestows Himself upon them as their God, they are under infinite obligations to devote themselves, and all that they are, have, and do to Him as His people. By His being their God, they are firmly bound, as well as powerfully excited, to love Him supremely, and to delight in yielding spiritual and universal obedience to Him. Because He is the Lord and their God, they are bound to keep all His commandments. And because it is of sovereign grace that He has been pleased to become their God, they are bound to obey His law as it stands in His covenant of grace—to obey it not that He may become their God, but because He already is their God. The covenant right which, according to His gracious promise, they have to Him as their God, gives Him an additional claim to them, and to all their love and obedience.

5. Their obligation to obey His law as a rule of conduct proceeds likewise from His being their redeeming God. In His love and pity He has redeemed them. From eternity He, according to the good pleasure of His will, has chosen them to everlasting salvation, and has devised the amazing scheme of their redemption. In the immensity of His redeeming love, and in the exceeding riches of His glorious grace, God the Father has sent His only begotten Son to purchase redemption for them, and His adorable Spirit to apply it to them.

He has appointed His only Son to answer the demands of His law as a covenant for them that they might be justified, and His Holy Spirit to write His law as a rule on their hearts that they might be sanctified. As means of attaining the inestimable benefits of eternal redemption, He has moreover favored them with the doctrines, promises, and ordinances of His blessed gospel. Thus the Father, Son, and Holy Spirit, one Jehovah, stands in the endearing relation of a redeeming God to all true believers; Christ the glorious Mediator stands in the relation of a near Kinsman, an incarnate Redeemer; and the Holy Spirit in the relation of a Sanctifier and Comforter to them. And while God the Father and Christ and the blessed Spirit stand in these and other endearing relations to believers, believers stand in all the correspondent relations to them.

Now from those relations an additional obligation to love and to good works arises which, instead of impairing, greatly strengthens all the other ties under which believers lie to yield evangelical and universal obedience. Because God graciously redeems them from the hand of all their enemies, and that with an infinite price and by infinite power, they are surely under the firmest possible obligations "to serve Him without fear, in holiness and righteousness before Him, all the days of their life" (Luke 1:74–75). The notion of a divine Redeemer implies that of a Creator. "Thus saith the Lord thy Redeemer, and He that formed thee from the womb, 'I am the Lord that maketh all things' " (Isaiah 44:24).

As God's being the Redeemer of His people, then, implies His being their Creator, in subordination to His glory in the redemption of them, so the obligation to obedience arising from His being their sovereign Creator is implied in, and strengthened by, the obligation flowing from His being their Redeemer. The redeeming grace of God in Christ is so far from lessening the force of the natural obligation under which believers as creatures lie to love and obey Him, that it increases this obligation in the highest possible degree.

The great God who is glorious in holiness has not resigned His right of sovereign authority over His saints by redeeming them from the law as a covenant, and from their spiritual enemies; but, on the contrary, He has hereby laid them under further and stronger obligations to universal obedience to the law as a rule.

The more illustrious the displays of His glorious perfections, and especially of His infinite goodness, are which He has afforded in their redemption, the greater are their obligations to obedience. When they consider that they have the righteousness of the incarnate Redeemer imputed to them to entitle them to eternal life, and His Spirit dwelling in them to make them meet for the perfection of it, they must surely acknowledge themselves to be under the firmest obligations possible to devote themselves entirely to the service and glory of their redeeming God.

In order to be satisfied of the truth of this, we need only to consider the new relations mentioned above, from which arises a set of new duties which no man is capable of performing, or has access to perform, unless he previously is a partaker of those relations. Of this class of duties are the faith, love, reverence, and worship which believers owe to Christ the adorable Mediator, to God in the relations of a Friend, Father, and God in covenant, and to the Holy Spirit dwelling in them as a Quickener, Sanctifier, and Comforter— also the duties which they owe to fellow-saints as members of Christ's mystical body. From those endearing relations, and the inestimable blessings issuing from them, believers cannot but be laid under new and peculiar obligations not only to perform these, but all the other duties required of them, in the law as a rule of life.

6. The holy will of God, revealed in His law as a rule of duty to believers, lays them under infinite obligations to obedience. The law in the hand of Christ is to His spiritual seed not only the rule, but the reason of their duty. They are bound not only to do that which is required in the law, and to leave undone that which is forbidden, but they must do what is commanded for the very reason that the Lord requires it, and abstain from what is forbidden because He forbids it. "Thou hast commanded us," says the holy Psalmist, "to keep Thy precepts diligently. Oh, that my

ways were directed to keep Thy statutes!" (Psalm 119:4–5).

To keep His commandments is, according to the phraseology of Scripture, to do His will. "He that doeth the will of God," says the Apostle John, "abideth forever" (1 John 2:17). And, says another apostle, "This is the will of God, even your sanctification" (1 Thessalonians 4:3). It is the will not only of God the Father, but of God the Son: "I have ordained you, that ye should go and bring forth fruit, and that your fruit should remain" (John 15:16). It is the will also of God the Holy Spirit, whom believers grieve, and even quench, when they do not study to advance daily in the love and practice of universal holiness.

The law as a rule is not only a transcript of the infinite purity of God's holy nature, but it is, at the same time, a declaration of His holy will respecting the duty which His people owe to Him. They are, then, under the firmest ties to keep His holy commandments because it is His will that they should keep them. His will declared in His law is infinitely, eternally, and immutably holy, and therefore, in connection with the other sources of obligation already mentioned, it lays believers under the highest possible obligations to perfect and perpetual obedience of heart and life to His holy law.

7. Once more, the obligation under which believers are to obey the law as a rule arises also from the inexpressible benefit or advantage of holiness to themselves. The law in the hand of Christ is not only holy and just, but it is good. It is good in itself and good for believers. It requires nothing of them but what is good for them to perform, and to endure nothing but what is suitable and advantageous to them; nothing but what is agreeable and delightful to the new and holy nature imparted to them in regeneration.

To be enabled, then, from principles of faith and love, and for the glory of God, to perform spiritual obedience to such a law is profitable, honorable, and delightful to real believers. It is profitable for them. "Godliness is profitable unto all things" (1 Timothy 4:8). "Godliness with contentment is great gain" (1 Timothy 6:6). "Charge them that are rich in this world ... that they do good, that they be rich in good works" (1 Timothy 6:17–18). "These things are good and profitable unto men" (Titus 3:8). To love the Lord their God with all their heart, soul, strength, and mind, and their neighbor as themselves, is the very perfection of their nature, the highest advantage of which it is capable.

Holy obedience to the law in the hand of Christ is also honorable to believers. "If any man serve Me," said our blessed Lord, "him will My

Father honor" (John 12:26). And again, "If a man love Me he will keep My words; and My Father will love him, and we will come unto him and make our abode with him" (John 14:23). What a high honor, what an exalted distinction is conferred on sinful worms of the dust when they are not only beautified with the holy image of God, but are advanced to intimate fellowship with Him! Conformity of heart and of life to the divine law is true honor.

To resemble Him who is the brightness of the Father's glory, and the express image of His person, is the honor and glory of a man. To yield obedience to the law of Christ is delightful also to holy souls. As they delight in the law itself, so they take pleasure in yielding spiritual obedience to all its holy commandments. Wisdom's ways are ways of pleasantness to them. Holiness is not only connected with happiness, but is itself happiness. A man is miserable in proportion as he is sinful, and happy in the same degree in which he is holy. In obedience there is a present and a great reward.

True holiness is the health and happiness, the peace and pleasure of the soul. It renders the external comforts of the believer doubly pleasant and his heaviest crosses light, his life valuable and his death desirable. The holy commandments are inscribed on his heart; and therefore, he is well pleased with the purity, spirituality, and goodness of them. He delights in meditating on them (Psalm 1:2), and especially on the holiness of them; he counts them an easy yoke, and he chooses and resolves to perform spiritual and perpetual obedience to them.

He knows by experience that he is happy in proportion as his inclinations, thoughts, words, and actions are holy; and that he is in his proper element only when he is exercising graces and performing duties. Now, seeing holiness is, in subordination to the glory of God, profitable, honorable and pleasant to believers themselves, and so is highly beneficial to them, they are bound to make continual progress in the love and practice of it. As they are bound to glorify God as their redeeming God, and, in subordination to this, to advance in the enjoyment of Him, so they are under strong obligations, in obedience to His holy law, to advance in conformity to Him and in communion with Him: for they cannot glorify Him but in proportion as they enjoy Him, and they cannot enjoy Him but by such conformity to His image as is the fruit of communion with Him.

Let every believer, then, endeavor diligently to advance in faith and holiness according to the law of Christ; for "blessed is the man that trusteth in the Lord, and whose hope the Lord is" (Jeremiah 17:7), and "blessed also is the man that feareth the Lord, that delighteth greatly in His commandments" (Psalm 112:1).

From what has now been said, we may warrantably infer that all they to whom the law of the Ten Commandments is given as the authoritative rule of their life have already received spiritual life as the beginning of life eternal. They have all been quickened by the Spirit of Christ, united to Him as their living Head, instated in His covenant of grace, and justified for His righteousness imputed to them. And so they have received already the beginnings of eternal life as the gift of God through Him. "He that believeth on the Son hath everlasting life" (John 3:36). And again, "Whosoever liveth and believeth in Me shall never die" (John 11:26).

The law as a covenant of works says to the dead sinner, "Do this and live; do this for life." The law as a rule of life, on the contrary, says to the living saint, "Live and do this; do this not for, but from life already received." All they, then, to whom the law as a rule of life in the hand of the Mediator is given already have, in their regeneration, received the beginning of eternal life prior to their being capable of performing the smallest degree of obedience to the law in that form.

They cannot obey the law as a rule of life otherwise than by working from life; but this supposes them to have life previous to such working, and as the principle of it. Christ lives in them, and they live by the faith of Him. Their spiritual and eternal life is the life of Christ, life which is wholly derived from Him; and the rule of it by which all its activity is to be regulated is the divine law as the law of Christ (Galatians 6:2). Regeneration and vital union with Christ are previously and absolutely necessary to the smallest act of acceptable obedience to the law as a rule of life.

Does the law as a rule of life oblige believers to yield even perfect obedience to its precepts? We ought not to infer from this that it can either justify them before God or condemn them. To justify or to condemn a man belongs to the law as a covenant, but not to it as a rule. To be under the law as a rule of life is the privilege only of believers who are already justified freely by grace through the redemption that is in Christ Jesus, and who are thereby placed forever beyond the reach of condemnation (Romans 8:1).

The law as a rule cannot justify believers for their obedience to it, for they were perfectly justified in the sight of God before they began their course of sincere obedience; and besides, their obedience is far from being perfect. Neither can it condemn them to eternal wrath for their disobedience; for in their justification they were delivered from condemnation before they began, strictly speaking, to disobey it. It can indeed adjudge them to endure the painful effects of paternal anger, but not to suffer the direful effects of avenging wrath (John 5:24).

The law as a rule can direct and bind believers even to perfect obedience, but it cannot either justify them to eternal life or condemn them to eternal death. Their tide to eternal life, and their security from eternal death, have been merited for them by the obedience and death of the last Adam; and they are secured to them by His intercession. This consideration should endear exceedingly the holy law as a rule of duty to the true believer, and should constrain him to rejoice in the thought that he is bound, and in the prospect that to all eternity he shall be bound, by the authority of it to perfect and perpetual obedience (Psalm 119:77; Revelation 22:3).

Hence also it is evident that the main reason why many true believers have but little holiness of heart and life is that they have much of a legal spirit still remaining in them. It is only with their renewed nature that they obey, or are capable of obeying, the law as a rule. Their unrenewed nature still cleaves to the law as a covenant. In proportion, then, to the degree of corruption remaining in them is that of their legal or old covenant spirit; and the more this prevails in them, the less holy they are. Evangelical or true holiness is a conformity of heart and life not to the law as a covenant of works, but to it as a rule of life standing in the covenant of grace.

Although believers, as we said above, are wholly delivered from the dominion of the covenant of works as a rightful sovereign, yet many times it is permitted to re-enter their consciences and usurp authority over them. At such times it will venture either to promise eternal life to them for their obedience, or to threaten eternal death to them for their disobedience. Now in exact proportion to the degree of their legal temper they are disposed to hearken to the voice of the law in their consciences; and as far as they regard the usurped authority of the law as a covenant of works, they so far disregard the high authority and obligation of it as a rule of duty.

Believer, you cannot advance in holy conformity to the law as a rule but in proportion as you, by the Spirit, mortify your legal temper. You may be eminently strict, exact, and uniform in your external performance of every duty; but in as far as a legal spirit prevails and influences your performance of them, they are so far unholy and unacceptable to God. He will accept none of your works but those which are done from evangelical principles and in an evangelical manner.

Nothing will more effectually retard your progress in true holiness than either to hope that you shall obtain heaven for your works of obedience or to fear that you shall be cast into hell for your sins. If you trust your habits of grace rather than the fullness of grace in Christ; if you derive your comfort from your lively frames and religious attainments rather than from Christ and the promises; and if you make either the good dispositions implanted in you or the good works performed by you the ground of your right to trust daily in Him for salvation, instead of trusting in Him upon the ample warrant afforded you by the offers and calls of the gospel, by doing so you will assuredly decline from holy and cheerful obedience to the law as a rule of life.

If instead of coming always as a sinner to the compassionate Savior, and placing direct confidence in Him for salvation to yourself in particular, you refuse to trust in Him except when you can bring some good qualification or work with you to recommend you to Him, you cannot advance in that holy obedience to His law which is the obedience of faith (Romans 16:26).

It is no less manifest from what has been said that the state to which believers are advanced upon their vital union with Christ is so far from being a state of liberty to commit sin that it is a state in which they are laid under the highest possible obligations even to perfect obedience. If all men are bound to keep the commandments of God because He is Jehovah, the redeemed are especially and still more firmly bound to yield all obedience to them because He is not only Jehovah, but is besides their God and Redeemer. None are under such high and strong obligations to holiness of heart and life as the ransomed of the Lord are.

He is their God in covenant, and this lays them under the firmest ties to be His obedient, holy people. He is their almighty and gracious Redeemer, and therefore they are not their own, but His, and are infinitely bound to glorify Him in their bodies and in their spirits, which are His (1 Corinthians 6:20). Why do the saints bitterly bewail the strength of their corruptions and the weakness of their graces, the innumerable sins of which they have been guilty, and the want of perfect conformity to the holy law of which they are sensible? Is it not because they feel their infinite obligations not to merely sincere, but even to perfect obedience?

And why do they, in their exercise of evangelical repentance, loathe themselves in their own sight for their iniquities and their abominations (Ezekiel 36:31)? Do they it not because they are enabled to account their want of that perfect conformity to the law to which they are bound an abominable defect? The wonderful grace of God displayed in their justification and deliverance from the law as a covenant of works, instead of leaving them at liberty to continue in sin, disposes and powerfully constrains them to depart from all iniquity and advance resolutely in universal obedience to the law as a rule of life. There is not a true believer in the world who does not know this by experience.

What has been advanced may also serve to throw some light on the doctrine of vowing to the Lord, and of the obligation which arises from a lawful vow. Believers are far from being left at liberty to vow or not to vow as they please. They are expressly commanded to vow to God, and also to perform their vows. "Vow, and pay unto the Lord your God" (Psalm 76:11). "Pay thy vows unto the Most High" (Psalm 50:14). It is clear from the context that the vows mentioned in this last passage are not legal and ceremonial, but spiritual or moral vows; vows which believers in all ages of the Church are bound both to make and to perform.

Isaiah, when predicting the conversion of multitudes in New Testament times, and especially in the millennial period of the Church, says, 'The Egyptians shall know the Lord in that day; yea, they shall vow a vow unto the Lord, and perform it" (Isaiah 19:21). Accordingly, the venerable Assembly at Westminster teaches that "vowing unto God is a duty required in the second commandment of the moral law" (Larger Catechism, question 108). All true converts, in every age of the Church, dedicate themselves, and all that they are, have, and do to the Lord; and in doing so they either expressly or implicitly vow to Him. That is to say, they solemnly purpose and promise that in dependence on promised grace, or that in as far as the Lord Jesus will according to His promises, enable them, they shall, all the days of their life, yield sincere and increasing obedience to His holy law as the rule of their duty.

They do not engage or promise to yield perfect obedience in their present state of imperfection, or to perform so much as a single duty in the strength of grace already received, but to perform in the strength of that grace which is promised, and which they trust will be given them, all necessary duties. This is not a particular, but a general vow. Neither is it a legal and ceremonial, but a spiritual and moral vow. It is the believer's baptismal vow which, if opportunities are afforded, he will be sure willingly, explicitly, and frequently to renew at the Table of the Lord.

Now, from this vow or promissory oath arises an obligation on the believer to do as he has said. He vows to perform nothing but what he was previously under the firmest obligations possible to perform; and therefore, though his vow cannot add to the authority of God in His law, nor, strictly speaking, strengthen those obligations to obedience which are already as strong as it is possible for them at the time to be; yet it is the source of a new, a distinct and a super-added obligation.

It is not, indeed, a primary source of obligation to obedience like those mentioned above; but still it lays the believer under a new and distinct obligation to fulfil his engagement. He engages or obliges himself, by his own voluntary act, to perform sincerely all those duties to which he is already bound by the law. And the more often he repeats his vow, the obligation arising from it becomes the firmer. If a lawful vow, with respect to things indifferent, founds an obligation, as generally seems to be allowed, much more, surely, must a lawful vow concerning necessary duties be binding.

The new obligation to necessary duties, arising from a deliberate and solemn vow to perform them, is not in the least inconsistent with those high obligations to them which flow from the other sources already explained. It is, indeed, associated with these obligations, but it is no disparagement to them.

Should any still be disposed to question if a lawful vow respecting moral duties can found a new and distinct obligation to perform them, I would only add that it either lays the believer who makes it under a new obligation or it does not. There can be no medium here. If it lays him under an obligation, it must be an obligation posterior to those considered above, and therefore a new and distinct one. If it lays him under no obligation, it will follow that lawful vows do not bind; if they do not bind or impose an obligation, they cannot be broken; and, if so, the saints in all ages have acted an unwise, yea, and a superstitious part when they have confessed and bitterly bewailed their breach of vows.

Many professors of religion in our day seem unwilling to vow to the Lord for fear that, by the breach of vows, they should increase the number of their sins. But this discovers both a want of knowledge and a want of sincerity. Matthew Henry, commenting on Isaiah 45:23, says well, "If the heart be brought into obedience to Christ, and made willing in the day of His power, the tongue will swear to Him, will lay a bond upon the soul, to engage it forever to Him; for he that bears an honest mind doth never startle at assurances."

In conclusion, believers are under every obligation not only to obedience to the divine law, but to free and voluntary obedience. They are bound to yield such obedience as cannot be performed under the law as a covenant of works, as cannot be performed from the principle either of slavish fear or of servile hope. They are under the strongest ties to yield voluntary obedience to the law as a rule of life. They are firmly bound, but it is to free obedience; to the obedience not of slaves or hirelings, but of sons and daughters.

The Lord Jesus says in His law to them, as on a particular occasion He did to His disciples, "Freely ye have received, freely give" (Matthew 10:8). With infinite willingness, He obeyed the law as a covenant for them in order that they, by His grace, might with sincere willingness and, in due time, with perfect willingness obey it as a rule. The law as a rule of life to believers has, as was said above, no threatening of eternal death, and no promise of eternal life annexed to it.

No obedience, therefore, is suitable to it but that which is free and voluntary, proceeding from love to God, delight in His will, and concern for His glory. In proportion, accordingly, as the saints are enabled to believe the astonishing love of God with application to themselves, and to contemplate the infinitely free grace manifested in redeeming them from the broken covenant of works, and in bringing them under the law of the hand of Christ, they yield free and unconstrained obedience to this law. Made a willing people in the day of the Redeemer's power, they obey willingly, and that not from legal motives, but from 'evangelical ones.

They study to do what the Lord requires because He commands them, and in order to please and honor Him. They hate all manner of sin because it is hateful in itself, and because He hates it. With holy abhorrence they forsake iniquity because He forbids it, and in order that they may not displease or dishonor Him. And though their obedience will not be absolutely free till it is absolutely perfect, yet the freeness of it will always be in exact proportion to the strength and frequency of their actings of faith and love.

When a man is habitually attentive to the manner as well as to the matter of every act of obedience, it is a good evidence that he is dead to the law as a covenant, and is brought under the obligation of it as a rule; that the law as a covenant has begun to be erased from his heart, and the law as a rule to be written on it.

CPSIA information can be obtained
at www.ICGtesting.com
Printed in the USA
LVHW021033100921
697438LV00011B/485